Table of Contents

Biography 4
Introduction 5
Dedication 6
Explanation of Title 7

Chapter One 8
Chapter Two 13
Chapter Three 31
Chapter Four 48
Chapter Five 58
Chapter Six 73
Chapter Seven 88
Chapter Eight 107
Chapter Nine 120
Chapter Ten 138
Chapter Eleven 156
Chapter Twelve 163
Chapter Thirteen 172
Chapter Fourteen 177
Chapter Fifteen 183
Chapter Sixteen 187
Chapter Seventeen 191
Chapter Eighteen 194
Chapter Nineteen 197

Additional Notes 202

Worksheets: From Chapter to Chapter 219
Worksheets: Chronology of Events 229

Historical Timeline 232
Some Useful Literary Terms 241
Selected Additional Reading 246
Selected List of Films about the South or Racism 248

Additional Material: 250
- The Detective Story 250
- The American South 252
- Race and Ethnicity 254

Biography

Tom Franklin was born in Dickinson, Alabama in 1963. He is the author of a collection of short stories, **Poachers**, of which the title story won the Edgar Allan Poe Award. He has written four novels, **Hell at the Breech**, **Smonk**, **Crooked Letter, Crooked Letter**, and **The Tilted World**. The third novel won the UK's Golden Dagger Award for Best Novel, the LA Times Book Prize for mystery/thriller, and the Willie Morris Prize for Southern Fiction. His most recent book, **The Tilted World** was co-written with his wife, the writer and poet Beth Ann Fennelly. He is a former Guggenheim Fellow. Tom Franklin lives with his family, which includes three children, in Oxford, Mississippi.

He holds the following degrees: BA and MA in English from the University of South Alabama (1990, 1995), and an MFA (Master of Fine Arts) from the University of Arkansas (1997). He is currently Associate Professor of Fiction Writing at the University of Mississippi.

In 2016 Tom Franklin was awarded the Berlin Prize from The American Academy in Berlin. The prize included a stipend and accommodations in Berlin.

The author has acknowledged that much of his own personal life, his family, the countryside he grew up in has found its counterpart in **Crooked Letter, Crooked Letter**. Larry, for example, is in many ways based on the author's own experiences as a student in high school. Cecil's jumping from a tree is similar to an incident that occurred in the author's life. Even Dr. Israel actually existed. To quote the author: "He was my father's doctor. He was a good man."

Writing the novel did not come easily, but he was able to complete the novel when he accompanied his wife to Brazil where she was a part of the Fulbright Visiting Scholars Program. Ironically, it was being away from his familiar surroundings that helped him to sharpen the contours of local color in his novel.

It was in the five months in Brazil when he wrote most of **Crooked Letter, Crooked Letter**. In the words of the author:

> The process of writing this book was a slow one at first. It began around 2003, my only idea [being] about brothers. When I decided on the title **Crooked Letter, Crooked Letter**, I realized it would have to be a crime novel because that title sounds like a crime novel title. It would also need to be set in Mississippi. I'd been thinking about two characters, a mechanic with no customers and a rural police officer. A pal of mine, David Wright, who's African-American, suggested I make the cop a Black guy. I tried it and liked it. He became Silas, the cop. The white guy became Larry, the mechanic. Gradually, as I worked, I realized they were half-brothers. As I say, it was a slow process, at first. I started around 2003 and stopped to write **Smonk** in 2004 and 2005, then came back to **Crooked Letter, Crooked Letter** after that and still didn't quite know what it was. It took shape over many years. I wrote most of it in Brazil, in about 5 months, which is typical of how I write.

The author has strived to blend his love of "high literature" such as the works of William Faulkner and Flannery O'Connor with the books he read as a boy: the horror novels of Stephen King or the fantasy novels of Edgar Rice Burroughs. Moreover, Tom Franklin has always been fascinated by crime fiction focusing on moral dilemmas, as in the works of Laura Lippman, George Pelecanos, Richard Price and Dennis Lehane.

Introduction

The history of the South has had a unique and tragic place in American history. The traumatic experience of the Civil War (1861 – 1865), the failure of The Reconstruction from 1865 to 1872, and the shadow of slavery and Jim Crow still hang over the South, and in more subtle and not so subtle ways over the rest of America. Southern writers since the end of the 19th century have especially focused on the problems of injustice and racism in various literary forms. We need only think of such writers as John Griffin, Flannery O'Connor, William Faulkner, Ernest Gaines, and Harper Lee. Tom Franklin's writing reflects this tradition. He feels himself closely tied to his Southern heritage and is especially appreciative of the uniqueness of Southern culture and language.

In an interview he said:

> *I think growing up in the South made me the person I am, and the writer I am comes from that. So, yes, the South's made me the writer I am. It taught me to listen to the cadences and rhythms of speech, and to notice the landscape. It also has this defeated feel, a lingering of old sin, that makes it sweet in a rotting kind of way. Much of it is poor, much is rural, and that's an interesting combination, a deep well for stories.*

quoted from an amazon.com interview: https://www.amazon.com/Crooked-Letter-Novel/dp/0060594667?ie=UTF8&ref_=ntt_at_ep_dpi_1

On the other hand, the author fears that being labeled as a Southern writer has its downside:

> *I feel less good about it [being characterized as a Southern writer] every year. I was happy about it for the first couple of books because I never thought I would - honestly - publish a book. And then I did. And being a Southern writer, there is kind of a built-in audience. But I'm feeling more and more pigeonholed by that. [...] Nobody in New York reads me. I mean, honestly, I think that, you know, that New York is so important in publishing. But if somebody's a Southern writer, I think it's harder to break through.*

quoted from an PBS interview on October 3, 2010: http://www.npr.org/templates/story/story.php?storyId=130303007

to pigeonhole to categorize

A talk given in Berlin by the author on November 17, 2016 is available at:
http://www.americanacademy.de/home/media/videos/accidentally-autobiographical-american-south-south-america

Notes:
"TF" is used to indicate a commentary or definition by the author.

Headwords in the annotations that are highlighted in gray should be part of a student's active vocabulary.

For Jeff Franklin
and
in loving memory
of
Julie Fennelly Trudo

M. I. crooked letter, crooked letter, I, crooked letter, crooked letter, I. humpback, humpback, I.

– How southern children are taught to spell *Mississippi*

humpback *Buckel*

Chapter One

The Rutherford girl had been missing for eight days when Larry Ott returned home and found a monster waiting in his house.

It'd stormed the night before over much of the Southeast, flash floods on the news, trees snapped in half and pictures of trailer homes twisted apart. Larry, forty-one years old and single, lived alone in rural Mississippi in his parents' house, which was now his house, though he couldn't bring himself to think of it that way. He acted more like a curator, keeping the rooms clean, answering the mail and paying bills, turning on the television at the right times and smiling with the laugh tracks, eating his McDonald's or Kentucky Fried Chicken to what the networks presented him and then sitting on his front porch as the day bled out of the trees across the field and night settled in, each different, each the same.

It was early September. That morning he'd stood on the porch, holding a cup of coffee, already sweating a little as he gazed out at the glistening front yard, his muddy driveway, the bobwire fence, the sodden green field beyond stabbed with thistle, goldenrod, blue salvia, and honeysuckle at the far edges, where the woods began. It was a mile to his nearest neighbor and another to the crossroads store, closed for years.

At the edge of the porch several ferns hung from the eave, his mother's wind chime lodged in one like a flung puppet. He set his coffee on the rail and went to disentangle the chime's slender pipes from the leaves.

Behind the house he rolled the barn doors open, a lawn mower wheel installed at the bottom of each. He removed the burnt sardine can from the tractor's smokestack and hung the can on its nail on the wall and climbed on. In the metal seat he mashed the clutch with one foot and brake with the other and knocked the old Ford out of gear and turned the key. The tractor, like everything else, had been his father's, a Model 8-N with its fenders and rounded hood painted gray but its engine and body fire-engine red. That red engine caught now and he revved it a few times as the air around his head blued with shreds of pleasant smoke. He backed out, raising the lift, bouncing in the seat as the tractor's big wheels, each weighted with fifteen gallons of water, rolled over the land. The Ford parted the weeds and wildflowers and set off bumblebees and butterflies and soggy grasshoppers and dragonflies, which his mother used to call snake doctors. The tractor threw its long shadow toward the far fence and he turned and began to circle the field, the privet cut back along the bobwire, the trees tall and lush, the south end still shaded and dewy and cool. He bush-hogged twice a month from March to July, but when the fall wildflowers came he let them grow. Migrating hummingbirds passed through in September, hovering around the blue salvia, which they seemed to love, chasing one another away from the blooms.

At the chicken pen he shifted into reverse and backed up, lowering the trailer hitch. He checked the sky shaking his head. More clouds shouldering over the far trees and rain on the air. In the tack room he ladled feed and corn into a plastic milk jug with the mouth widened, the brown pellets and dusty yellow corn giving its faint earthy odor. He added a little grit, too, crushed pebble, which helped the chickens digest. The original pen, which his father had built as a Mother's Day gift somewhere back in Larry's memory, had run twenty feet out for the length of the left side of the barn and adjoined a room inside that had been converted to a roost. The new pen was different. Larry had always felt bad that the hens lived their lives in the same tiny patch, dirt in dry weather and mud in wet, especially when the field surrounding his house, almost five acres, did nothing but grow weeds and lure bugs, and what a shame the chickens couldn't feast. He'd tried letting a couple run free, experiments, hoping they'd stay close and use the barn to roost, but the first hen made for the far woods and got under the fence and was never seen again. The next a quick victim of a bobcat. He'd pondered it and finally constructed a scheme. On a summer weekend he'd built a head-high moveable cage with an open floor and attached a set of lawn mower wheels to the back end. He dismantled his father's fence and made his own to fit against the outside door to the coop, so that when the chickens came out they came out in his cage. Each morning he latched an interior door and, weather permitting, used the tractor to pull the cage into the field, onto a different square of grass, so the chickens got fresh food – insects, vegetation – and the droppings they left didn't spoil the grass but fertilized it. The chickens sure liked it, and their egg yolks had become nearly twice as yellow as they'd been before, and twice as good.

<u>He came outside with the feed. Storm clouds like a billowing mountain loomed over the northernmost trees, already the wind picking up, the chime singing from the porch.</u> Better keep em in, he thought and went back in and turned the wooden latch and entered the coop, its odor of droppings and warm dust. He shut the door behind him, feathers settling around his shoes. Today four of the wary brown hens sat in their plywood boxes, deep in pine straw.

"Good morning, ladies," he said and turned on the faucet over the old tire, cut down the center like a donut sliced in half, and as it filled with water he ducked through the door into the cage with the non-setting hens following like something caught in his wake, the tractor idling outside the wire. He flung the feed out of the jug, watching for a moment as they pecked it up with their robotic jerks, clucking, scratching, bobbing their heads among the speckled droppings and wet feathers. He ducked back into the coop and shooed the setting hens off and collected the brown eggs, flecked with feces, and set them in a bucket. "Have a good day, ladies," he said, on his way out, turning the spigot off, latching the door, hanging the jug on its nail. "We'll try to go out tomorrow."

---

chicken pen structure to hold chickens
to shift umschalten

to ladle to fill with a large spoon
jug Krug
grit small granule
to digest verdauen
pebble small stone

to adjoin to connect with s.th.
roost a place for chickens to sleep
patch Stück Land
to lure locken

bobcat wild cat found in North America
to ponder to think about s.th. carefully

to dismantle to take apart
coop cage for chickens

to latch verriegeln

droppings Kot
to fertilize düngen
yolk the round, yellow inner portion of an egg

to billow to swell out
to loom (here:) sich auftürmen
em (slang) them

wary cautious
plywood Tischlerplatte
pine Kiefer
faucet (AE) Wasserhahn

to duck (here): to move through s.th. with the body lowered
non-setting not sitting on or producing an egg
wake Schlepptau
to idle to let the motor run without being in gear
jerk sudden movement
to bob to rapidly move up and down
speckled with spots
feces ['fi:si:z] (formal) droppings
to shoo to say "shoo" and wave away
spigot faucet

to tap to hit lightly
sink *Waschbecken*
whiskers (here): the hairs resulting from shaving
chubby somewhat fat
choppy not evenly cut

nursing home *Pflegeheim*
attendant (here): person who takes care of old people in a nursing home
to swipe to wipe

bay section in a garage where cars are repaired
to crumble to slowly fall into pieces
trim decoration at the edges

firearm *Schusswaffe*

to don (formal) to put on
khaki [ˈkɑːki] brown-yellow

to scramble to mix together

charger *Ladegerät*
to squish (here): to walk noisily on s.th. thoroughly wet
to crank (here): to start up

battered badly damaged
to wrench off to pull off with force
to crank (here): *kurbeln*
to toss to throw carelessly
to shift *umschalten*
drive the position of an automatic transmission for driving forward
box fan large fan in a square, metal casing
job (here): repair
to prop open (here): to open und place a thin piece of wood or metal underneath to keep the door open

Back inside the house he blew his nose and washed his hands and shaved at the bathroom mirror, the hall bathroom. He tapped the razor on the edge of the sink, the whiskers peppered around the drain more gray than black, and he knew if he stopped shaving his beard would be as gray as the beards his father used to grow during hunting seasons thirty, thirty-five years before. Larry had been chubby as a kid but now his face was lean, his brown hair short but choppy as he cut it himself, had been doing so even before his mother had gone into River Acres, a nursing home nowhere near a river and mostly full of blacks, both the attendants and attended. He'd have preferred somewhere better, but it was all he could afford. He splashed warm water on his cheeks and with a bath rag swiped his reflection into the steamy mirror.

There he was. A mechanic, but only in theory. He operated a two-bay shop on Highway 11 North, the crumbling white concrete block building with green trim. He drove his father's red Ford pickup, an early 1970s model with a board bed liner, a truck over thirty years old with only 56,000 miles and its original six-cylinder and, except for a few windshields and headlights, most of its factory parts. It had running boards and a toolbox on the back with his wrenches and sockets and ratchets inside, in case he got a road call. There was a gun rack in the back window that held his umbrella – you weren't allowed to display firearms since 9/11. But even before that, because of his past, Larry hadn't been allowed to own a gun.

In his bedroom, piled with paperbacks, he put on his uniform cap then donned the green khaki pants and a matching cotton shirt with LARRY in an oval on his pocket, short sleeve this time of year. He wore black steel-toed work shoes, a habit of his father's, also a mechanic. He fried half a pound of bacon and scrambled the morning's eggs in the grease and opened a Coke and ate watching the news. The Rutherford girl still missing. Eleven boys dead in Baghdad. High school football scores.

He detached his cell phone from its charger, no calls, then slipped it into his front pants pocket and picked up the novel he was reading and locked the door behind him and carefully descended the wet steps and squished over the grass to his truck. He got in, cranked the engine and reversed and headed out, raindrops already spattering his windshield. At the end of his long driveway he stopped at his mailbox, tilted on its post, a battered black shell with its door and red flag long wrenched off. He cranked down his window and reached inside. A package. He pulled it out, one of his book clubs. Several catalogs. The phone bill. He tossed the mail on the seat beside him, shifted into drive and pulled onto the highway. Soon he'd be at his garage cranking up the bay door, dragging the garbage can out, opening the big back doors and positioning the box fan there to circulate air. For a moment he'd stand in front by the gas pumps, watching for cars, hoping one of the Mexicans across at the motel would need a brake job or something. Then he'd go inside the office, prop open the door, flip the CLOSED sign to OPEN, get a Coke from the machine in the corner, and click the lid off in the bottle opener. He'd sit behind his desk where he could see the road through the window, a car or two every half hour. He'd open the low drawer on the left and prop his feet there and tear into the package, see which books-of-the-month these would be.

But four hours later he was on his way back home. He'd gotten a call on the cell phone. His mother was having a good day, she told him, and wondered might he bring lunch.

"Yes, ma'am," he'd said.

In addition to lunch he wanted to get a photo album – one of the nurses, the nice one, had told him those helped jog her memory, kept more of her here, longer. If he hurried, he could get the album, go by Kentucky Fried Chicken, and be there before noon.

He drove fast, unwise for him. The local police knew his truck and watched him closely, often parking near the railroad tracks he passed daily. He had few visitors, other than midnight teenagers banging by and turning around in his yard, hooting and throwing beer bottles or firecrackers. And Wallace Stringfellow of course, who was his only friend. But always unnerving were the occasional visits, like yesterday, of Gerald County chief investigator Roy French, search warrant in hand. "You understand, right," French always said, tapping him on the chest with the paper. "I got to explore ever possibility. You're what we call a person of interest." Larry would nod and step aside without reading the warrant and let him in, sit on his front porch while French checked the drawers in the bedrooms, the laundry room by the kitchen, closets, the attic, on his hands and knees beaming his flashlight under the house, poking around in the barn, frightening the chickens. "You understand," French usually repeated as he left.

And Larry did understand. If he'd been missing a daughter, he would come here, too. He would go everywhere. He knew the worst thing must be the waiting, not being able to do anything, while your girl was lost in the woods or bound in somebody's closet, hung from the bar with her own red brassiere.

Sure he understood.

He stopped in front of the porch and got out and left the truck door open. He never wore his seat belt; his folks had never worn theirs. He hurried up the steps and opened the screen door and held it with his foot as he found the key and turned the lock and stepped into the room and noticed an open shoe box on the table.

His chest went cold. He turned and saw the monster's face, knowing it immediately for the mask it was, that he'd owned since he was a kid, that his mother had hated, his father ridiculed, a gray zombie with bloody gashes and fuzzy patches of hair and one plastic eye that dangled from strands of gore. Whoever wore it now must have found the mask French never had, hidden in Larry's closet.

Larry said, "What – "

to flip to quickly turn

to prop to support

to jog to activate

to bang by to pass by making a lot of noise
to hoot to shout loudly

county Kreis
search warrant Durchsuchungsbefehl

nod nicken

laundry room room for the washing machine and dryer
attic Dachboden
to beam to shine a light in a certain direction
to poke around to search around for s.th. hidden

to bind, bound, bound to tie with a rope
bar Stange
brassiere [brəˈzɪr] (formal) bra

porch Veranda

to ridicule [ˈrɪdɪkjuːl] to make fun of s.th./s.o.
gash long, deep cut
fuzzy covered with short, fine hair
to dangle to hang loosely
gore thick blood from a wound

Chapter One

The man in the mask cut him off in a high voice. "Ever body knows what you did." He raised a pistol.

Larry opened his hands and stepped back as the man came toward him behind the pistol. "Wait," he said.

But he didn't get to deny abducting the Rutherford girl last week, or Cindy Walker twenty-five years ago, because the man stepped closer and jammed the barrel against Larry's chest, Larry for a moment seeing human eyes in the monster's face, something familiar in there. Then he heard the shot.

When he opened his eyes he lay on the floor looking at the ceiling. His ears were ringing. His belly was quivering in his shirt and he'd bit his lip. He turned his head, the monster smaller than he'd looked before, leaning against the wall by the door, unable to catch his breath. He wore white cotton gardening gloves and they were shaking, both the one with the pistol and the one without.

"Die," he croaked.

Larry felt no pain, only blood, the heart that beat so rapidly pushing more and more out, bright red lungblood he could smell. Something was burning. He couldn't move his left arm but with his right hand touched his chest, rising and falling, blood bubbling through his fingers and down his ribs in his shirt. He tasted copper on his tongue. He was cold and sleepy and very thirsty. He thought of his mother. His father. Of Cindy Walker standing in the woods.

The man against the wall had sunk to his haunches, watching from behind the mask, eyes shimmering in the eye holes, and Larry felt a strange forgiveness for him because all monsters were misunderstood. The man moved the pistol from his right hand to the left and reached and touched the gory mask as if he'd forgot it was there and left another smudge of red, real among the paint, on its gray cheek. He wore old blue jeans frayed at the knees and socks stretched over his shoes and had a splotch of bright blood on his shirtsleeve.

Larry's head and face had filled with a rattlesnake's buzz and he heard himself whisper something that sounded like silence.

The man in the mask shook his head and moved the gun from one hand to the other, both gloves now stained red.

"Die," he said again.

Okay with Larry.

Chapter Two

Silas Jones was his name but people called him 32, his baseball number, or Constable, his occupation. He was himself the sole law enforcement of Chabot, Mississippi, population give or take five hundred, driver of its ancient Jeep with its clip-on flashing light, licensed registrant of its three firearms and Taser, possessor of a badge he usually wore on a lanyard around his neck. Today, Tuesday, it lay on the seat beside him as he returned from afternoon patrol. On a back road shortcut toward the town, he glanced out his window and saw how full of buzzards the easterly sky had grown. There were dozens of them, dark smudges against darker clouds like World War II photographs he'd seen of flak exploding around bomber planes.

He braked and downshifted and did a three-point turn and pulled onto a small dirt road. He looked for signs of a dog or deer hit by a car or four-wheeler and saw nothing except a box turtle on the pavement like a wet helmet. Might be something near the creek, a mile or so down the hill, hidden in the trees. He shifted into first and nosed the Jeep into the mud and slid and yawed over the road until he found its ruts. He let the steering wheel guide itself until the road curved around a bend in the woods and he began the slow process of braking in mud. When he'd stopped it was in front of an aluminum gate with a yellow POSTED: NO HUNTING sign, signature of the Rutherford Lumber Company. The signs were everywhere in this part of the county (and the next) – the wealthy Rutherford family owned the mill in Chabot as well as thousands of acres for timber farming. Sometimes higher-ups, always white folks, got to hunt whitetail deer or turkeys on prime plots. But out here, these acres were mostly loblolly pines ready to be cut, orange slash-marks on some trees, red flags stapled onto others.

Silas got out and his sunglasses fogged. He took them off and hung them in his collar and stretched and smelled the hot after-rain and listened to the shrieking blue jays, alone at the edge of a wall of woods, miles from anywhere. If he wanted, he could fire his .45 and nothing or nobody in the world would hear other than some deer or raccoons. Least of all Tina Rutherford, the nineteen-year-old college student, white girl, he was both hoping and hoping not to find under the cloud of buzzards. Daughter of the mill owner, she'd left home at the end of summer, headed back north to Oxford, to Ole Miss, where she was a junior. Two days had passed before her mother, worried, had phoned. When her roommates confirmed that she'd never arrived, a missing persons report had gone out. Now every cop in the state was looking, especially those around here: forget everything else and find this girl.

Silas searched through a wad of keys for the one with a green tag and let himself in the gate and drove through and parked on the other side and closed the gate and locked it behind him.

Chapter Two

to float through (here): to drive through quietly

to angle to tilt
trunk *Stamm*
to bump to move rapidly up and down
jurisdiction area of responsibility
to requisition to request
clunker (coll.) old car in need of repair
faint barely visible
tailgate back door
to crackle to make small, sharp sounds

vine *Kletterpflanze*
to clear-cut to completely cut down
shelved with rows of mushroom with rows of fungus growths up and down the trunk

hill tropic i.e. tropical-like hill
charged *geladen*

snare-roll like the sound of a snare drum (*Schnarrtrommel*)

hollow (AE) valley
to set off (here): to cause to make noises
cattail a marsh plant
reeds *Schilfgrass*
slough [sluː] swamp
wake (here): movement of water behind s.th. swimming
bloop sound of a bubble
faded the colours and print now faint
cove small bay
turn bend in a stream
to litter to throw away empty bottles, cans, or wrapping

Back in the Jeep, he cranked down his window and floated through identical pine trees, tall wet bitterweed in the middle of the road wiping the hood like brushes at a carwash.

Where the land slanted down the trees had angled their trunks gracefully like arms bent at the elbow. He bumped and slid along half hoping he'd get stuck. Since much of his work in his rural jurisdiction involved dirt roads, he kept requisitioning the Chabot town council for a new Bronco. Kept not getting it, too, stuck with this clunker that, in a past life, had been a mail truck – you could still see a faint US POSTAL on its little tailgate.

His radio crackled. "You coming, 32?"

Voncille. If Silas was the Chabot police force, she was City Hall.

"Can't, Miss Voncille," he said. "Got something I want to check out here."

She sighed. If he wasn't there to do it, she'd have to put on the orange vest and direct traffic at the mill entrance for the early shift change.

"You owe me" she said. "I just got my hair done."

He rogered and hung the radio on his belt and shook his head at what he was about to do to his good leather boots.

He slowed to five miles an hour. When the road ended at the bottom of the hill he braked but kept moving, his own private mud slide. The Jeep turned by itself and he turned with it and soon had it stopped. He took his cowboy hat off the seat beside him and got out and pushed his door to and passed into the trees and descended the hill, digging his heels in the wet carpet of leaves, slipping once and grabbing a vine, which rained a pail's worth of water on him. Prettier land down here and, too steep to clear-cut, trees other than pines. The trunks were darker in the rain, some shelved with rows of mushroom or layered in moss. The air grew cooler the lower he went and at the bottom he brushed at his shoulders and emptied his hat, the hill tropic behind him, its odor of rain and worms, dripping trees, the air charged as if lightning had just struck, squirrels flinging themselves through patches of sky and the snare-roll of a woodpecker a few hollows over, the cry of an Indian hen.

He picked his way along the water's edge, setting off a series of bullfrogs from the cattails and reeds. Cane Creek was more like a slough, he thought. It hardly moved at all, its blackberry water stirred only by the wakes of frogs or bubbles from the bottom or the bloops fish made. Among floating leaves and dark black sticks, liquor bottles and their reflections and faded beer cans and theirs had collected in coves and turns, and he wondered who the hell would come all the way out here to litter. He fanned his face again, insects like toy planes propellering madly through the high branches. Might just be a bobcat, he thought. Come down to the creek to die. That old instinct: hurt, head for water.

Chapter Two

He thought of his mother, dead eight years. The time the two of them lived in a hunting cabin on land owned by a white man. No water in the place, no electricity, no gas. They'd been squatters there for less than a week when a one-eared tomcat appeared on the porch just past dark, scrotum big as a walnut. They shooed it off but morning found it lying at the steps with a twitching mouse in its jaws. My Lord, his mother said, that cat's applying for a job. They hired it and it insinuated itself all the way onto his mother's bed, where she said it warmed her feet. They moved from that cabin a few months later and the cat moved with them. It would live with them for years, but then, just before he left to go to Oxford his senior year, the cat disappeared. By the time he noticed, his mother said it had been gone nearly a month.

"Where?"

"Just off, baby," she said.

"Off?"

She was washing clothes in the sink, still in her hairnet from work. "To die, Silas," she'd said. 'When an animal's time come, it goes off to die."

The underbrush thinned as he went, the air hotter, muggier, and suddenly the trees had thrown open their arms to a high white sky, a burst of glowing logs and schools of steaming toadstools and clouds of gnats, wet leaves sparkling like mirrors and a spiderweb's glowing wires. A mosquito whined past his ear and he slapped at his arms and neck, going faster, leaves plastered to his boots, aware of a sharpness to the air, now a sweet rot.

Something fifty yards ahead began to lurch toward him. He stopped and thumbed the quick-release of his sidearm as other things moved as well, the earth floor stirring to life. But the thing veered away flapping into the air, just a buzzard, feet hanging, and then others were winging their duffle bodies over the water or waddling up the bank.

The odor grew worse as he stepped closer to where the land gave over to swamp. Farther down more of the birds lined the bank like crows on steroids, unfeathered necks and heads and some with faces red and tumored as a rooster's, some stepping from one scaled claw to the other and some with their beaks open.

He hoped not to have to shoot any as he mushed along fanning the air with his hand. Here he was two years as Chabot's law and he'd never fired his pistol except at targets. Practice. Never for real. Not even a turtle on a log.

Another of the ungainly birds heaved itself from the bank and kicked the swamp face, breaking its own image, and flapped up to the knuckled low branch it stood clasping and unclasping with its feet. He remembered somebody, Larry Ott, telling him that once a flock of buzzards took to roosting in a tree, the tree began to die. He could smell why. He took a ripe breath and went on as the limbs closed in again. He ducked a low vine, wary of snakes. Cottonmouth-moccasins, his mother used to call them. Mean ole things, she'd say.

---

squatter person living in building without permission

scrotum Hodensack
to twitch to make sudden, small, convulsive movements
jaw Kiefer
to insinuate oneself into s.th. to slowly move into a certain place

senior year last year of high school

muggy schwül

toadstool a kind of mushroom
gnat [næt] small fly that bites

rot decay
to lurch to make a sudden forward movement
quick-release safety switch

duffle thick
to waddle watscheln
swamp Sumpf
on steroids with drugs that strengthen the muscles
tumored i.e. with ugly growths
scaled schuppig
claw Klaue
beak Schnabel
to mush (here): to walk over wet land
law (here): law officer
ungainly clumsy
to heave oneself to lift oneself, especially when heavy
face (here): surface
knuckled (here): with small swellings
to clasp to hold tightly
to take to doing s.th. to start doing s.th.
ripe (here): deep
limb branch
wary cautious
ole (coll.) old

lump (here): loose pile
plaid *bunt kariert*
grown-up (here): ready for picking
lodged stuck
knee (here): part of the root of a tree that grows above the water in a swamp

decomposition *Verwesung*
to key to press the keys

secluded *abgelegen*

charred black from burning

disability (here): monthly compensation for a disability (*Körperbehinderung*)
allegedly *angeblich, vermeintlich*
weed (coll.) marijuana
to sting, stung, stung (coll.) to catch

barring except for
to flip on s.o. (coll.) *verraten*

simple assault not a serious physical attack

crackhead person who smokes crack

trespasser s.o. who enters a property without permission
to discern (formal) to determine

to prize to remove with difficulty
to mushroom to expand

Big and shiny as a black man's arm, and a mouth as white as the cotton he pick.

Silas took off his hat. In the distance, three or four lumps in rags of plaid clothing, lodged in the water among a vista of cypress trees and knees and buzzards black and parliamentary and all the flies a world could need. A large shadow passed him and he looked overhead where more buzzards circled yet, some at near altitudes not colliding but seeming to pass through one another, their wings and tail feathers sun-silvered at the tips. His mouth was dry.

These early birds had been at work awhile, and the heat hadn't helped. From this far off, and at this level of decomposition, an ID should have been impossible. But Silas shook his head. Keyed his radio.

It was the plaid, he'd later tell French.

A few days back Silas had been called out to a secluded area behind a grown-up cotton field off Dump Road. An old Chevy Impala burning. The driver of a passing garbage truck had seen smoke and radioed it in.

Silas knew the car from its charred vanity plates, M&M, Morton Morrisette's nickname. He'd played second base to Silas's shortstop in high school. After graduation M&M had worked for a dozen years at the mill until he hurt his back; now he got a small disability and, allegedly, sold weed on the side. Because he was smart and careful, and because he avoided narcotics, he'd never been stung by the police. Watched, yes: French and the county narcotics investigator managed to keep their eyes on nearly every known or suspected dealer in the county, but barring violence or a complaint, or someone flipping on him, they'd had to let him be, and M&M had sold his marijuana to trusted locals both black and white since the early 1990s.

Regarding the burning car, Silas had called French – for anything higher than simple assault, he had to notify the chief investigator. French arrived quickly and took over and within twenty-four hours had found an elderly woman who'd seen a man matching the description of a well-known crackhead in the car with M&M. French and the narcotics investigator had been watching this man – Charles Deacon – for a while and used this occasion to swear out a warrant. But thus far they hadn't found him. Or M&M either, for that matter. While Silas had gone back to his patrols, looking for trespassers on Rutherford land, writing tickets, directing traffic, moving roadkill, French had searched M&M's house and discerned that somebody, presumably M&M, had been shot there and then moved. Though the place had been carefully wiped down, they'd still found a few blood specks and prized from the wall a .22 bullet, mushroomed so badly from impact that it would likely be of no use. They did not, however, locate the gun. As for drugs, they found nothing but a pack of Top rolling papers, not even any shake. A few days later, they'd found M&M's plaid fedora snagged in a tree near a creek miles away, in Dentonville.

But since the Rutherford girl's disappearance, everybody had back-burnered Deacon and all but forgotten M&M.

Silas was sitting on a fallen log upwind from the body. Even here, the edge of the swamp, he could see how swollen M&M's face was – the size of a pillow, blacker than he'd been while alive and grotesque and pink where the skin had split, eyes and tongue eaten out, much of his flesh torn by the buzzards, a long lazy line of entrails snaking away in the water.

Silas thought he smelled cigarette smoke and was about to turn around when someone tapped him on the back.

"Shit," he said, nearly coming off the log.

Standing behind him, French set his investigator's kit down. "Boo," he said.

"That ain't funny, Chief."

French, a former game warden and a Vietnam vet, laughed and showed his small sharp teeth. He was late fifties, tall and thin, pale green eyes behind his sunglasses and close-cropped red hair and matching mustache. He had a blade for a chin and ears that stuck out and that he could move individually. Said his nickname in Nam had been Doe. He wore blue jeans and a tucked-in camo T-shirt that showed a Glock 9 mm in a beefy hand, aimed at the viewer. YOU HAVE THE RIGHT TO REMAIN SILENT, his chest said, FOREVER. The pistol on his belt was a dead match to the one on his shirt.

He said, "M&M?"

Silas flapped his hand toward the body. "What the buzzards and catfish done left of him."

"You go out there?"

"Hell naw."

"Good."

Above all, the CI hated having his crime scenes disturbed. He bent to see Silas's face and smirked. "You go puke in that water yonder the catfish'll eat it."

Silas ignored him, looked up at what sky showed through the trees and swirling buzzards. He thought of M&M when they were kids, how every time you bought a candy bar at recess he'd be there asking for a piece. If not for school lunches, he and his red-eyed sisters would've starved.

French sat with a Camel hanging on his bottom lip and slipped off his boots and set them side by side on the log and pulled on a pair of waders, adjusting the suspenders.

"Watch out for gators," Silas said.

French smushed out his cigarette on the log and put the butt in his shirt pocket and pulled on a pair of latex gloves.

"I shall return," he said and rose and walked off like a fisherman, not even pausing as the swamp began, slogging out, lowering with each step as if descending a staircase, his wake gently dissolving behind him.

---

disappearance *Verschwinden*

entrails organs inside the body

game warden *Jadgaufseher*
vet (coll., AE) veteran

blade *Klinge*
Nam (colloquial, AE) Vietnam
camo (coll.) camouflage
beefy thick and strong

dead match exact copy

naw (slang) no

to smirk *grinsen*
to puke [pjuːk] (coll.) to vomit

to swirl to move in circles
recess (AE) *Pause*

Camel™ brand of cigarette
waders rubber boots attached to waterproof trousers
suspenders *Hosenträger*
gator (coll., AE) alligator
to smush (coll.) to crush
butt the unsmoked end of a cigarette

to slog out to move forward with great difficulty
to dissolve to disappear

caw sound a crow makes

unperturbed *gelassen, unbeirrt*
to slosh around to move about in water

to work one's way up the ladder *sich hocharbeiten*
to shrug off (here): to remove by moving your shoulders
to flex to move about

to dump to get rid of
thunk (dialect) thought
brung (dialect) brought
to thow (Southern dialect) (throw) **s.o. off** to cause s.o. to come to the wrong conclusion – "Thow" for "throw" is used several times in the novel.
honcho (ironic) boss

coroner public official who determines the cause of death
to bumble to walk awkwardly
to curse *fluchen*
pigeon-toed *mit einwärtsgerichteten Füßen*
pucker a slightly, round, forward position
milk shake milk mixed with ice cream
to sniffle to inhale noisily
sinus [ˈsaɪnəs] *Nebenhöhle*

spine *Rückgrat*
wangdangler (vulgar) penis

Gone try. (coll.) Going to try.
chubby rather fat
denim blue cotton cloth as used for jeans

lip (here): narrow, projecting strip
yall (southern dialect) you all

Overhead, crows were swirling, too, their caws something Silas had been hearing awhile, saying whatever crows said.

Near the body and in water to his waist, the chief bent, seemingly unperturbed by the smell or sight. He fished his digital camera from his pocket and began to take pictures, sloshing around to get every angle. Then he stood for a long time, just looking. From Game & Fish, he'd got on at the sheriff's department and worked his way up the ladder to his current position. Rumor was he might run for sheriff when the present one retired next year.

After a while he came back and sat on the log and shrugged the suspenders off and kicked out of the waders, flexing his feet.

"How deep's it get out there?" Silas asked.

French grunted, pulling on his boots. "Deep enough to dump a body, somebody thunk. All this rain brung him up."

"You figure his hat floated all the way to Dentonville?"

"Upstream?"

"Somebody trying to thow you off then."

"Be my guess, honcho. I'd say we dealing with above-average criminal intelligence."

"That eliminates Deacon."

"Maybe."

French pulled his boots on and rose and took more pictures from the bank, shook out another Camel.

Soon the birds went all aflutter again and a pair of paramedics and the coroner came bumbling out of the trees slapping their arms, cursing. One of the EMTs was Angie, a pretty, light-skinned girl, petite, slightly pigeon-toed, that Silas had been seeing a few months now, getting more exclusive by the week. Thing he liked best about her was her mouth, how it was always in a little pucker, off to the side, always working, like she had an invisible milk shake. She sniffled, too, from bad sinuses, and weird as it was, he found it cute.

Tab Johnson, her driver, an older white man who always seemed to be shaking his head, was doing so now, chewing his Nicorette gum.

Angie stood behind Silas and touched her shoulder to his back and he leaned into her thinking of the night before, her on top and her face buried in his neck, her slow hips and breath in his ear. Now her hand was going up his spine. She smelled like her bedsheets and suddenly what she called his "wangdangler" moved his pants. She sniffled and he looked down at her, over his shoulder.

"You coming over tonight?" she asked.

"Gone try."

She moved her hand. Here came the coroner, a young chubby white man in a denim button-down, glasses on forehead. Had a few years on the job. He'd ridden out with Angie and them and came between the two with his bag and his shirt out at the back and walked to the lip of the land, shading his eyes with his hand.

He said, "I pronounce it dead. Yall go ahead."

"Yuck," Angie said, glancing up at Silas. "You couldn't a found this on second shift?" She stuck out her tongue and headed down the bank, snapping on a pair of rubber gloves, fastening a surgical mask to her face.

Now the reporter who had the police beat and a couple of deputies were coming down the hill, and Silas took the occasion to walk around some more, hoping to find a cigarette butt floating, a thread snagged in a spiderweb. And to avoid seeing them roll the pieces into the body bag.

A couple of hours later, back at the office, he sat brooding. He and M&M had fallen out of touch when he left in high school and now he wished he'd stayed in better contact. Maybe he could've done something. But who was he kidding. M&M wouldn't have had anything to do with a constable. He'd be polite, that was all. No friendly visits. No fishing.

Silas was at his computer, deleting e-mails, but paused at one from Shannon Knight, the police reporter, called "follow-up question." He opened the e-mail and pecked out an answer. Even though he'd found the body, he knew Shannon would interview French as well, and he would be the one quoted in the paper.

Silas sat back in his chair. He shared the one-room building of the Chabot Town Hall with Voncille, the town clerk, her desk to the left by the window that faced trees. She got the good view, she said, because she'd been here longer than him and the mayor combined, plus neither of them was ever at his desk. Fine with Silas. Except for when he left the seat up in their shared bathroom, he and Miss Voncille got along fine. They were Chabot's only full-time employees, their benefits coming through the mill. Morris Sheffield, the mayor, part-time, kept a desk in the back; he was a real estate agent with an office across the lot. He bopped in Town Hall once or twice a day with his BlackBerry and loose tie and loafers with no socks. He and Silas were both volunteer firefighters and only saw each other at monthly office meetings and the occasional fire.

"You okay, hon?" Voncille asked, rolling her chair back. Her desk was behind a cubicle wall she'd bought herself. She had blue eyes and a pretty, fat face and looked at him over her reading glasses. She was white, early fifties, divorced a couple of times. Her stack of stiff red hair seemed unperturbed by her morning of directing traffic.

"Yes, ma'am," he said. "I will be."

"Poor ole M&M," she said. "Didn't yall play ball together?"

"Back in the day we could turn the double bout as good as any two boys anywhere."

"Yall still talk? I mean before."

"Not really."

She bunched her shoulders, both understanding and disapproving at the same time. But who did he see but other cops and the people he arrested? Just Angie. Who else did he need?

---

yuck expression to indicate disgust

police beat being assigned to cover crime stories

to brood to think a lot about s.th. upsetting

to peck out to type with two fingers

town clerk (AE) person in charge of the records of a town

through the mill i.e., from the taxes of the owners of the sawmill
real estate agent *Makler*
lot parking lot
to bop in (coll.) to casually appear
loafers shoes you can slip your feet into

unperturbed (here): unaffected

bout (coll.) about

to bunch (here): to raise

Chapter Two

to prop up to support

diner small restaurant
convenience store small market

mill crowd employees of the sawmill
to make out to have sex with s.o.
to knock out of gear to accidentally disconnect the engine from the gearbox (*Gangschaltung*)
gully deep channel formed by running water
vagrant person without a home and job
kudzu climbing plant that grows rapidly

feral wild
to rove to roam
fleet *flink*
spirit ghost

DUI tally number of people caught driving while drunk
county seat *Kreisstadt*
high cotton (southern AE) sensational
spate amount

tanker railway car that transports liquids
rumbling making low, rolling sounds

shed simple, single-story building

skidder tractor for hauling logs
to untusk (here): *entladen*
limber flexible
plank *Brett*
to creosote to preserve with chemicals
maintenance *Wartung*
accountant *Buchhalter*

per se really

emphysemic (humorous) sickly

Voncille was back to work and Silas leaned forward. Out the window by his desk, propped up with an old Stephen King book, were Chabot's other buildings: Mayor Mo's real estate, the post office, a bank that was more of a credit union for the mill, a diner/convenience store called The Hub, an IGA grocery store and a drugstore, both going out of business because of the Wal-Mart in Fulsom. The third-to-last establishment, the Chabot Bus, was an old yellow school bus on blocks that had been converted into a bar, a counter at the back end and a few plastic tables and chairs inside and several more outside. Silas met Angie there for drinks a couple of times a week, later in the evening, after the mill crowd had gone home. The first time they met there, by accident, they'd closed the bar then made out in his Jeep until they knocked it out of gear and nearly rolled off into the gully before he pulled the emergency brake. Looking out the row of bus windows, you saw the last two buildings, empty offices with boarded windows. Silas checked them nightly for vagrants and crackheads. You saw, too, that Chabot had been built on the edge of a gully filled with kudzu, that snaky green weed nothing could kill. Somebody kept throwing trash in the gully, which brought raccoons and feral cats, roving stretches of ink in the leaves at night, fleet as spirits.

Chabot didn't have an ATM; the nearest was eleven miles north, in Fulsom. Cell phones worked in Chabot sometimes and sometimes they didn't. Because Gerald County, wet, was bordered on two sides by dry counties, the DUI tally was high. Fulsom was the county seat and, with its Wal-Mart, high cotton compared to Chabot's little spate of stores. Chabot's one barber had died, and his son had come and dismantled the building a piece at a time and carried it off in his pickup truck. Now its lot was vacant, an explosion of wildflowers and weeds, and if you wanted your hair cut, you went to Fulsom or did it yourself.

Because of the gully, Chabot's buildings all faced east, like a small audience or a last stand: out Town Hall's front windows, across the road and beyond strings of railcars and tankers, the tall, rumbling city of the Rutherford Lumber Mill. It blocked the trees behind it and burned the sky with smoke, one giant metal shed after another, smokestacks with red bleeping lights, conveyor belts and freight elevators below, log trucks, loaders and skidders beeping backward or grinding over sawdust to untusk limber green logs soon to be cut to planks and treated or creosoted for poles. The mill boomed-gnashed-screeched and threw its boards and sparks and dust and exhaled its fumes sixteen hours a day, six days a week. Two eight-hour shifts and a six-hour maintenance shift. Its offices were a two-story wooden structure a hundred yards past the mill, two dozen people there, accountants, salesmen, secretaries, administration. Some even got company trucks, big green Ford F-250s with four-wheel drive.

Not Silas. He wasn't a mill employee per se, so he got what Chabot could afford. His Jeep, purchased at auction, was over thirty years old. It had an emphysemic air conditioner and a leaky master cylinder, an addict to both Freon and brake fluid. Not to mention oil. Its odometer had stopped on 144,007. When he complained it was an old mail Jeep, Voncille said, "Count your blessings, 32. You lucky the steering wheel's on the right, and by that I mean left, side."

Around one, French called to say he was at The Hub across the parking lot. Did Silas want anything?

"*Hell* naw," he said and the chief laughed and hung up.

A few minutes later he came in the front door with a greasy brown bag and a Coke and took Mayor Mo's desk and uncrinkled the sack and removed an oyster po'boy.

"Where's his highness?"

Silas raised his chin. "Out buying land."

"Roy," Voncille said, leaning around her cubicle, pictures of her kids push-pinned over nearly every inch of it. "I don't see how you can eat from the same place every day."

"Hell," he said, chewing, "ain't got no choice. I done arrested somebody or other in ever goddamn joint in the county. Busboys, dishwashers, waitresses, fry cooks, owners, silent partners. Marla" – the cook at The Hub – "she's got a get-out-of-jail-free pass up to and including premeditated murder, long as she keeps feeding me. I gotta eat."

"What about Linda?"

Chewing. "Time she gets off work she don't do nothing but sit in front of the TV watching reality."

When he finished his last bite he wadded the paper into a ball and threw it into the wastebasket by Silas's desk. He slurped the rest of his Coke and got his Camels and shook one out.

"Don't you light that," Voncille called.

French lit it anyway, grinning at her sigh, the way she stapled harder.

"FYI," he told Silas. "Paid me a visit to Norman Bates other day."

Silas glanced over. "Who?"

"From *Psycho*," Voncille said. "He means Larry Ott."

French blew a ray of smoke. "Always do it with a missing person, especially a girl. You know. The usual suspects."

Silas frowned. "You think Larry had something to do with the Rutherford girl?"

"*Larry*?"

Silas regretted saying it. "I was in school with him's all. Knew him a little way back when."

"He didn't play ball, did he?" Voncille asked.

"Naw. Just read books."

"Horror books," French said. "His house is full of em."

"Find any dismembered bodies?"

"Nah. I'll run by his shop a little later. See if I can spook him some more. Went this morning but he wasn't open yet."

"What time?" Silas asked.

He thought about it. "Twenty minutes ago."

to creak (here): to move with a creak (*Knarren*)	

"Shop wasn't open"

The CI shook his head.

Silas creaked back in his chair and folded his arms. "You ever know of him *not* being open during business hours?"

"So what. He ain't had a customer in I don't know how long. Don't matter if he's in or not."

there's being there, is

"Yeah, but that ain't never stopped him from there's what I'm saying. Monday through Saturday, regular as clockwork. Don't even take lunch usually."

to recline to lean back
ankle *Fußknöchel*
holster leather case that holds a pistol

"Guess who's the detective now," French said, reclining in the mayor's chair. He stretched out his legs and adjusted his ankle holster with the opposite foot. "You ever see that other movie Alfred Hitchcock did, Voncille?"

"Which one?"

"*The Birds*?"

"Long time ago."

younguns (coll.) children, young persons

"All them buzzards and crows this morning reminded me of it. Seen it at the drive-in, when we was younguns. After it was over my little brother says, 'You know what? I wish that really would happen. With birds like that. Just going crazy. We could find us some football helmets and a bunch of guns and ammo and go on the road, just killing birds and saving people.'"

ammo (coll.) ammunition

barely *kaum*

Silas barely heard. He was thinking of how, not long after he'd returned to south Mississippi, Larry Ott had called and left him a message on his home phone.

"Miss Voncille," Silas said. "You went to Fulsom High, didn't you? Did you know Larry Ott?"

"Not really hon," she said. "Just of him. He was a few years behind me."

to wink *zwinkern*
to snort to noisily breathe through your nose to show you are amused

The CI winked at Silas. "You ever go out with him, Voncille?"

"Just the once," she said. "I was never heard from again."

French snorted. "We wish."

puddle *Pfütze*
spongy *schwammig*
breed race
7 i.e. Highway 7
kitty (coll.) *Kasse*
to gnaw [nɔː] **at s.o.** to continuously trouble s.o.

Silas had been driving north on Highway 11 for ten minutes before he realized he was heading toward Larry Ott's garage. It was early afternoon, the rain gone at last, puddles steaming in the road, a spongy dog of some unidentifiable breed shaking water from its fur. He ought to be over on 7, watching for speeders, getting his quota for the week, make a little cash for the city kitty, but something was gnawing at him.

landline *Festnetz*

Larry's first phone call had been nearly two years ago. Silas didn't use his landline much and had gone a couple of days without noticing the answering machine had been blinking.

to mash (here): to push with force

"Hello?" the voice said when he mashed the button. "Hello? I hope I got the right number. I'm looking for Silas Jones. If I got the wrong number I apologize."

He had stared at the phone. Nobody called him Silas anymore. Not since his mother died.

Chapter Two

"Silas?" the recording went on. "I don't know if you'll remember me, but this is Larry. Larry Ott? I'm sorry to bother you, but I just wanted to, um, talk. My number is 633-2046. "Silas made no move to copy it down as Larry cleared his throat. "I seen you was back," he continued. "Thank you, Silas. Good night."

He'd never returned Larry's call – if Larry had phoned him at Town Hall instead of home, he would've had to.

But then, instead of taking the hint, Larry tried again. Eight-thirty, a Friday night, couple of weeks later, Silas had stopped in for a change of clothes, on his way to eat, a date with some girl. Before Angie. When the phone rang he picked up and said, "Yeah?"

"Hello? Um, Silas?"

"Yeah."

"Hey."

"Who's this?"

"It's Larry. Ott. I'm sorry if I'm bothering you."

"Yeah, I was just heading out." The heat trickling from his chest. "What's up?"

Larry hesitated. "I just wanted to, you know, say welcome back. To the crooked letter."

"I gotta go," Silas said and hung up. He'd sat on the bed for half an hour, the back of his shirt stuck to his skin, remembering him and Larry when they were boys, what Silas had done, how he'd beaten Larry when Larry said what he said.

Silas felt clammy now as he drove. Since leaving he'd known Larry was ostracized, but it wasn't until he'd returned to lower Mississippi that he heard everything that had happened.

He rolled the Jeep up behind a log truck and slowed, the rag stapled to the longest pole fluttering. Taillights were fine, tag good. He eased over in the opposite lane and mashed the accelerator and the Jeep backfired. Piece of shit. He tooted his horn as he passed the truck, leaving clouds of ugly black smoke, and the driver blew his air horn back.

French was right that Ottomotive Repair hadn't had a local customer – or any customer, really – since Larry's father had died and Larry'd taken over. Silas could testify: in all the times he'd driven past on his way to Fulsom, he was yet to see anyone get their car fixed. Nobody but Larry there, that red Ford. Still, he showed up to work every day, waiting for somebody on his way to someplace else, somebody who didn't know Larry's reputation, to stop in for a tune-up or brake job, the bay door always raised and waiting, like something with its mouth open.

Larry was taller now, thinner. Silas hadn't seen him close but his face looked thin, his lips tight. Used to be, his mouth always hung open, giving the impression he was slow. But he wasn't. He was smart. Knew the weirdest shit. Once told Silas a king cobra could grow to over sixteen feet long and raise eight or nine of those feet

---

to clear your throat *sich räuspern*

to trickle to flow (the sweat from the heat) slowly in a small stream

gotta (slang) have to

clammy uncomfortably damp
to ostracize *ausstoßen*

tag (here): license update
to ease over to move slowly into a certain direction

to toot the horn *hupen*

to testify (here): *bestätigen*

reputation *Ruf*
brake job repairing the brakes

king cobra large cobra that can grow to 18 feet (5.5 meters)

to bottleneck to become narrow

to sprout sprießen
posted with signs saying trespassing is not allowed
vintage of former styles
stock Inventar
busted (coll.) broken
shingled covered with shingles (*Shindel*) from the roof
to sag to hang down
to buckle to become bent
to cater to s.th. to provide some special service for people
quickie (coll.) quick sex
fading slowly losing color

stint short period of time

to quit (here): to leave

occasional gelegentlich
to front to direct towards the front

caster small wheel

to squeal quietschen
knock sudden, loud sound
cinder block Schlackenstein

quaint pleasingly old-fashioned
trim decoration along the edge of s.th.
to flake off to come off in thin layers
laundry detergent Waschmittel
to pull in to drive in

into the air. Imagine it, he'd said. Like a giant swaying scaled plant from another time looking down at you right before you died.

Silas passed the Wal-Mart and then the arrowed sign to Fulsom's business district. Soon the road bottlenecked down to a two-lane and the businesses became sparse, the sidewalks cracked, sprouting weeds, buildings posted, windows and doors boarded. He passed what used to be a post office. He passed a clothing store that had gone so long without customers it'd briefly become a vintage clothing store without changing stock. Building on his right was an ex-Radio Shack, windows busted or shot out and the roof fallen in so thoroughly the floor was shingled, the walls beginning to sag and buckle. The only businesses still open on this end were a cheap motel that catered to quickies and Mexican laborers and the garage he was approaching, OTTOMOTIVE REPAIR painted on the side in fading green letters.

Larry's pickup, as French had said, wasn't in its usual spot, the bay door closed. Silas slowed. He signaled and turned into the garage lot and came to a stop by the gas pumps, as if he wanted to fill up. This the closest he'd been to the shop since . . . well, he'd never been this close. The two antique pumps hadn't worked in years, though, and looked like a pair of robots on a date. In raised, white-painted numbers on metal tape readouts were the prices when they'd last been used: .32 regular and .41 ethyl.

Silas switched the Jeep off, his eyes settling on the rectangle of dead grass by the shop where, except for a stint in the army, Larry had parked every day since he quit high school. The same truck. Driving the same miles to and from the same house. Same stop signs, stop lights. Nothing to show but dead grass.

Inside the shop, he knew, there was a red toolbox, a pump handle jack, creepers against the wall, drop lights hanging from the ceiling. Occasionally as he drove past, Silas had seen Larry leaning on his push broom watching cars. Silas would front his eyes as if he had someplace important to go. Other days Larry would have rolled his toolbox out on its casters so he could watch traffic as he wiped his wrenches and sockets with a shop rag. Sometimes he'd wave.

Nobody waved back. Nobody local anyway. But say you were from out of town, you were passing through with your brakes squealing, a bearing singing, a knock in the shocks, maybe. Say you'd been worried about breaking down when you saw the white cinder block shop, quaint, green-painted trim flaking off, the building itself the color of powder laundry detergent, maybe you'd slow down and pull in. You'd notice the gas pumps and smile (or frown) at the prices. You'd see no other customers and count yourself lucky, for by now Larry would be walking outside pulling a rag from his pocket, his name on his shirt. Short brown hair, cap pulled too low over his ears.

Lucky you.

But you wouldn't know his reputation. That, in high school, a girl who lived up the road from Larry had gone to the drive-in movie with him and nobody had seen her again. It had been big news, locally. Her stepfather tried to have Larry arrested but no body was found and Larry never confessed.

Silas looked at his watch then sat a moment longer. He had known Cindy Walker, too. The missing girl. In a way, Larry had introduced them.

He glanced up the road.

Where the hell was Larry? Probably sitting at home, reading Stephen King. Maybe he finally took a day off. Or gave up.

But still the gnawing. What if some relation of the current missing girl, Tina Rutherford, dwelling on Larry's reputation, had taken it upon himself to pay Larry a visit?

Look at you, 32 Jones, he thought. You done ignored the poor fucker all this time and now all the sudden you care?

"32?" The radio.

"Yeah, Miss Voncille?"

"You need to get over to Fourteenth and West. It's a rattlesnake in somebody's mailbox."

"Say what?"

"Rattler," she repeated. "Mailbox."

"Was the flag up?"

"Ha-ha. Mail carrier reported it. It being, you know, in the box? That makes it a federal crime."

"How you know that?"

"32," she said. "You only been in that uniform two years. You know how long I been setting in this chair?"

"So it's happened before?"

"You don't even want to know. I'll call Shannon."

He signed off, glad Voncille would contact the police reporter. Anytime he got his picture or name in the paper, it raised his profile, which might boost his salary at evaluation time. Enough good PR he could be a black Buford Pusser, maybe run at sheriff himself in ten years.

He could head over to Larry's house later, he thought, cranking the Jeep. But then he got a better idea and flipped his cell phone open.

"32," Angie said. "You ain't got another decomposing corpse, do you?"

"Hope not," he said. "What's going on?"

Not much, she reported. Wrapping up a one-car on 5, no injuries except the dead deer. Trooper had already split. Tab and the guy who'd hit the deer were field dressing it, planning to split the meat. "Tab say you want a tenderloin?"

"Angie," he said. "You know Larry Ott?"

Her phone crackled. "Scary Larry?"

"Yeah. Feel like following a hunch?"

"May be, baby. Tell me more."

I need yall to run out there when you got a minute. Little dirt road in Chabot, off Campground Cemetery Road."

"I know where he stays. How come?"

---

current *aktuell, gegenwärtig*
to dwell on s.th. to think a lot about s.th.
to take it upon yourself to do s.th. to decide to take a course of action

mail carrier mailman

to sign off (radio) to say goodbye and disconnect
to boost (coll.) to increase
evaluation time time when a person's job performance is judged

to crank to start up

to wrap up (coll.) to finish up
one-car one car accident
trooper state trooper – policeman who works for the state police force
to split (coll.) to leave
to dress (here): to remove the innards and prepare for cooking
to split (here): to share
tenderloin the best meat
to crackle *knistern*
hunch feeling s.th. is true

"Just when you got a minute. See if the place looks clean. It ain't far from where yall at now."

"Hang on," she said.

He pulled to the edge of the highway and waited for a log truck, the Jeep shaking as the truck thundered past with its logs bouncing.

"Angie?"

"All right," she said. "But 32?"

"Yeah?"

"This means you going to church with me on Sunday."

"We'll talk," he said. "And save me that tenderloin."

He could cover his jurisdiction one end to the other, Dump Road to the catfish farm, in fifteen minutes if he stuck his light on and hauled ass, like today, and soon he'd neared Fourteenth Avenue. Silas thought of it as White Trash Ave., a hilly red clay road with eight or ten houses and trailers clustered along the left side and Rutherford land on the right, fenced off and posted every fifty yards, an attempt to keep the rednecks from shooting deer and turkeys in the woods. Wildlife was good for the mill's image. You rode through the pines braking for deer, sometimes fawns on clumsy legs, rare red foxes, bobcats, you almost forgot for a moment the trees were a crop.

He patrolled through here once or twice a week, different times, keeping his eye on an Airstream trailer out behind one of the houses, half blocked from the road by a shed. The way the trailer's windows were boarded up, its door padlocked, made him think it might be a crystal meth lab but, without probable cause – a neighbor complaining, an explosion – he couldn't check it out.

Every time he cruised past, the white residents frowned from chairs on their porches, thin tattooed bleach-blond women with babies on their laps, strained-looking grandmothers in housedresses smoking cigarettes, garbage in the yards, clotheslines with sheets lifting in the wind, sheer panties, nylons. In one yard was an old Chevy Vega, no hood, bitterweed growing through the engine block, windows broken, the trunk open – he'd seen a dog sitting in there once with its tongue out. Seen a goat on a rope, too, cast-off car parts speared by grass, fishing lures dripping from the power lines. An old camper shell used for a chicken coop and chickens and guinea hens running wild in the weeds. A duck in a kid's wading pool. Kids revving four-wheelers in the deep grass. He didn't know what it was about white folks and four-wheelers, but every damn house seemed to have one.

And the dogs.

Each place yielded half a dozen, rarely any known breed, mostly just Heinz 57s, a throng of unneutered, collarless barking mongrels waiting for his Jeep whenever he rounded the curve at the bottom of the hill, chasing him until the woods picked back up.

Here they came now, the whole furious, joyful tide of them, parting as he rode through, barking alongside the Jeep, three or four big dark ones loping along with bass voices, a few mediums and several small yappers. He saw the postal Jeep up ahead, newer model than his, nice paint job, parked to the side of the road in the shade, its flashers on. He knew the driver, a woman named Olivia. They'd met in the Chabot Bus and gone out a couple times, but she had two young boys. Silas wasn't much for kids and she wasn't much for a man who didn't swoon over her children. On one of their dates they'd discussed White Trash Ave., which he'd confessed to calling it, and she'd told him it was the bane of her route, she refused to get out and deliver any package to those white folks' doors because of the dogs. Instead, she'd blow her horn, which she knew pissed them off, and if nobody came, she'd just put a notification in the box, saying come to the post office. And why didn't he like children?

Olivia was out of her vehicle now, standing with four other women, all white, one holding a baby. Shannon hadn't gotten there yet. In the nearest yard, its grass to their knees, three boys, two crew cuts and a mullet, stood watching. One had a BB gun and another a plastic bow and arrow set.

Silas coasted to a stop and killed his engine, the dogs gathering at his door, one little biddy one that jumped so high it kept appearing in his window.

"Get down," he said, fingering his Taser, which, like his pistol, he'd never used.

"Sellars," a woman called, "get them damn dogs."

The boy with the BB gun, shirtless, dirty face, came to the Jeep and started kicking at them, allowing Silas to push his door open. The boy with the mullet joined him and helped drive the dogs back.

"Hey, 32," Olivia said.

"Hey, girl." He approached the crowd, carrying his camera, the women looking him up and down, him touching the brim of his hat.

"Hey," one young woman said. "I'm glad you here." She wore cut-off jeans and a tank top over a sports bra. She was barefooted. Attractive. Maybe twenty-two, -three years old. Tattoos on both forearms and one peeking from the low neck of her tank and another, a green vine, tracing up out of her jeans. You couldn't help but wonder where it started. "My name's Irina Mott."

"Hey, Mrs. Mott. 32 Jones."

She tilted her head and squinted cutely in the sun. "Just Irina."

"It's her mailbox," Olivia said.

"Her snake-of-the-month club arrived early," said another young woman, pierced nose, black eyeliner.

"Yeah," Irina said, "but I'd ordered a copperhead."

Olivia pointed to the mailbox, askew on its post and the address flaking off. "I'm driving along, and I start to open it and the next thing I know it's buzzing like a hornet's nest. I open it a crack more and heard something whop the door from the inside and I closed it right back."

Silas regarded the mailbox, then thumped its flag and heard the buzz start inside, like a tiny motor. "Can somebody get me a shovel?"

---

yapper (coll.) small dog

to swoon over s.th./s.o. to feel delighted about s.th./s.o.
to confess to admit
bane (here): horrible place
to refuse *sich weigern*
to piss s.o. off (slang) to anger s.o.

to gather *versammeln, sammeln*

brim *Krempe*

tank top sleeveless, collarless shirt

to peek (here): to be just visible
tracing out seemingly climbing out
to squint to almost shut the eyes

eyeliner make-up put around the eyes

askew not level, tilted
to flake off *abblättern*
crack (here): just a bit
to whop to beat

to thump to hit hard

to switch hips to change from one hip to the other TF	
to prompt to suggest	
to reckon to consider as a possibility	
to stall to try to delay taking action	
grit small pieces of sand or stone	
to bunch itself up to gather up in a pile	
to herd to bring together	
to lunge to suddenly move forward	
to cling, clung, clung to hold tightly	
to inflate and deflate to expand and then cause to reduce in size	
blur an unclear shape	

"Edward Reese," a fat woman said to one of the boys watching from the yard. "Run get one, hear?"

He disappeared around the house, dogs following him, tails wagging.

"What time you last open it?" he asked Irina.

"Last night, bout dark. Put my phone bill in."

"Yall got any idea who might've done this?" he asked.

The women frowning at one another, the one with the baby switching hips.

"Ex-husband?" Silas prompted. "Angry boyfriend?"

"Hell, Officer," Irina said. "It's three of us divorced girls live here. And between us? How many candidates you reckon, Marsha?"

"Oh Lord. You got to narrow it down."

"Angry's one list," Irina said. "Jealous is another. Then there's the biggest list of all."

"The crazy list" Marsha said. "Not to mention the all-of-the-aboves."

The boy came running up with the shovel and held it out, handle first.

"Thanks, son," Silas said, glancing down the road. He thought about stalling for Shannon. "Yall ladies back up."

"You ain't got to tell us twice," Marsha said.

Silas handed Olivia the camera and stood off to the side and with the spade end pulled the door open, the buzzing louder, sliding grit. The dogs were barking again.

"Careful," Olivia said.

He moved and peered in, not getting too close, the women behind him, looking around his back. The snake had bunched itself up in the rear of the box, triangle head flattened and low, angry slits for eyes, its tongue flicking.

"Look," Irina said. "It's done pissed on my phone bill."

"It stinks," one of the boys said, trying to herd the dogs.

"Diamondback," Silas said. Olivia handed him the camera and he made a few more pictures, then gave it back. Taking a breath, he eased the shovel in front of the box. The snake lunged and struck the metal and Irina screamed and when she grabbed his arm Silas jumped.

"Shit," he said. Then said, "Sorry," noticing the kids.

He eased the shovel up again, Irina still clinging to his arm. The snake struck and he pinned its neck against the edge of the box and then yanked it out and flung it on the ground where it coiled to a pile, inflating and deflating and its tail a blur and rattle rising.

"Yall watch out now," he said, the dogs closing in. "And try to get them dogs back."

"Shoot it," one of the boys said as he and the others began to kick the dogs away.

"No need for that." He moved the spade to its neck, its body wrapping itself up the pole. Pinning the head, he put his heel on the shovel and pressed it against the pavement and sawed at its head until it hung by a shred of skin, the body flopping and writhing, rattle still buzzing.

"Is it dead?" a boy asked.

"Yeah. But yall be careful." Suddenly he heard Larry's voice when he said, "That head'll still kill you. Them fangs is like needles."

"Can I have the rattles?" the mullet boy asked.

Silas looked at the women.

"Fine with me," the fat one said. "His birthday's next month." She winked to let him know it was a joke, and he bent to work cutting the dry cartilage off with the shovel and kicked it out of the snake's range. The boy picked it up and smelled it, then ran off shaking it, the other boys and the dogs following.

With the shovel, Silas scooped the diamondback, two feet long and heavy, still moving a little, and carried it across the road and flung it over the bobwire fence into the woods. Olivia left, declining to take the wet envelope, but Silas stayed around, getting statements awhile, making notes, thinking Shannon might come yet, trying not to flirt too much with Irina. He found himself telling the story about the time he tried to run over a snake, big brown cottonmouth with yellow stripes on it. In that very Jeep yonder. This after he'd just got back down here from Oxford.

"Oxford," Irina said.

"Hush," Marsha said, "and let him finish."

"You can't just roll over no snake and go on," Silas said, tipping back his hat, "cause that'll just make em mad. You gotta back over it and spin your tires if you want to kill it." That's what he was trying to do, he said, braking in the middle of the road, backing up, trying to stop on it. When he had its tail under his back driver-side tire, the snake biting the rubber, he popped the clutch. But instead of spinning out dead, the moccasin spun up, alive, into his wheel well. Silas drove forward leaning out with the door open, waiting for it to drop, to fall out from under his Jeep. "It never did," he said.

"Shit," Irina said. "What happened?"

It died up in there. In the rocker panel. Smelled bad for two months. Hottest part of the summer. Sometime," he said, "driving along, I swear I can still smell it."

The women were smiling.

"Served you right," Irina said.

When he glanced at his watch his smile left. He'd have to hurry to make it back to Chabot for the five-thirty shift change. He couldn't miss it again. Miss Voncille's hair was at stake.

"Ladies," he said, touching the brim of his hat, presenting Irina with one of the cards he'd paid for himself. "Call if yall remember anything else."

"Oh we will," Irina said.

Fifteen minutes later he stood on the road in front of the railroad tracks, in the orange vest and his sunglasses, so sweaty his hat was

shred small piece
to flop to move about loosely
to writhe [raɪð] to twist

fang sharp tooth

cartilage Knorpel
range Reichweite

to scoop to pick up with a shovel or large spoon
to decline to refuse

to pop the clutch to suddenly release the clutch (*Kupplung*)

wheel well the part of a car or truck that surrounds a tire

rocker panel the part of a car or truck under the door sill (*Türschwelle*)

to be at stake *auf dem Spiel sein*

a shade (here): a bit
to grumble to make a low, rolling sound
to drone to make a buzzing sound

hard-hat hair hair flattened by a safety helmet
cab part of truck where the driver and passengers sit

to screw up (slang) to ruin
to pitch to be the pitcher on a baseball team
to be discharged to be officially allowed to leave a position or job
frat fraternity (*Verbindung*)
to man (here): to watch over s.th., to be in charge of s.th.
hamlet small village
police work *Polizeiarbeit*
to blare to make a loud, unpleasant sound

foreman person in charge of a group of workers
to slam to push down heavily

to cast *werfen*
to lean on s.th. (here): to press down on s.th.
to spit, spat, spat *spucken*
to dig out (here): to get s.th. out with difficulty

heavy, his uniform a shade darker where it stuck to his belly. To his left the mill grumbled and droned and saws screamed out like people burning in a fire. He blew his whistle and held up his hands for both lanes of cars to stop, then stepped off the hot pavement and waved on the line of pickups waiting to leave the mill yard, dirty men with hard-hat hair lighting cigarettes in their air-conditioned cabs, some heading over to the Chabot Bus for a beer, which Silas wouldn't mind doing himself.

His cell phone began to buzz. He wasn't supposed to answer during the shift change and stood fanning the trucks on, the drivers in cars on the highway glaring at him as if he'd chosen to be out here screwing up their day, as if this had been his life's goal, the reason he'd destroyed his arm pitching college baseball and joined the navy and then, discharged, gone to the police academy in Tupelo and spent ten years babysitting students at Ole Miss, breaking up frat parties, manning the gate at football games, giving DUIs, years of preparation to come ruin their day. He thought this job would be different. *Constable*, the Internet ad had said *of a hamlet*. He'd had to look up *constable* and *hamlet*, but he liked both words and the job had promised police work, flexible hours, a vehicle.

More horns blared and he waved harder, each driver creeping his truck over the raised tracks. To further complicate things – a loud whistle from the north – here came the two-thirty freight train from Meridian, forty-five minutes late, rounding the curve under its storm of smoke and slowing as it readied to stop and be loaded with logs and poles. Blowing his whistle, Silas stepped in front of an oncoming truck, a big Ford F-250, with his hand up, and the driver, who happened to be the mill foreman, slammed on his brakes then rolled down his window.

"You could've let me through," he said. "Shit, 32, I'm going fishing."

Silas bit down on his whistle as the train approached, its shadow casting him in a moment of shade.

"God damn it," the foreman said and leaned on his horn.

Silas ignored him and took off his hat and spat out the whistle so it hung at his chest on its string, fanned himself with the hat. His cell was buzzing again. Fuck it, he thought and dug it out. Mayor Mo wanted to fire him for talking on the phone, let him.

"32?" It was Angie.

"Yeah?"

The phone crackled. "32," she said again. "We at Larry Ott's house like you said?"

"Yeah?"

"Oh my God," she said.

Chapter Three

The first thing he noticed was that they didn't have coats. It was just after dawn in March 1979, a Monday, Larry's father driving him to school and dragging a fume of blue exhaust behind his Ford pickup. The spring holidays had come and passed, but now a freakish cold snap had frozen the land, so frigid his mother's chickens wouldn't even leave the barn, the evergreens a blur outside the frosted truck window and him lost in yet another book. He was in eighth grade and obsessed with Stephen King and looked up from **Salem's Lot** when his father braked.

The pair of them was standing at the bend in the road by the store, a tall, thin black woman and her son, about Larry's age, a rabbit of a boy he'd seen at school, a new kid. He wondered what they were doing here, this far out, before the store opened. Despite the cold the boy wore threadbare jeans and a white shirt and his mother a blue dress the wind curved over her figure. She wore a cloth around her hair, breath torn from her lips like tissues snatched from a box.

His father passed without stopping, Larry turning his head to watch the boy and his mother peer at them from outside.

Larry turned. "Daddy?"

"Ah dern," said his father, jabbing the brakes. He had to back up to meet them, then he leaned past Larry on the truck's bench seat (an army blanket placed over it by his mother) and rattled the knob and they were in in a burst of freezing air that seemed to swirl even after the woman had shut the door. They were all forced together, Larry against the boy on one side and his father on the other, uncomfortable because he and his father almost never touched, awkward handshakes, whippings. For a moment the four sat as if catching their breath after a disaster, the truck idling. Larry could hear the boy's teeth clacking.

Then his father said, "Larry, thow a log on that dad-blame fire. Warm these folks up."

He turned the heater to "Hi" and soon the black boy beside Larry had stopped shivering.

"Alice," said his father, pulling onto the road, "introduce these younguns."

"Larry," the woman said, as if she knew him, "this is Silas. Silas, this is Larry."

Larry stuck out his calfskin glove. Silas's slender brown hand was bare, and despite the quick soul shake it gave, Larry felt how cold his skin was. If he gave him one of his gloves, they could each have one warm hand. He wanted to do this, but how?

They smelled like smoke, Silas and his mother, and Larry realized where they must live. His father owned over five hundred acres, much of it in the bottom-right corner of the county, and on the southeast end, a half a mile from the dirt road, if you knew where to look, was an old log hunting cabin centered along with a few trees in a field

bump (fig.) small, raised surface	
bare (here): very simple	
woodstove Holzofen	

can (slang) part of the body you sit on	
the like something like this	

awkward (here): *unangenehm*	
tap water water that comes out of a tap (*Wasserhahn*)	
pipe *Leitung*	
to steal, stole, stolen a look at s.o. to secretly look at s.o.	
to pretend *so tun als ob*	
grade (AE) *Klasse*	

vice assistant	
mill (here): *Fabrik*	
to spike (here): to drive a volleyball sharply downward with a hard blow	
to field a grounder (baseball) to catch a baseball that has been hit by a batter so that it rolls on the ground	
to fire to throw the ball with full force	
dodgeball *Völkerball*	
to swish to move quickly in the air	
to swipe to quickly catch	
fierce aggressive	
smoothly *reibungslos*	

inappropriate *unpassend*	

oddity strangeness	

to mumble *nuscheln*	

to occupy *besetzen*	

a few acres across, just a little bump on the land. Bare furnishings inside, dirt floor, no water or electricity. Heated by a woodstove. But when had they moved in? and by what arrangement?

His father and the woman called Alice were talking about how cold it was.

"Freeze my dad-blame can off," his father said.

"Mm hmm," she said.

"You ever seen the like?"

"No, sir."

"Not even in Chicago?"

She didn't answer, and when the silence became awkward, his father turned the radio up and they listened to the weatherman saying it was cold. it was going to stay cold. Leave your tap water running tonight so your pipes wouldn't freeze.

Larry stole a look at the boy beside him and then pretended to read his book. He was terrified of black kids. The fall after the summer he turned eleven he had entered the seventh grade. Recent redistricting of county schools had removed him from the public school in Fulsom and forced him to go to the Chabot school, where 80 percent of the student population (and a lot of the teachers and the vice principal) were black, mostly kids of the men who worked in the mill or cut trees or drove log trucks. Everything Larry couldn't do – spike a volleyball, throw a football or catch one, field a grounder, fire a dodgeball – these black boys could. Did. They manipulated balls as if by magic, basketballs swishing impossibly, baseballs swiped out of the air, fierce-eyed boys hurling and curving through their lives as smoothly as boomerangs. None read, though, or understood Larry's love for books. Now he glanced over and saw Silas's lips tense and his eyes moving across Larry's page.

"What grade you in?" Larry asked. Silas looked at his mother.

"Tell him," she said.

"Eighth," he said.

"Me, too."

In Fulsom his father dropped the boys off at school, Alice climbing out and then Silas, Larry aware how unusual, inappropriate, it was for black people to be getting out of a white man's truck. As he slid across the seat Larry glanced back at his father, who faced the road. Silas had disappeared – probably as aware as Larry of the oddity of their situation – and Larry stepped past the woman called Alice, seeing for the first time, as she smiled at him, how lovely she was.

"Good-bye," she said.

"Bye," he mumbled and walked off with his books. He glanced back, once, and saw his father saying something, the woman shaking her head.

At lunch in the cafeteria he looked for Silas among the black boys who occupied the two center tables but didn't see him. He had to be careful because if they caught him looking they'd beat him up later.

As usual, he sat with his tray and milk a few feet down from a group of white boys. Once in a while they'd invite him over. Not today.

His mother picked him up that afternoon, as usual, and, as usual, quizzed him about his day. She seemed surprised about their morning passengers. She asked where they'd been standing.

"They didn't have coats," he said. "They were freezing."

"Where do they live?" she asked.

He sensed he'd said too much already, though, and said he didn't know. For the rest of the ride, his mother was quiet.

Wherever Alice and Silas lived, they were there the next morning, same place, same time. His father pulled the truck over and the smell of woodsmoke blew into the cab with the icy wind and soon they all rode silently side by side. Larry opened **Salem's Lot** and held it so that he was sure Silas would notice. It was the best part, where the girl came back as a vampire, floating there at Ben's window.

Wednesday and Thursday passed, each day the colored people waiting, his mother picking him up in the afternoon and quizzing him on the morning trip. Did the woman seem friendly to his father? How did his father act? Was he stiff, the way he could be, was, most of the time? Or was he –

"Why do you care?" Larry asked. She didn't answer.

"Well? momma?"

"I don't care," she said. "I'm just curious about your day."

"I think," he said, worried he'd hurt her, "they live in that old place down in the southeast acreage."

"Do they," his mother said.

At supper that night he could tell something was wrong. She'd told Larry to feed the chickens when he'd already done it and his father had to be reminded to say the blessing. Now neither of his parents spoke as they sat around their dining table and passed squash and meat loaf. And just before she rose to gather their dishes, his mother announced that she would drive Larry to school the following day, in her car.

His father glanced at Larry. "How come, Ina?"

"Oh," she said. "This morning that gas man's coming and I can't talk to him. You've got to tell him to come every week, every week, and make sure he understands. Besides – " She took the dishes to the sink and returned to the table. "I've got some things to return at Bedsole's."

His father nodded, then looked at Larry before pushing back from the table and bending into the refrigerator for a Budweiser and opening it with his pocketknife on the way to his chair to watch the news.

"Carl?" His mother set a pie plate down, a little hard.

"Enjoyed it," he called back.

As Larry dried the plates his mother handed him, he understood that he had betrayed a trust between himself and his father, and the next morning, in his mother's Buick, she turned at the bend in the

tray *Tablett*

cab *Kabine, Innenraum*

stiff *steif, unlocker*

curious *neugierig*

acreage *area of land that is several acres*

to remind s.o. *jmd erinnern*
blessing *(here): Tischgebet*
squash *Flaschenkürbis*
meat loaf *Hackbraten*
to announce *ankündigen*

gas man *man who refills the gas tank*

Budweiser *a brand of American beer*

to betray a trust *Vertrauen missbrauchen*

Chapter Three

drawn pale and thin	

road where Alice and Silas waited, shivering, holding on to each other. As his mother slowed, Larry saw Silas push away from Alice, just as he would have done. Her drawn face pretty despite how the cold made her lips tiny, her skin the color of coffee the way women drank it, her hair in a scarf but her eyes large and frightened.

"Honey," said Larry's mother, "Roll your window down, please."

crank *Hebel*

Without looking away from the woman, Larry turned his window crank.

glass the car window

"Hello, Alice," his mother called as the glass descended.

"Miss Ina," Alice said. She stood very straight. Silas had stepped back, turned his face away.

Larry's mother reached over the seat behind them and withdrew a paper grocery bag. From it she took two heavy winter coats, old ones from their hall closet, one of hers for Alice and one of Larry's for Silas. "These should fit," she said, funneling them out the window,

to funnel to push through a narrow space
to poke at s.th. to quickly push into s.th.

Larry's hands poking at the coats, warm from the car's heater, from the heat of their closet before that and before that the heat of their bodies, now going out to the bare black fingers in the cold.

Alice held her coat, didn't even put it on. For a moment Silas glared at both Larry and his mother. Then he stepped back.

to glare to stare angrily

"You've never minded," Larry's mother said to Alice, looking hard at her, "using other people's things."

Then she pressed the accelerator and left them holding their coats in Larry's side mirror.

accelerator *Gaspedal*

In a moment his mother touched his knee. "Larry."

He looked at her. "Ma'am?"

"Roll up your window," she said. "It's freezing."

They were never there again, Silas and his mother. And now Larry and his father, who'd had little to say before, rode the miles of dirt road and two-lane blacktop without a word, just the heater blowing on their feet and the radio's agricultural report and the heater blowing on their feet.

blacktop road with a tar surface

He understood that Carl liked most everyone except him. From an early bout of stuttering, through a sickly, asthmatic childhood, through hay fever and allergies, frequent bloody noses and a nervous stomach, glasses he kept breaking, he'd inched into the shambling, stoop-shouldered pudginess of the dead uncles on his mother's side, uncles reduced to the frames of their boxed photographs now, whom Carl wouldn't have on the walls. One uncle, Colin, had visited when Larry was five or six years old. At supper the first night Uncle Colin had announced he was a vegetarian. Seeing his father gape, Larry assumed that word, whatever it meant, meant something awful. "Not steak?" his father asked. "Nope." "Pork chops?" "Never." His father shaking his head. "Surely chicken?" "Rarely," the smiling uncle said, "Which doesn't mean rare. Oh," he went on, picking at his cornbread, "I'll eat me a piece of fish once in a while. Tilapia. Nice mahimahi." Carl Ott by this point had put down his fork and knife and glared at

bout short period

to inch into (here): to slowly grow into
to shamble to walk in an awkward manner
stoop-shouldered with the shoulders hanging down
pudginess being short and slightly fat

to gape to stare with your mouth open
to assume *annehmen*
nope (coll.) no
pork chop *Schweinekotelett*

rare almost raw

his wife, as if she were to blame for the crime against nature sitting at their table.

Also, Uncle Colin was the only person Larry had ever seen wear a seat belt, as they rode to church (where he would refuse the communion saltine and grape juice). The seat belt irked his father more than Uncle Colin's not eating meat, because, though his father never said it, Larry knew he considered seat belts cowardly. Larry had become an expert at reading his father's disapproval, sidelong looks, his low sighs, how he'd shut his eyes and shake his head at the idiocy of something. Or someone.

"Yall look just alike," Larry's mother said at dinner on Uncle Colin's last night, looking from her brother to her son.

Larry saw that Carl was sawing at his venison. "My little doppelgänger," Colin said.

Carl looked up. "What'd you say? Your little what?"

Uncle Colin tried to explain that he hadn't just referred to his sexual organ, but Carl had had enough and left the table.

"Doppelgänger," he said, glancing at Larry.

Rather than his father's tall, pitcher's physique and blond curls and dark skin and green eyes, Larry got Uncle Colin and his mother's olive skin and straight brown hair and brown eyes with long lashes which, attractive on women, made Larry and Uncle Colin soft and feminine, seat belt users who ate tilapia.

In addition, Larry was mechanically disinclined, his father's expression. He could never remember whether counterclockwise loosened a bolt or what socket a nut took, which battery cable was positive. When he was younger, his father had used this disinclination as a reason not to let him visit the shop, saying he might get hurt or ring off a bolt, and so, for all those Saturdays, all those years, Larry stayed home.

Until his twelfth birthday, when his mother finally convinced Carl to give Larry another chance, and so, anxious, afraid, in old jeans and a stained T-shirt, Larry accompanied Carl to Ottomotive on a warm Saturday. He swept and cleaned and did everything Carl told him to and more. He liked the shop's rich, metallic smell, the way oil and dust caked on the floor in crud you had to scrape off with a long-handled blade, a thing he enjoyed for the progress you witnessed, the satisfaction of driving the blade under the moist scabbery and shucking it away. He also liked cleaning the heavy steel wrenches and screwdrivers, the various pliers and Channellocks and ball-peen hammers, the quarter- and half-inch ratchet and socket sets, the graceful long extensions and his favorite socket, the wiggler. He loved wiping them dry on red cotton shop rags and placing them in a row and sliding the oily-smooth drawers shut. He liked lifting cars by pumping the hand jack and letting them down by flipping the lever, the hydraulic hiss. He liked rolling creepers over the floor like large, flat skateboards to stand them against the back wall, liked

---

to blame s.o. jmd die Schuld geben

to irk annoy

cowardly feige, memmenhaft
disapproval Missbilligung

venison deer meat

pitcher (baseball) player who throws the ball to the batter
physique [fɪˈziːk] body build
lashes Wimpern

disinclined (here): unfähig
counterclockwise entgegen dem Uhrzeigersinn
bolt Bolzen
nut Mutter
shop (here): Werkstatt
disinclination (here): Unfähigkeit
to ring off to ruin the thread (Gewinde)
stained with marks that are hard to remove

anxious besorgt, ängstlich
to accompany begleiten

to cake to harden
to scrape off to remove s.th. from the surface with a sharp instrument
blade Klinge
moist feucht
scabbery crust
to shuck away to throw away
extension Verlängerung

hand jack Wagenheber

crate Kasten	
to stack to pile up	

to relish to take pleasure in s.th.
odd unusual
to spin, spun, spun to turn quickly

beaded with small round beads (*Kügelchen*)
slot narrow opening
quarter, dime, nickel 25 cents, 10 cents, 5 cents
rack framework upon which articles are placed

to assemble to gather
revelation *Offenbarung*

to gather versammeln
carburetor Vergaser

to chuckle to laugh quietly
minute [maɪˈnuːt] extremely small

hood Motorhaube
convertible Kabriolett

dang (coll.) milder form of "damn"

friction Reibung

sieved pan pan with small holes to let a liquid through
vat large container
foul awful
to peel back (here): to suddenly move back

to spin, spun, spun out to turn uncontrollably
it was (dialect) there were
to go amiss to go wrong
valve Ventil

---

how the drop lights hung from their orange cords, liked using GoJo to clean his hands.

But he loved best when the Coca-Cola truck had left six or seven or eight of the red and yellow wooden crates stacked by the machine, the empties gone and new bottles filled with Sprite, Mr. Pibb, Tab, orange Nehi, and Coca-Colas, short and tall. Larry never had to be told to fill the Coke box. He relished unlocking the big red machine, turning the odd cylinder of a key and the square lock springing out. When you spun this lock the entire red face of the machine hissed open and you were confronted with a kind of heaven. Long metal trays beaded with ice were tilted toward the slot where they fell to where your hand waited. The rush of freezing air, the sweet steel smell. The change box heavy with quarters and dimes and nickels. Taking bottles from the cases, he'd place each one in its rack, considering the order, taking care not to clink.

He learned to keep out of sight for most of the day as Cecil Walker, their closest neighbor, and other men began to assemble for what was, to Larry, always a revelation: his father telling stories, something he never did at home. In the late afternoon, as more fellows got off from the mill, they began to arrive in their pickup trucks, sometimes with a knocking tie rod, sometimes a whine in their engine block, sometimes just to listen to Carl at his worktable, the men gathered three, four deep, watching the mechanic place a carburetor on a clean shop rag.

Passing his bottle, Cecil would ask, "Carl, what was that you's saying other day, about that crazy nigger – ?"

And Carl would chuckle while he selected a tiny screwdriver and start the story. Loosening the carburetor's minute screws, he would tell how Devoid bought this little red used MG Midget in Meridian and was driving it home to Dump Road when, along about time he passes Ottomotive, its hood unlatches and flies open. Carl pointing with his screwdriver. "Right out yonder there. The car's a convertible, top folded back. Did I mention that? and Devoid, he has him a Afro, size of a dang peach basket. One of them black power fist combs sticking out of it.

"Now he's got the top down cause he liked the way the wind friction felt against his hair, he said. and while he ain't never confirmed it, that very nest of hair probably saved his life as that damn MG's hood unsprang at fifty–five miles per hour there on the highway. I seen it happen. Swear to God." Carl dropping the parts into a sieved pan and lowering the pan into a vat of ink-black, foul-smelling carburetor cleaner. "Hood peeled back, hit the rim of the windshield and bent and knocked ole Devoid right on the head, pop! The Midget spun out, lucky it was no other cars nearby, and Devoid luckier still to finally get it stopped there in a dust cloud."

Talking the whole time, raising the sieve from the cleaner and setting the pan over a clean shop rag to dry, pausing only if something went amiss at his fingertips, a spring stuck in some valve, say,

Attending this need might take five seconds, ten, a minute. He might have to excuse his way through the men and get a tiny socket or a different pair of pliers or maybe talk to the screw, "What's got you stuck?" or he might just grimace, but then, however long it took (never long), the problem solved, he'd go on as if he'd never stopped.

" – got that MG stopped out in front there. Ole Devoid come staggering out fanning dust and holding his head a–yelling, 'Call a got-dog am-bu-lance!' Had a line of blood dripping off his nose. A cussing up and down the chart, got damn this and got damn that, son-of-a-bitching shit hell damn. Crazy nigger," he'd say, laughing, "Sold me the car on the spot, for two hundred dollars cash. I closed the hood and wired it shut and give him a ride home in that very car, him hunched down the whole time, worried bout that hood. I asked him did he want a motorcycle helmet but he said no, it'd never fit over his hair."

All the men would be laughing and Cecil, drunk, a cigarette in his mouth and another behind his ear, laughing the hardest, would say, "You something else, Carl. Tell when you asked him about his name."

Carl bending low over the table, close to the carburetor. "Yeah, I did. Said one time, 'Devoid That's a hell of a name. You know what it means?' and he said, yeah, he'd looked it up. 'Barren. Empty. A wasteland.' In school said his nickname was 'Nothing.' "

"You something else," Cecil would say, shaking his head. "Tell em about that dog, Carl," and Carl would launch off into the funeral of so-and-so's daddy where they was all standing around the grave out in the middle of nowhere, ten, fifteen miles to the nearest blacktop. "Somebody's eulogizing the hell out of M. O. Walsh – that's who it was – lying through his teeth telling what a gentleman he was, when from out behind us we hear a gunshot. Pop! Next thing we heard was a little ole dog go a-yipping and I bout bust out laughing when that got-dang dog come a shooting out the woods bleeding from the side. It run right through us all and through the tombstones a–yipping fore it went on down the road. I leaned over and said, 'fellows, when my time comes, I want me a *three*–*dog salute*.' "

The men laughing, Cecil hardest of all. They'd have Coca-Colas or beer and jaws fat with tobacco. They'd spit and wipe their lips with the backs of their hands. Most in baseball caps. White T-shirts. All in steel-toed boots. The confluence of pickup trucks framed in the door and the two big electric fans pushing the hot air around and cigarette smoke curling high in the rafters like ghosts of bird nests, the men sniping from Cecil's bottle. Carl drinking, too, and Larry, hidden, listening, the stories weaving his imagination and the sounds of his father's voice into what must have been happiness, as his father's hands lifted the rebuilt carburetor to its waiting car, a clean rag over the intake manifold, the giant hands with the care of a surgeon fitting a heart back into its chest, turning the screws and reattaching the fuel line and listening with his head cocked as the owner climbed into the driver's seat with the door open and one leg out gunned it on

---

to attend a need to take care of s.th. not functioning properly

to stagger to walk almost falling
got-dog milder form of "God damn"

to cuss (coll.) *fluchen*

to hunch down to sit in a lower position

barren *öde, dürr*

to launch off into s.th. to energetically begin with s.th.
funeral *Beerdigung*
to eulogize (formal) to speak in high praise of s.o.

to yip to bark sharply
bout (coll.) about
tombstone *Grabstein*
fore (coll.) before

to spit, spat, spat *spucken*
confluence (formal) coming together

to curl to move in circles
rafters *Dachsparren*
to snipe (coll.) (here): to sneak a drink TF
to weave, wove, woven (fig.) to form, to create

surgeon *Chirurg*
cocked tilted to one side

Chapter Three

wing nut Flügelmutter

gasoline Benzin

stump what remains of a tree after the trunk has been cut through
to bounce (here): to move along on an uneven road
to swing, swung, swung to cause to move from side to side
its i.e. Mississippi

restroom (AE) toilet

betrayal Verrat

fly ball (baseball) a ball hit by a batter that is high above the ground
barehanded mit bloßen Händen
chain-link fence Maschendrahtzaun

to grumble to complain

jumbled (fig.) in a confused state
safety i.e. safety switch
yoked resting on his shoulder like a yoke (Joch) on an ox's neck TF
camouflage coat Tarnjacke

to glimpse to get a quick look at s.th./s.o.
to sneak around herumschleichen
deck porch
to cock up to bend up
strap Träger

to mess with s.o. sich mit jdm anlegen

command while Carl regulated its gasoline flow and, at last, placed the air filter over the carburetor and tightened the wing nut as the engine raced and the air smelled of gasoline and Carl stood back, arms folded, nodding, the shadows of men behind him nodding, too, and Larry watching, from behind the Coke machine, Cecil saying, "Carl, tell that one about that old nigger used to preach on a stump – "

Now, as he and his father bounced over Mississippi on the way to school, as they swung in and out of its shadows and rose and fell over its hills, Larry worried he'd lost the privilege of Ottomotive forever. They were pulling to the corner by the gymnasium where he got out. Before he closed the truck door each day, he'd say, "Bye, Daddy. Thanks for the ride."

"Have a good one," his father would say, barely a glance.

In the coming days he'd see Silas across the playground, in his class as he passed on his way to the restroom. In the cafeteria Silas sat with a group of black boys, laughing with them, even talking now and again. A betrayal, to Larry. For hadn't Silas been his doppelgänger? He'd see him out in the field by the trees, playing baseball, catching fly balls barehanded, his shoes, which looked too big for him, over by the chain-link fence.

Then, one Sunday afternoon in late February, Larry's mother off doing church volunteering, his father at work (even on Sundays, coming home from church and putting on his uniform and grumbling about all the money they spent, how he had no choice but to work), Larry set off down the dirt road they lived on, his lockblade knife in his back pants pocket and carrying a Marlin .22 lever action, one of his father's old guns. Since his tenth birthday, he'd carried a rifle with him in the woods. Some days he shot at birds and squirrels halfheartedly, rarely hitting anything, and if he did, just standing over it a minute, two, staring, and then leaving it lying, his feelings jumbled, somewhere between pride and guilt. But today he kept the safety on and carried the rifle yoked over his shoulder. He wore his thick camouflage coat, camouflage cap and pants, his fur-lined boots. He left no footprints in the frozen mud. Most days he would have gone east, along the dirt road, toward the Walker place. Cecil Walker lived there with his wife and his fifteen-year-old stepdaughter, Cindy, whom Larry hoped to glimpse. In summer he'd sneak around the house, through the woods, and watch as she'd stretch a towel out across the boards of their deck and take the sun wearing a bikini, flat on her back in a pair of huge dark glasses, one brown leg cocked up, then turning onto her belly, slipping a finger beneath the shoulder straps, one, the other, to lie on her breasts, Larry's heart a bullfrog trying to spring out of his chest. On colder days she came outside to smoke, stretching the long cord of their telephone out the door, not talking loud enough for Larry to hear. She'd only said a handful of words to him, and some days, the days when Cecil would come outside and mess with her, telling her get off the phone, put out that cigarette,

Larry imagined her coming to him for help, and some days, as she lay in the sun or smoked another Camel, he wished she'd see him where he hid, at the edge of the woods, watching.

But not today.

Today he went west, through the wire of a fence into the woods. At night sometimes in these cold stretches you'd hear noises like gunshots. It wasn't until he'd come, once, to a tree snapped cleanly in half, that he realized the cold would break them. The young ones, the old. A tree enduring another freezing night suddenly explodes at its heart, its top half toppling and swinging down, scratching the land with a horrible creak, broken in half and turning like a hanged man, its leaves beginning to brown at the edges first as the days and nights passed.

Walking, he wondered if they still lived out there, Silas and his mother. He worked his way south, making little noise, and carefully descended the rocky berm and picked through a tangle of briars at the bottom and into deeper woods.

Having a black friend was an interesting idea, something he'd never considered. Since the redistricting he was around them constantly. The churches were still segregated if the schools weren't, and sometimes Larry wondered why grown-ups made the kids mingle when they themselves didn't. He remembered two years before, how, in the hall on his first day at the Chabot Middle School, a white boy had come up behind him and said, "welcome to the jungle."

Other white boys would speak to him on occasion, usually if they were alone with him, or passed him on the playground away from their friends. Larry hurried through the halls, not making eye contact because it was safer, his nose in his handkerchief or a book, the new kid who was never quite accepted. In groups, the white boys laughed at him though they'd sometimes let him tag along, the butt of jokes but grateful to be included. The black boys were aggressive to him, bumping him as he passed, knocking his books off his desk as if it were an accident, tripping him on his way to the bathroom.

In the sixth grade, near the end of the school year, he found himself swinging with a white boy named Ken on one side of him and another, David, on the other. Both their fathers worked in the mill and both were poorer than Larry – he knew this because they got free lunches. Swinging, Larry kicked his legs as he flew forward, going higher, higher, the classroom building up the hill from the playground, a gray two-story structure with second-story fire escapes where teachers, all black, stood smoking and laughing, out of earshot.

Below them to the right a clump of skinny black girls with Afros and short shorts were standing and sipping short Cokes from the machine in the gym and sharing a bag of Lays, not really watching the boys, just talking about whatever black girls talked about, once in a while breaking out in high, cackling laughter and cries of "You crazy!" that Ken would imitate so they couldn't hear.

stretch (here): area of land
to snap to break with a loud noise

to endure durchmachen
to topple to finally fall down
creak Knarren

berm slope, incline TF
to pick (here): to move along carefully and slowly
briar [ˈbraɪər] Dornstrauch
to consider in Erwägung ziehen
to segregate divide along racial lines
to mingle to mix

middle school school with grades 5 to 8

on occasion bei Gelegenheit

to tag along to join a group without the others really wanting you to join
butt the person about whom jokes are made
to bump to push your body against s.o.
to trip s.o. to purposely cause s.o. to fall

to swing, swung, swung (here): to move forwards and backwards on a swing (Schaukel)
second-story first-story in Germany
fire escape a metal staircase outside a building to be used in an emergency when there's a fire
out of earshot too far away to be heard
clump small group
to sip to drink small amounts of s.th.
gym gymnasium
cackling with a loud, unpleasant sound
a (dialect) are

Chapter Three

to snap back to say angrily

retort quick, witty reply

sibling Geschwister

sneaker shoe for sports or casual wear

simian connected with monkeys or apes

teefs (dialect) teeth
to thank (dialect) to think
to whiz to rush

to drill (here): *bohren*
garden hose *Gartenschlauch*

to neck to kiss

eager *eifrig*

to scale to climb s.th. high
dorm dormitory (*Studentenwohnheim*)

titties (vulgar) breasts
pussy (vulgar) female sexual organs
to swoosh to move quickly through the air

to clench to hold tightly

trajectory curved path of an object that has been fired or thrown into the air
to struggle *sich bemühen, abquälen*

to cast an evil look at s.o. to look at s.o. in a way that shows you have an evil intention
to bite (here): to accept an offer that might be a trick

David said, "Them nigger girls sound like a bunch of monkeys," in a low voice.

"You a nigger," Ken snapped back, and Larry laughed.

"Yo momma is," David said, the standard retort of the year.

"Yo daddy," Ken said.

"Yo sister."

"Yo brother," and on until you got to the distant relatives, step-siblings, and great aunts.

Ken grew bored of naming relatives and, swinging forward, pointed with his sneaker toward the black girls. "Look at monkey lips," he said. This was their nickname for Jackie Simmons, a small dark-skinned girl with big teeth and lips. "She's so dark you can't see her at night less she smiles at you."

Larry laughed and said, "Jackie Simian."

"What?" Ken said.

"You see them big teefs in the dark," David said in dialect, "you'll thank it's a drive-in movie you be watching."

Going back and forth, whizzing past one another, the boys began to discuss the drive-in movie theater on Highway 21, Ken saying he'd seen a show called *Phantasm* there. Larry knew the movie from his magazines. It was about two brothers who broke into a funeral home. Ken was telling about this steel ball that flew around with a blade sticking out that would drill into your head and spray blood like a damn garden hose.

"When yall go?" he asked Ken, who said his older brother would sometimes take him and David with him and his girlfriend, let them sit in the front seat while his brother and his brother's girlfriend necked in the back. Ken and David discussed other movies they'd seen, *Dawn of the Dead*, which Larry had also read about and was eager to see, where zombies tore people apart and ate them as they screamed, and one called *Animal House*, how John Belushi from *Saturday Night Live* scaled a ladder to spy on girls in a dorm room pillow fighting and taking their clothes off –

"You seen their titties?" Larry asked.

"Shit," Ken said, "pussies, too."

"We go all the time," David said, swooshing past. "Me and Ken going Friday night, too, ain't we."

"Hell yeah."

Larry clenched the chains. "Yall think I could go sometime?" he asked, moving his neck to see David behind him, beside him, above.

David and Ken, swinging opposite trajectories, like a pair of legs running, had to struggle to make eye contact.

"My brother ain't gone take you," Ken said and David laughed, like what a stupid question.

"It's one way you might could go," David said, and even though Larry saw him cast an evil look at Ken, he couldn't help biting.

"How?"

"You got to join our club."

"Yeah," said Ken.

"How do I join?"

A moment passed, the boys swinging.

"You got to call Jackie 'monkey lips,'" David said. "To her face."

A bell rang up at the school and the teachers began to grind out their cigarettes.

"Watch this," David said, kicking his legs harder, so hard, going so high, the chains in his fists slackened on his upswing and he bounced hard in the rubber seat and swung back and the chains snapped again and as he flew forward he leapt from the swing, seat flapping in his wake, and sailed a long time over the ground – his shirt flying up and his arms out, feet dangling – and landed dangerously close to where the group of black girls was giggling about something.

They jumped and screamed as David skidded and dusted them with playground sand.

"Boy, you crazy," one said, brushing sand from her backside, almost laughing.

"He go break his neck," another said.

Up at the school, the teachers had paused before going in, watching.

Before Larry knew it Ken had sailed out, snapping his chains, flapping the swing, airborne, the girls backing up as he landed fancy, doing a somersault and rolling to his feet with his hands out like, "Ta-da."

"Them white boys crazy," another girl shrieked, the group moving farther away, but everybody, David, Ken, the girls, and the teachers, looking at Larry now, as he kicked his legs harder and harder, getting ready. He thought that if he did a good one, better than anybody else, they might let him go to the drive-in, he imagined telling his daddy about it, where you going boy? To the drive-in movie with my friends, in a car.

He went back, kicked, up, kick, back, the girls waiting, Ken and David watching. He thought if he could land in the center of them, scatter them, what a story it would make, he thought of going inside with Ken and David who'd tell everybody how far Larry Ott flew and how he sailed like a missile into the nigger girls.

He'd jump the next time, as a couple of teachers went into the upstairs door, Larry swinging back, needing more altitude, now the black girls turning, Larry forward, kicking, thinking, wait, but then the second bell rang and a teacher waved her arm, come on in, as the playground began to empty. When he jumped only Ken saw, David having given up, too, and Larry sailed out, his legs running, arms behind him.

He yelled, "monkey lips!" and landed on the wrong foot and half-ran, half fell to a hard stop, tumbling in his own dust, winding up on his stomach with his breath knocked out, rolling over, opening his eyes to the high white sky latticed with leaves. The face that appeared above him, a moment later, was Jackie's. He was aware of how quiet the playground had become with everybody inside, how far his yell had carried. Ken and David had stopped and were looking back.

"What you call me?" Jackie asked.

He couldn't catch his breath. He couldn't answer.

"Tell me, white boy."

He opened his mouth.

But she'd turned. She walked away, through her friends who were putting their hands on her back, casting their furious eyes back at Larry. Ken and David hurried off, not even looking at him. Larry pushed up on his elbows, lungs on fire, tears stinging the rims of his eyes, sorry for saying it, seeing the door open at the end of the building and Mrs. Tally, a black teacher, coming out, meeting the girls, just as Ken and David went inside.

"You know what that white boy call Jackie?" one said.

Mrs. Tally knelt in front of Jackie and said something, then sent her and the other girls inside. Larry was on his knees when she came over, her legs blocking the school from his view.

"Ain't that girl got enough problems in this world without a white boy calling her that?" she asked.

He couldn't look up. "I'm sorry."

"I'm not the one you need to say that to. You will apologize to Jackie."

"Yes, ma'am."

"I ought to call your daddy," she said, walking away. "But what good would that do?"

He returned to his classroom, where he, Ken, and David were the only white boys mixed in with two white girls, eight black boys, and nine black girls. Mrs. Smith, black, too, shook her head and pointed him to his desk and they finished their world history lesson.

After a time Mrs. Smith told them to read ahead and left the room. Larry, who hadn't yet dared to look up, was focused on a paperback copy of **The Shining** on his desk when a heavy world history textbook suddenly hit him on the side of his head. He flinched as the book slid off his shoulder onto the floor, felt like his ear had been torn off, and he lowered his head into his arms, folded over his desk. The black girls and boys began to snicker.

"White boy," a girl named Carolyn hissed. One of Jackie's friends, heavy-set and light-skinned. Mean.

He ignored her.

"White boy! Brang me that book."

His head throbbed but he didn't look up.

"White boy. YOU," she called, and Larry felt all their eyes crawling over him. He heard Ken and David, across the room, begin to laugh, and then the white girls, both of them, giggled. The black boys were hooting, and then somebody else threw a book. Then somebody else. Larry kept his head on the desk, smelling his own sour breath in the pages of **The Shining** as more and more books pounded him. He knew somebody was posted at the window, where Mrs. Smith was outside, smoking and talking to another teacher.

Monkey Lips, he thought as more books pelted him. *Monkey Lips, Monkey Lips, Monkey Lips.* Then, *Nigger nigger nigger nigger.*

A desk leg screaked the floor and somebody slapped the back of his head. "Boy, you better answer me fore I whoop yo ass."

"Whoop his ass, Carolyn," a big black boy called.

Nigger nigger nigger nigger.

She grabbed his scalp, bunched his hair and squeezed it, pulled his head up, the laughter louder, without the nest his arms had made. Some part of him hoped the white boys would rally for him, admire him for what he'd said, but they were laughing and pointing at him, as were the two white girls, and he knew this was not going to happen any more than the drive-in movie would. Carolyn twisted his head harder, and Larry pushed at her arm but she had his hair and he told himself not to cry. Then she slammed his head down, hard, onto his desk. Everybody laughed so she did it again.

He stole a sideways look and saw her face. He'd never been that angry. He didn't think he had the ability to summon such anger, or the right. With her other hand Carolyn grabbed his arm and twisted it so he fell out of his desk, **The Shining** landing beside him on the floor.

Still holding his arm, she put her foot on his neck and pushed. "Carolyn!" somebody hissed. "Mrs. Smith coming."

In a flash he was let go and black hands were grabbing books. He'd just pulled himself back into his desk when the teacher walked in, chewing a stick of gum, and said, "What's all this noise?"

She looked over the room, everybody miraculously in their desks, focused on their world history books. When her eyes settled on Larry, she stopped.

"Lord, child," she said. "You need to comb your hair. And why you so red?"

The class exploded into laughter as Larry sank his head back onto his desk.

Even today, more than a year later, carrying his rifle through the woods, the memory shamed him. He'd gotten a belt whipping from his father that night – for tearing his clothes jumping out of the swing, *Clothes I work hard to buy.* He'd apologized to Jackie the following day, gone up to her and mumbled, "Sorry," but she'd just walked away, leaving him alone.

Now, as he made his way toward the cabin where Silas and his mother were staying, the woods had begun to thin, and as he came to the edge of the field with his .22, he looked over the frozen turnrows and saw the dark elbow of smoke from the cabin's stovepipe.

He knelt, a fallen log at the tree line like a wall, the bramble cross-stitching his face so they'd never see him from the windows. He knew the cabin, had been there before, had pushed open its door on leath-

---

posted placed in a position to warn others when s.o. comes
to pelt to attack by throwing things

to screak to slide on s.th. making a harsh, shrill noise
to slap to hit with the open hand
fore I whoop yo ass (dialect) before I hit you on the backside
to bunch to gather together

to rally for s.o. to defend s.o., to support s.o. in trouble

to slam to push with force

to summon *aufbringen*
the right *das Recht*
to twist *verdrehen*

in a flash immediately

belt whipping *Tracht Prügel mit einem Gurt*

turnrow land at the side of a field where a plow can be turned
tree line edge of the forest
bramble *Brombeerstrauch*
cross-stitching i.e. the stalks of the bramble crossing each other

Chapter Three

hinge Scharnier
fissure long, deep crack
to mortar to apply cement in the space between the logs

to shore to support, to hold up

woodbox box to hold firewood
cockroach Küchenschabe

to lug to carry s.th. heavy
to resume to begin again

six o'clock to his high noon on the opposite side of the house
white oak a kind of oak (*Eiche*) (*Quercus alba*)
stricken (fig.) damaged
to sneak up to s.th./s.o. to move up quietly to s.th./s.o. without being noticed
limb [lɪm] branch

thermal cap cap for cold weather

habit Angewohnheit
to hesitate zögern
to envelop [ɪnˈvɛləp] to cover

to shrug to move your shoulders up and down

barrel Lauf
bark Rinde

cause (coll.) because
deer Rotwild

to reckon (coll.) to think, to suppose
to borry (dialect) to borrow

er hinges and peered into the dust and dark where fissures of light showed how poorly the logs were mortared. There'd been little else to see. A wooden table and a couple of single beds hunters used, a wash pot. The stove in the back corner with its iron door opened and its pipe a straight line to the roof, shored around the top with bent, blackened patches of aluminum. A woodbox coated in dust that held only dead cockroaches and rat droppings when he raised its lid.

He wondered now, watching the cabin, if Silas did his homework by firelight? You'd have to lug water from the creek on the other side of the field, where the trees resumed. Larry wondered if he could get closer, if he should circle the edge of the woods to the point nearest the house, six o'clock to his current high noon. From here was about a hundred yards to there, all open field, just one white oak stricken against the sky like an explosion. Be better at night. They didn't have a dog or he'd know it by now. If he came back tonight, he could sneak up and look right in the window.

"Hey," said a voice behind him.

He turned with the rifle. It was Silas, his arms full of limbs. Firewood.

The black boy dropped the wood and raised his hands like a robber. For a moment that was how they stood, Silas in the coat Larry's mother had given him and one of Larry's old thermal caps his mother must've thought to put in the pocket.

Silas opened his mouth. "You gone shoot me?"

He moved the rifle. "No," he said. "You scared me is all. Sneaking up like that."

"I ain't sneak." Silas lowered his hands.

"Sorry," Larry said. He put the .22 against a tree and hesitated, then came forward to shake Silas's hand. His father's habit. Silas hesitated, too, then, perhaps because they were alone in the woods, no school around them, they shook, Silas's fingers again enveloped Larry's gloves.

For a moment they looked at each other, then knelt together to pick up the wood. Larry stacked his limbs onto the top of the pile Silas held. Silas shrugged a thanks and stepped past Larry and went to the edge and stopped. He looked back over his shoulder.

"What you doing out here?"

"My daddy owns this land." Larry turned to where the gun stood, barrel up, against the bark of a pine tree. "I was hunting."

"You kill anything?"

He shook his head.

"Cause I ain't heard no shots."

"I'm hunting deer," Larry said.

"I had me a gun I could kill some of these squirrels. Let momma fry em."

Larry's hand in its glove reached for the .22.

"You reckon I could borry that one?" Silas said. "I bet your daddy got twenty-five more ain't he."

He did, he had several guns. Larry brought this one because it didn't kick and wasn't as loud as the others, twelve- and twenty-gauge shotguns or higher-caliber rifles.

"How yall get to town now?" Larry asked.

"Momma got a car."

"How'd she get it?"

"I don't know. How your daddy get his truck?"

"Paid for it."

They stood. Silas looked toward the cabin then dropped the wood again and turned, pointed to the .22. "Let me shoot it."

Larry looked toward the house. "Won't your momma hear?"

"She workin."

"I thought she worked the early shift. Piggly Wiggly."

"She do. Then she work the late shift at the diner in Fulsom. Here go," he said, stepping forward and taking the gun from Larry who never even tried to stop the black boy. "How you do it?" Silas asked.

"It's already one in the chamber," Larry said. "All you got to do is cock it and shoot."

"How you shoot?"

"You ain't never shot?"

"I ain't never touch no gun," Silas said. He held the rifle by its stock and forestock, as if it were a barbell without weights.

Larry raised his arms and mimed how you'd aim the gun. "Which hand are you?"

"Say what?"

"Right-handed or left. I'm right."

"Left."

"So you're opposite me. See that hammer there?" Larry pointed. "Cock it back."

Silas did, and Larry watched him raise the rifle to his right cheek. "Lay your face on the wood," he said.

"Cold," Silas said.

"Now close your left eye and look with your right down the barrel. See that little sight? Put that on whatever you want to hit."

Silas aimed at something across the field, closer to the cabin than Larry liked, and then shot and the echo slapped through the trees.

"It ain't loud," Silas said. He lowered the rifle and peered toward where he'd fired.

"That's how come I like it."

"Can I shoot it again?"

"Go on."

"How many bullets you got?"

"Cartridges. This one shoots cartridges. Twenty-two longs."

"It shoot twenty-two times?"

Larry had to smile. "No, this gun's a twenty-two caliber. It shoots long or short cartridges. I got longs today."

"How many you got?"

"Enough."

---

to kick (here): to move back sharply (a firearm) when firing

diner [ˈdaɪnər] (AE) small restaurant

chamber back end of the barrel into which the cartridge is inserted
to cock to push back the hammer

stock the back part of a rifle or shotgun you hold to your shoulder
forestock wooden part under the barrel to hold on to with your hand
barbell (sports) long metal bar with weights on each end
to mime (here): to demonstrate

sight little, upright, narrow piece of metal on the barrel used to aim at s.th. – Usually there's a front and a back sight.
to aim zielen
to slap (here): to make a sharp sound

bullet Kugel
cartridge Patrone

to pull the trigger *den Abzug betätigen*

to work (here): to lower and raise
to lever [ˈlevər] to make use of the lever
to snap to move suddenly
spent used
hull *Hülse*
reverence great respect
to retrieve to get back

to pan (here): to slowly move the barrel from one side to the other

to go numb [nʌm] to lose all sense of feeling
even quitt

to eject to throw out

to strike, struck, struck (here): to cause a reaction
to blurt out to say suddenly without thinking
to display to show
array collection

pointer tip

to quit to stop

to discern (formal) to make out
began to gather its folds (fig.) began to bring everything into darkness

Silas raised it again and sighted down the barrel and pulled the trigger.
Nothing happened.
"Work the lever," Larry said, miming.
Silas levered the rifle and his head snapped when the spent hull flew out of the side.
"Now see how it's cocked? It's ready to shoot again, so be careful."
Holding the rifle with a kind of reverence, Silas bent to retrieve the hull.
"It's hot," Larry said, but Silas picked it up with his fingers and then cupped it in his palm.
"What you do with these?"
Larry shrugged. "Throw em away."
Silas put the cartridge to his nose. "It smell good."
"Gunpowder."
"Gunpowder."
They watched each other.
Then Silas raised the rifle again and panned it over the field, past the house, all the way back around to Larry, and held it on him. For a moment Larry saw into the perfect O of the barrel and followed it to Silas's opened eye and went numb.
"Now we even," Silas said.
Then he moved the gun, continued his pan until he stopped on a pine tree and shot. He levered the rifle and this time caught the ejected hull. It clinked against the other in his palm. Then he put them both in his coat pocket, and it struck Larry with a wave of sadness, a boy saving the hulls as something valuable.
"Go on keep it," Larry blurted out. "The rifle."
Silas when he smiled displayed an array of handsome teeth. "For real?"
It was the first time Larry had seen him smile. "I got to get it back, though. Pretty soon, okay? Promise?"
"I'll just shoot me a few these squirrels," Silas said. He sighted something high in a tree. "You got the bullets? The cartridges?"
Larry unzipped his coat pocket and brought out both of the small white boxes and held them out to the black boy. Silas took them reverently and transferred them to his own coat pocket. Larry showed him how to load it and gave him pointers about aiming and shooting, the same lessons his father had given him. By the time he finished telling Silas how to clean the rifle, the sky outside the woods had reddened and the limbs were darker and the smoke from the cabin had quit.
"Oh man," Silas said, grabbing all the wood he could gather in one hand, gun in the other. "That fire go out my momma kill me dead."
With sticks pointing in every direction he raced toward the sun, and only when Larry could no longer discern the rifle barrel from sticks of firewood did he himself turn and walk back into the forest where night had already begun to gather its folds. He felt welcomed

by it and full of air. The last thing he did was pull at the fingers of his gloves, removing the left one, the right, and erect a stick the shape of a Y in the cold mulch beneath the leaves. On each peg he left a glove.

to erect to fix in an upright position
mulch decaying leaves
peg short, round piece of wood to hang s.th. on

Chapter Four

"Bad," Angie's voice said of Larry Ott's condition. They'd arrived, she reported, on scene to find him lying on his back in a puddle of blood. Single gunshot wound to the chest, pistol in his hand.

He could hear the siren. "He gone make it?"

"Don't know yet." Breathless.

"Was anybody else there? Sign of a fight?"

"We ain't see nobody and the place ain't look like no struggle. We left his gun on the floor."

Silas switched ears with his cell phone. In his headlights the slick blacktop two-lane ribboned up and down the razed hills like film unspooling, the Jeep riding the land.

"Anything else?" he asked.

"Not that we noticed. We was kinda busy, though."

"I know you was, sweetie. Thanks for going."

"You coming to the hospital?" she asked, and he knew she'd hang around if she could, maybe get a coffee with him in the cafeteria.

"Naw, I'm going on over to Lar – to Ott's, get a look around."

"See you tonight at the Bus?"

"Might be hard."

"Damn, I hope so."

He laughed. "It ain't no telling how late I'll be out there."

Next he called French, in his office in Fulsom. The chief was chewing.

"You shitting me," he said.

"Naw I ain't. Shot in the chest."

"Rains it pours, don't it." French sounded annoyed. "How'd they know to go out yonder?"

Silas slowed for a log truck in front of him on the road, its longest tree with limbs that still bore a few shivering pinecones. "I sent em."

A long beat. "You sent em."

"Yeah."

French waited. "Well?"

He hesitated, aware of the word he was about to use. "On a hunch."

"A *hunch*? What are you, Shaft?"

Silas fed him the chain of events.

"Shit, 32," French said. "Track a cloud of buzzards to a floater in the morning and follow a 'hunch' to attempted murder in the afternoon. You after my job or something?"

Silas signaled and passed the log truck, waving an absent hand out the window. "Just a pay raise. But Ott might be more than attempted murder."

"Right." Chewing. "Maybe we'll get lucky and he won't make it."

"That a oyster po'boy, Chief?"

"Shrimp, smart-ass." He belched.

"Damn, I can smell that shit through the phone."

Chapter Four

"I'll go to the hospital," French said, "get a look at the victim. You boogie on over to your friend's and I'll get there when I can. And don't touch nothing."

He rogered and hung up, relieved not to have to go see Larry.

By now it was darker and he turned on his lights, passed a run-down house with an old black man under his porch light in a rocking chair smoking a cigarette. Silas waved and the man waved back.

Though Larry's shop was on the outskirts of Fulsom, he lived near the community of Amos, just within Silas's jurisdiction. People from larger towns always thought Chabot was small, but it was a metropolis compared to Amos, Mississippi, which used to have a store but even that was closed now. The one paved road and a few dirt ones, a land of sewer ditches and gullies stripped of their timber and houses and single-wides speckled back in the clear-cut like moles revealed by a haircut. The train from Meridian used to stop there, but now it just rattled and clanged on past. Amos's population had fallen in the last dozen years, and most people remaining were black folks who lived along Dump Road. Silas's mother had lived there, too, for a while, in the trailer the bank had repossessed. Since her passing the population had declined to eighty-six.

He thought of M&M. Eighty-five.

He slowed at a little bridge, saw the sign. WELCOME TO AMOS. A little farther he turned left onto Larry Ott Road – since 9/11, for response to possible terrorism, every road, even dirt ones, had to be named or numbered. In this case, the sign was always gone because teenagers kept stealing them.

Silas braked, signaled, and turned, his lights sweeping Larry's beat-up mailbox into sight and back out as he tunneled through the darkness with his high beams, a road he hadn't seen for over two decades. A quarter mile farther he passed the old Walker place, where Cindy Walker, the girl who'd disappeared, had lived, the house nothing but a slanting shanty in weeds, roof sinking, windows boarded up, porch fallen in. Somebody had stolen the concrete block steps.

His tires slid on the dirt and he slowed, fishtailing, righting, looking for other tire tracks and seeing the ambulance's and a truck's, probably Larry's, intersecting and coming apart like something untwining. Dirt roads were a blessing when it came to investigating a crime scene. Silas had worked a few cases with French, couple burglaries and assaults and one murder about a year ago, watched French use his black magnetic powder to lift prints, his distilled water and cotton balls to collect blood samples. It was nothing like movies or television where they dug moths out of the victim's mouth with tweezers. Mostly it was just being careful and looking, a hair in the sink, a fingernail snagged in a rug.

He stopped at Larry's house under a clearing sky. No stars yet but half a bright yellow moon lodged in the trees across the field. He pulled on a pair of latex gloves and got out and aimed his flashlight. A lot of mud, lot of footprints.

---

victim Opfer
to boogie (slang) to move quickly

relieved erleichtert

outskirts an area far from the center

metropolis [məˈtrɑːpəlɪs] large, important city

sewer [ˈsuːər] **ditch** large and deep hole for waste water
to strip to completely remove
single-wide small mobile home
speckled back spotted TF
clear-cut area of land where all the trees have been cut down
mole pigmented mark on the skin (Leberfleck) or a small growth
to reveal to expose to view
to clang to make a loud, ringing sound
to remain to stay
to repossess (here): wieder in Besitz nehmen
passing milder form of "death"

to signal blinken
back out in another direction
beam Strahl

decade period of ten years

shanty small, primitive house
to fishtail to drive with the back end of the car or truck moving uncontrollably to the left and right
tire tracks Reifenspuren
to right (here): to get under control again
to intersect to come together
to untwine to come apart
blessing Segnung
assault bodily attack
to lift (here): to copy
print fingerprint
blood sample Blutprobe
tweezer Pinzette
to snag to be caught

to lodge to fix

Chapter Four

to muck up (coll.) to ruin

evidence *Beweise*

buck (slang) dollar

rocking chair *Schaukelstuhl*
cushion a kind of pillow to sit on

grip part of a pistol you hold in your hand when shooting

resumed itself returned to its former state
recliner soft, comfortable chair whose back can be pushed back

disinfectant a liquid cleaner that kills germs
mildew *Schimmel*

shotgun house house with a hallway from front to back to which all rooms are connected

to pile *stapeln*
tucked corners with the bed sheet folded under the corners of the mattress
paneled covered with thin boards of wood
paperback *Taschenbuch*

circular *Rundbrief*

stack pile
to frown *die Stirn runzeln*

Larry's truck was parked by the driveway, its door closed. He wished it was light so he could see better. It was too easy to muck up a crime scene in the dark, never knew what you'd step on. Not a bad case for waiting till morning. Of course the fresher the evidence was the better, especially fingerprints. But he didn't have a kit for that kind of detective work, and it wasn't his job anyway. That's why they paid French the big bucks, fourteen an hour.

He checked out the truck first. Driver window down. He laid the back of his hand on the hood. Cold. Rain had gotten in the cab but he didn't close the window, knew it was better to leave things the way they were.

He turned, glad the rain had stopped, but before he went to the house he clicked off his light and stood breathing the night air, listening to the far cry of a whip-poor-will and the pulse of crickets all around.

The house, small, wood, painted white, had a raised foundation and railed front porch, screened windows across the facade. He scraped mud from his boots on the bottom step of the sidewalk that led to the porch and walked up the steps. He paused a moment. There was a rocking chair with a cushion and he imagined Larry here each evening, the other half of the porch empty.

He pulled the screen door open and held it with his hip, turned the front doorknob with two fingers, this among the best places for prints. It was unlocked and he creaked it into the room with the heel of his hand and ran his light over the floor and saw it reflected in the puddle of blood. Pistol off to the side, bloodied grip.

He stepped in, located the switch and turned on the light and the room resumed itself, clean in its corners and dusted. An ancient television, a recliner with a TV tray folded against the wall. Kitchen to the left. He knelt by the pistol, not touching it. Twenty-two, looked like.

Breathing deeply, he stood. Smelled disinfectant and mildew. Only here once and he still remembered it. He closed the door, careful not to step in the blood, and crossed the room to where the dark hall stretched out of sight. He switched on the light. There were three bedrooms and one bathroom, door at the end. A shotgun house. He remembered the first room as Larry's as he walked along the wall, the gun cabinet halfway down the hall empty of rifles and shotguns, piled instead with mail and books.

In Larry's room he turned on the light, neat bed, tucked corners, paneled walls. Shelves full of the books Larry had read as a kid. Stephen King hardbacks. Tarzan paperbacks, Conan the Barbarians. Harlan Ellison. Louis L'Amour and others, lots of them he'd never heard of. In one corner there was another pile of yellowing mail. Hundreds of catalogs and sales circulars. A whole stack of Book-of-the-Month Club catalogs. Another of the Doubleday Book Club. The Quality Paperback Book Club. Several stacks of old *TV Guides*. Silas creaked the closet open and frowned at a row of suits and shirts, clothes of a boy on one end and growing longer down the rod, a man on the other. A stack of uniforms on the floor, LARRY on the shirt.

In the bathroom he flipped past his reflection in the medicine cabinet mirror. No prescription drugs. Just a tin of Bayer aspirin rusting on the metal. Tube of toothpaste. No dental floss.

Toilet bowl was clean of the ring Silas's had, which meant you needed to use some Comet or something. Even had one of those blue disinfectant things. Behind its curtain, the shower was clean, drain a little rusty, few hairs. Head & Shoulders, nub of soap.

Moving through the rest of the house he opened drawers and looked under beds but found nothing surprising. He left all the lights on and went out the back door and down the steps. He stood in the dark, listening to the birds and bugs. Out here wasn't what you'd call a backyard: it was more of a back field. His cone of light showed more footprints and he found an unmarred section of ground and walked to the gate and stopped.

There it was.

The barn.

He stood leaning on the gate and saw himself years ago, the day he'd come here. No grown-ups, no teachers, no other girls or boys, black or white, just him and Larry. He remembered following Larry through the house, past the gun cabinet, rifles and shotguns standing in their racks. Remembered going out the back door and over the huge yard, rolling open the doors and going inside the barn. They'd climbed on the tractor and caught lizards – anoles, Larry had called them. Then quickly added, "But some people call em 'lizards,' too." They "incarcerated" (Larry's word) the anoles in an aquarium Larry found in a dark cluttered room Silas didn't enter. They found what Silas proclaimed a cottonmouth-moccasin but Larry called a chicken snake woven around the rafters under the eaves, and Larry took its tail and unwrapped the snake as it snapped at him and shot out its tongue.

He grabbed it behind its neck and held it, enormous and gray, patterned with darker green ovals, longer than either boy. Did Silas want to hold it? Hell naw. It had a bulge like a softball in its stomach and Larry said it must've eaten a rat or something. He said there were big rats in the barn. Silas said why didn't they keep the snake incarcerated, too, and they did, in a gallon jar, alongside their aquarium. Silas had said, "Like a reptile house," and Larry had said, "A herpetarium."

Now, Silas took a deep breath and remembered the watermelon aroma of cut grass. He played his light over the yard, mown close, then turned back to the barn and followed the beam of light to the bay door and rolled it open. He slipped inside the dark, recalling the snake in the mailbox and trying to remember if snakes hung around after dark. His flashlight threw the tractor's shadow on the far wall and then probed the ground, no boards, just soft dirt. Rat waddling away. The same lawn mower handle sticking out, wrapped in black

rod *Stange*

to flip past to rush past

prescription drug *verschreibungspflichtiges Medikament*
dental floss *Zahnseide*

drain *Abfluss*
nub small piece

cone *Kegel*
unmarred (here): not touched, not disturbed

grown-up *Erwachsene(r)*

rack *Gestell, Ablage*

lizard *Eidechse*
anole a lizard that can change color
to incarcerate (formal) to imprison
cluttered covered untidily with things

chicken snake non-poisonous snake
to weave, wove, woven (here): to twist
eaves lower edge of the roof that overhangs the wall

to grab *greifen*

bulge swelling

herpetarium (formal) a place to keep reptiles
to mow, mowed, mown *mähen*

to probe *erforschen, prüfen*
to waddle to walk with short steps and moving from side to side

electrical tape. A chain saw hanging on a nail. He saw a door on the left side and heard movement within it. A stirring.

His heart beat faster. For a latch the door had a slab of a two-by-four nailed in the wall. He moved his light to his right hand and slid his .45 from its holster with his left, easing up on the door. That smell. What was it? For a moment he imagined it was a body. Aiming the pistol with a stiff arm, he used the flashlight to turn the latch down, and when he did, the door swung open and the noise stopped.

He poked his head in and a hen fluttered in his light and he yelped and his pistol discharged and set all the other birds aflight.

"Shit," he said, laughing.

The chickens agreed.

He was waiting on Larry's porch listening to the wind chime when Angie called, said she and Tab were headed to the Bus, if he wanted to join them. If he could he would, he said.

A while later French's Bronco came bouncing up, blinding him with its lights and pulled to a stop beside his Jeep. The CI got out adjusting his sidearm, holding a plastic bag with something in it. He went to the back of his Bronco, careful where he stepped, and raised the shell and lifted his heavy black investigator's kit out and joined Silas on the porch. He had a cigarette hanging from his lower lip and set the bag down.

"How is he?"

"Not dead," French said. He held up a bag with keys, a wallet, and cell phone in it and exhaled smoke from his nose and shook his head at, perhaps, the general nature of things. "Lost a shitload of blood."

"So I seen."

French pointed to the concrete walkway heading over the yard, a series of small sneaker prints, in blood, going away from the house, each dimmer than the one before.

"There's Angie."

Silas put his hat on and crossed the porch with his own light, fanning it out into the yard. People often covered their fingerprints, he knew, and destroyed bloody clothing and hid weapons. But they rarely thought of the simplest and oldest evidence in the world, footprints. Or tire prints.

French knelt at the end of the sidewalk with his light, reading the runes and ruts, a cigarette smoking in his fingers. Silas came to the top of the steps.

French turned his light. "Hold up your boot sole toward me."

Silas did.

"Yeah, this would be you."

French reached in his shirt pocket and withdrew a clump of thick rubber bands. "Put these on your feet," he said and watched as Silas stretched the bands over the thickest part of his foot. French also had them over his own shoes. Any foot without a band wouldn't be law enforcement and would require investigation.

Chapter Four

"Sorry, Chief," Silas said.

He ashed his cigarette in his palm and blew it into the wind. "You will be when I make you mold these motherfuckers."

Not bothering to put out his smoke, French hefted his investigator's kit and Silas followed him inside. The CI pulled out a chair from under the kitchen table and set the plastic bag and kit there and stood, pushing his hands in the small of his back until it clicked.

In the living room they stared at the floor, Angie's sneaker prints over the rug. The blood had dried to the color of molasses and the room had an unpleasant tang. French picked up the pistol by its barrel – it left a smear of blood – and examined it, ejected the cylinder. "Twenty-two," he said. "Fired once." He turned it. "Serial number's bout rubbed off." He replaced it and stood. "Sheriff Lolly took Ott's gun privileges away. After his daddy got killed. He ain't even supposed to have any firearms at all."

"Took em away how?"

"Just did it."

They went to the gun cabinet in the hall, gazed down at its stacks of old magazines on the green lining. French opened the drawer at the bottom, more mail. "Maybe Ott moonlit as a postman."

"Where'd they go?" Silas asked. "All the guns?"

"County auctioned em off, I expect."

"So where'd he get that pistol?"

"If it was his? Pawnshop. Gun show. It's a old model, could've had a dozen owners. I'll run a trace, but it'll be a dead end."

He fished his camera from his pocket.

"Bullet entry was straight in," he said, clicking through the pictures, Silas moving to see. Shots of Larry's pale face, obscured by the oxygen mask. The chief did a miniature slide show, shots of Larry on a table in his mechanic's uniform, bloodied at the chest. Larry's shirt being scissored off, an IV going into his arm, close-ups of the wound, tear marks and blackened skin.

"My guess?" French said. "Self-inflicted."

More shots, his pants being cut off, his egg-white legs, people in scrubs and masks, the keys and wallet, cell phone, money fanned out, close-up of Larry's driver's license.

"Could've surprised a crackhead," Silas said.

"Maybe." French still studying the pictures. "But he still had his wallet on him. And see the burns here? On his shirt, skin. That indicates a close-range shot, inches, probably."

He left Silas at the table and walked over to the television, an ancient mahogany cabinet model with an actual knob you turned. He looked behind the console.

"I believe our victim here's the last resident in Mississippi without a remote control. Or cable." He walked to the window and fingered the flat wire that ran from the back of the TV out the window, up to the antenna. "No answering machine. Ain't got a computer, either."

"So?"

---

to mold (here): *einen Gipsabdruck machen*
motherfuckers (vulgar) (here): tire tracks, footprints, etc.
smoke cigarette
to heft to carry s.th. heavy
small of the back the lower part of the back

tang strong, sharp smell
to eject to cause to spring out
cylinder The cylinder contains the cartridges and revolves at each firing.
serial number factory identification number

to gaze at s.th./s.o. *jdn/etwas anstarren*
lining soft inner covering
to moonlight, moonlit, moonlit (coll.) to have a secret, second job
county county government
to auction s.th. off *etwas versteigern*

pawnshop *Leihhaus*
to run a trace to research the archives
dead end (fig.) *Sackgasse*

to obscure to make difficult to see

IV putting blood, medication, or nutrients into a person's body intravenously
self-inflicted done by the victim or patient himself/herself

scrubs special clothes worn for operations
close-range from a short distance

to indicate *hinweisen, andeuten*

knob *Knopf*
console the cabinet of the TV

remote control *Fernbedienung*

old-timey shit (vulgar) old-fashioned equipment	
rotor any part of a machine that rotates	

"Unusual fellow. A frozen in the 1960s kind of character. For instance," he said, "you ever go in his shop? It's old-timey shit. Turns his rotors by hand. No power tools. Uses a hand jack. Go in Koen's up the road yonder and he's got air ratchets, uses compressors and computers and shit. Engine light comes on, power window stops working, fuel injectors clogged, replace the fucking computer. That's all they do now. Just take one computer chip out and put another one in. It's all computers now."

clogged *verstopft*

"Larry Ott don't need to upgrade if he ain't got any business."

They stood looking.

Silas said, "Maybe he can't get cable out here."

dish parabolic antenna for satellite reception

"He could get a fucking dish."

"Guess he reads books instead."

"Reads books."

They stood looking over the room.

"Chief," Silas said. "Maybe you right." He crossed to a shelf and picked up something he hadn't seen yet, a DIRECTV brochure that listed the advantages and channels.

spine back of a hardcover
knuckle *Fingerknöchel*
it's (dialect) there are

French came over beside him and touched the spine of one of the books with his gloved knuckle. "Into horror and shit. It's a lot more of these in that first bedroom. More in all the bedrooms but the parents'. More books I bet you than in the rest of the county combined. Including the library."

French went down the hall but Silas remained for a moment. He remembered this book, could see it in Larry's hands as Larry described the plot. For a moment he and Larry were out in the woods, walking, carrying their rifles.

cept (coll.) except

Silas found French in Larry's parents' bedroom, the CI opening drawers. He stopped at the one piled with a woman's clothes. "Cept for that front room this place don't look no different than it did when I was last here last week. My guess is he ain't touched this particular room since his momma went to the home."

home *Pflegeheim*

"Ain't nothing weird about that."

"I didn't say it was weird. My stepsister's mother died and she won't let nobody go in there except for her. Sometimes she stays in there singing Boz Scaggs songs, so don't get me started on weird."

Back in the kitchen French opened the refrigerator.

"Here's something," he said.

Silas looked past him, a case of Pabst Blue Ribbon beer among the eggs and containers of fast food. One can missing.

"Larry's been a nondrinker his whole life. His daddy died in a drunk-driving accident."

"Maybe he started."

"Maybe."

to poke around to search by pushing about
satchel bag with a long strap that you carry over your shoulder

French went to the table and examined the surface, then took a towel from the top of the kit and spread it out and began to poke around in the black leather satchel. It reminded Silas of an old-time country doctor's bag, but bigger; he'd envied this kit, but when he requisitioned the town council for a less expensive set, they'd denied the request.

French was rewinding a tape on his recorder/video camera, his head in a cowl of smoke. "You remember how to mold?"

"Yeah."

"It's some packets in my case. Hardener, too. Go get ever print you don't know. Front and back."

Silas carried the aerosol can of dirt hardener, three wooden frames, and three of the prepackaged molding kits outside. The kits were plastic bags of water, about the size of a bag of powdered sugar, with a smaller pack of cement inside you could feel sloshing around. He put the stuff on the porch and, with his light, began to examine the tracks of his Jeep, French's Bronco. The rain had pretty much obliterated any other vehicles' tracks. There were several footprints, full and partial. He ignored his own and Angie's, but found one near the front of the walkway. He set the frame around it and got one of the bags from the porch. He pushed on it until he found the cement pack inside and squeezed with his thumbs, began to knead the bag, mixing the cement and water. Then he sprayed the mud with the hardener and tore open one end of the bag and began to pour it carefully over the footprint. In the rear he found another set of footprints and repeated the operation.

When he came back in French had bagged the gun and was lifting prints.

"Here," he said. "Label these."

They spent nearly an hour cataloging the prints, French saying he imagined they were all Larry's. Then the chief used distilled water and cotton balls to get blood samples but found no blood other than the big patch on the living room floor. And that on the pistol. Finally they went down the hall and out the back door and stood looking at the barn as the night screamed with its birds and frogs and bugs.

"You look in there?" French said, aiming his cigarette at the barn.

"Yeah. Got bushwhacked by a flock of hens."

French snorted.

In the barn the chickens were making their noises. French probed the dark, dusty corners with his Maglite, looking for freshly disturbed dirt, loose boards, blood, hair, or the thing you'd only know once you saw it.

"Looks the same," he said. He went in the feed room and opened the chicken roost door and aimed his light.

They looked awhile longer then went back out and lifted the heavy concrete molds and set them in French's Bronco. Then the chief X'd the door with yellow tape, and they stood in the shadow of the barn, the CI emitting bursts of smoke that hung in the still air like sheets on a line. Silas thought he heard an owl somewhere and remembered Larry telling him you called baby owls "owlets."

"Tomorrow," French said, "I'm gone head up to Oxford. Talk to the sheriff. Interview some of the Rutherford girl's friends. Boyfriend.

to requisition to make an official request for s.th.
to deny a request *eine Bitte abschlagen*

cowl (fig.) loose covering for the head as worn by monks
it's (dialect) there are
ever (dialect) every

aerosol *Spraydose*

to slosh around to move about with a splashing movement

to obliterate to completely remove

to squeeze to press together
to knead [niːd] *kneten*

to label *etikettieren*

to bushwhack s.o. (coll., AE) to make a sudden, surprise attack from a hidden position
to probe (here): to examine

to emit (formal) to send out
sheets *Bettwäsche*
line *Wäscheleine*

Maybe a professor or two." He dropped his cigarette and crushed it out with his foot, picked it up. "In the morning, after your traffic, why don't you run back out here. Get a better look around. It's probably more tracks you can get molds of. Just do a general walk-around. I think Ott has like three hundred acres left."

"You think this might be connected with the Rutherford girl?"

"I ain't ruling it out," French said. "But you been wanting some real police work? Here's your chance."

They taped the back door of the house and went around the side. On the front porch, Silas reached in to turn off the lights. Then he waited as French taped the door and locked it and tossed him Larry's keys and cell phone. "Get these back when you're done. And let me know if you find anything."

"Right."

"When he wakes up, we'll go talk to him."

In the yard, French hoisted his bag into the back of his Bronco. "Keep them other two mold kits," he said. "You might need em tomorrow."

"Okay. You want me to call Shannon?"

"Naw. She'll find out soon enough." He stretched. "I'm going home."

Silas put Larry's stuff on the kitchen table of his trailer and laid his gun belt beside it, glad to be free of its weight. The handcuffs, flashlight, extra clips. He opened the refrigerator and drew a Budweiser from the nearly empty twelve-pack and got a glass from the drying rack by the sink. During his navy stint he'd drunk beer in several countries including England, where they drink it warm, or Belgium, where they have specialized glasses for each type, or Brazil, where the beer comes in giant bottles you split with your table mates, drinking from small glasses. He'd kept the latter habit here, but only in private. In the Bus, he drank from bottles because people would think a glass affected. He took the short water glass he liked and the bottle into the living room and set them on the coffee table. He sank back in the old sofa and pulled off his boots to let his socked feet breathe. He couldn't afford a washer or dryer and usually took his clothes to Angie's on the weekends.

He popped off the beer cap and filled the glass and drained it then poured the rest of the bottle in and put the empty on the coffee table and looked across the room to where his and Larry's keys lay side by side. He finished the beer and got the last one from the fridge and went down the hall unbuttoning his shirt with one hand. In his room he sat on the bed, unmade, and looked at his nightstand, over which he'd thrown a white T-shirt.

He glanced at his watch. Eleven p.m. Maybe he'd call Angie, say he was too beat to meet her. He filled his glass and drank then set it and the bottle on the floor and lay back and pulled the T-shirt from his nightstand and looked at the answering machine. The light was blinking. He reached over and pressed PLAY.

"Silas?"

Chapter Four

He sat up.

"I'm sorry to bother you." Larry Ott's voice said. "I know you're busy, but please call me back when you can, even if it's late. It's Monday morning, and I'm at the shop." As Silas listened, he gazed across the shag carpet that had been here when he'd bought the place and that he kept meaning to rip up. In the closet, behind his two extra uniforms, where he wouldn't have to look at it, was the Marlin lever-action .22 rifle.

Larry recited his shop number, slowly, as if he were giving the code to disarm a bomb. Then he said, "Please call back, even if it's late. It's kind of important, but I don't want to say it over the phone. Thank you."

Call back, even if it's late.

Well, it was late, wasn't it, Larry. Too late.

---

shag carpet carpet made of wool with long threads
to rip s.th. up zerreißen

to recite (here): to say slowly and carefully
to disarm entschärfen

Chapter Five

Larry woke before his mother knocked. It was a Saturday, the first day of summer, school out and three long months of freedom ahead of him. He dressed quickly in the clothes he'd chosen the night before, an old T-shirt and blue jeans with the knees out, perfect for getting dirty. He stuck his lockblade knife in his back pocket and tied his sneakers and was down the hall and out the front door before anyone saw him. He hopped onto his bicycle where he'd leaned it by the porch and kicked away pedaling. He flew down the driveway through the trees, dodging puddles and watching for snakes. He passed the Walker place, Cecil on the porch with a cup of coffee and a cigarette that he raised. Larry waved back and kept going, skidding to a stop before the mailboxes, theirs and the Walkers'. Without dismounting he opened the little door and pulled out the letters and circulars; he got Cecil's, too, glancing at it. Where Larry sometimes had mail, comic books or magazines, things he'd ordered, Cindy Walker never did. The Walkers usually only got junk.

Cecil was gone when he rode back by and he left their circulars on the porch. At home he laid his father's mail on the kitchen table and took his seat. In a moment the back door closed and his mother came in the kitchen with several eggs in her apron.

"You scared me," she said.

"Sorry."

She began to lay the eggs on the counter and noticed the mail. "Did your funny books come?"

"No, ma'am."

"Maybe Monday."

Because it was warm, she was barefoot. She lit a match and touched it to the burner and a flame bloomed to life, smell of natural gas, piped from the big metal tank in the backyard, filled once a month by a truck.

"How was your breathing last night?" she asked, rinsing the eggs.

"Fine. Good."

"Good." She was opening drawers, lighting another burner. "You want fried?"

"Yes, ma'am."

Something banged in the back of the house and they exchanged a look. Then the television clicked on and the newscaster's voice grew louder as Carl raised the volume, part of his morning ritual, watching the news and reading the mail while he ate.

A moment later he came into the kitchen tucking his green short-sleeved uniform shirt into his blue jeans, another sign of Saturday – the rest of the week he wore matching green pants. He often grumbled about having to work on Saturday, but Larry knew he preferred it to being here. And on any other Saturday Larry would have been anxious to go with him.

But not today.

"Good morning, Daddy," he said, once a commercial came on, the television visible only from Carl's end of the table.

His father was spreading the mail in front of him. "Morning."

His mother appeared at Carl's elbow with a ceramic coffeepot and poured his cup full.

"Thank you." He reached for the sugar and poured a huge amount in.

She lingered at his elbow. "Honey?"

He sipped and noticed them both looking at him, the usual Saturday ritual, the two of them teaming up on him, asking without words if Larry would be able to go to the shop today.

Today, though, Larry was relieved when his father looked back at the letter in his hand and said, "Got a busy one, Ina. Two transmissions and a carburetor. He won't do nothing but get in the way."

Behind them, the frying pan on the stove began to sizzle.

"Okay, Daddy," Larry said.

"Maybe next week," said his mother. One thing Carl had made clear long ago, to both of them, was that no meant hell no from the get-go.

In a moment his mother set Larry's eggs before him and he salted them and ate them quickly and his bacon, too. When he finished he felt his father's eyes on his plate and said, "Can I be excused?"

"What you tell your momma?"

"Enjoyed it."

"Go on."

He went down the hall toward his room but heard his father call, "Hey, boy?"

He hurried back. "Yes, sir?"

"You stay outside today. Cut the grass."

Which meant *Don't read all day*.

"Yes, sir."

He went down the hall and picked up the paper sack of trash, heavy with last night's beer bottles, and carried it outside and put it in the back of his father's truck, where Carl would throw it in his trash can at the shop.

He was lugging the push mower out of the barn when Carl drove past in the red Ford and slowed to a stop, lowering his window.

"Don't run over no sticks with that mower," he called. "I just sharpened the blade."

"Yes, sir."

He waved as his father drove away, then turned to face their three-acre yard, the house centered in it and the barn back by the trees. Half a day's work, at least.

"Dern," he whispered.

Might as well get it done with. That way he could salvage the second half of the day and not get in trouble. He added gas to the mower and checked the oil. It cranked on his first pull and he began

commercial *Werbung*

to spread *ausbreiten*

to linger to stay somewhere longer than usual

to team up on s.o. to join up with a person or persons to better oppose another person

relieved *erleichtert*
transmission *Getriebe*

to sizzle to make the sound of food frying

from the get-go (coll., AE) from the very beginning

trash (AE) garbage (AE)

to lug to drag s.th. heavy
push mower a mower you push by hand

blade *Klinge*

to salvage (here): to still have s.th. positive left from a bad situation
to crank (here): to start up
pull i.e. pull of the cord to start the motor

to mangle to badly damage

to fail s.o. to disappoint s.o.

to resemble *ähneln*

good-natured well-intentioned
ambush surprise attack from a hidden position

to abandon (here): to no longer use

mumblety-peg a game in which each player flips a knife from various positions so that the blade will stick into the ground
wheelie riding a bike balanced on the rear wheel
blacksnake rat snake, non-poisonous
hognose *Heterodon simus*, a harmless snake
pillowcase *Kopfkissenbezug*

creek *Flüsschen, Bach*
rod *Angelrute*
reel *Angelrolle*
tackle *Angelausrüstung*

to bait to place a bait (*Köder*) on a hook
cork (here): *Schwimmer*
bass [bæs] *Barsch*
sinker a weight for sinking a fishing line

to push it along the edge of the driveway, shooting grass, small rocks, and mangled sticks out the side, glad again that the eighth grade was over. Next year he'd go to the ninth, in Fulsom, the only public high school in the county.

As he pushed the mower, he thought how Alice's car must have come from Carl, but Larry knew not to say more about it. He'd failed Carl before by not understanding that the black woman and her son had been their secret. He should have known that men do not discuss with their wives (or mothers) the business that is their own.

Since he'd given Silas his .22, he now carried a Model 94 lever-action .33 that, of all their guns, most closely resembled the .22. Though his mother couldn't have named a difference if you'd lain the rifles side by side, his father would have noticed if Larry began to carry a gun without a lever, a pump shotgun, or one of the single-shot or automatic rifles.

For the past spring, whenever he'd been able to, Larry would race through the woods with this rifle, toward the cabin. Each time Silas would jump out with the .22, a good-natured ambush, Larry understanding that Silas would have been waiting for him no matter how long it took him to get there, the black boy always breaking into his big grin.

As it had grown warmer, as the school year had progressed, Silas had abandoned the coat and gloves from Larry and Larry saw he now wore better clothes, his mother (with her two jobs, a waitress in the Fulsom Diner and a cafeteria worker in the grocery store) buying them at the TG&Y. The boys would shoot their rifles, play mumblety-peg with Larry's knife, play chase, war, cowboys and Indians, climb trees. With Silas on Larry's bike, racing back and forth, doing wheelies, skidding, Larry ran along behind with his stick, looking for snakes sunning on the road. When they found one – a blacksnake, a hognose –Larry would pin its head to the dirt with the stick and grab the snake behind its neck, holding it as it wrapped itself around his wrist and shot out its tongue. Silas always kept his distance as Larry stuffed the snakes into the pillowcase he carried.

In April they began to fish in the creek on the other side of the cabin. In one of the rooms in their barn, Larry's father had several rods and reels on nails on the wall, and a giant tackle box, and as long as he was careful, Larry was allowed to use the equipment.

As they walked, loaded down with rods and reels, the tackle box, their rifles, Silas asked if Larry was going out for baseball this year. Larry said he wasn't, he'd never played, had never even considered it.

"How come?"

"I ain't no good."

At the creek's widest point, he showed Silas how to bait a hook, throw the cork out, catch and clean a fish. How to use artificial bait, rubber worms, broke-back minnow, Snagless Sallys, silver spoons, plugs. But these were for bass, which were few in the creek and hard to catch, and so mostly they used corks and sinkers, for this was what the big gray catfish that sucked along the bottom of the creek preferred. Larry had tried to get Silas to take their first stringer of these fish home to his mother, several pounds, but Silas said he couldn't.

"Why not?" Larry was sitting on the creek bank, watching his cork, the water roiling and bubbling as the fish pulled at the stringer. Silas, fascinated at what they'd hooked from the creek, raised the stringer to gape at the prehistoric faces, their wide mouths, flat heads.

"Why not?" Larry asked again.

"Momma. She say I ain't supposed to play with you."

"Why?"

Silas just shrugged. The catfish croaked, and Silas splashed them into the water.

"What's that?"

Larry smiled at him. "That's how they talk."

He pulled them up again.

"Careful of that long fin there," Larry said. "It'll stick you."

Silas lowered his face to the catfish's. "What you saying, Mr. Catfish?"

"Is it cause I'm white?" Larry asked.

"What?"

"Why your momma don't want you to play with me?"

"I don't know."

"She didn't tell you?"

"She just say, 'Don't you go near that boy.' Made me promise I wouldn't."

"How come?"

"I done said I don't know."

Larry was puzzled. It had to be his color. What else could it be? He'd known his own father would disapprove. He would never tell Carl about the friendship, but wouldn't it be different for Silas? Wouldn't a black woman be happy her son had a white friend? They'd given them coats, a car. He'd assumed the anger that black folks felt was a reaction to white people's attitude toward them. *Yall started it.* But if somebody white was willing to befriend somebody black, offer them gifts, even a place to live, shouldn't the blacks be grateful?

"You ever tell her about that rifle?"

"Hell naw. I keep it hid."

"How come?"

"Cause she'll make me give it back."

"I do need it back," Larry said. "Fore my daddy goes looking for it. Here," he said, offering his knife. "I'll trade you this."

"A knife for a gun?"

"Please?"

"Tell me one them stories," Silas said.

He meant a Stephen King story. Larry had lent Silas books, but the black boy said he didn't like reading, homework was enough. Weren't lights in the cabin anyhow. Just an oil lamp and candles. A flashlight.

---

stringer (here): a wire onto which fish that have been caught are attached

to roil to move turbulently
stringer (here): fishing line

to gape at s.th./s.o. to stare at s.th./s.o. with your mouth open

to croak to make a low, rough sound

to assume *annehmen*
attitude *Haltung, Einstellung*

to trade *tauschen*

interstate exit an exit on the Interstate Highway System
to surround umgeben, umzingeln

to thread (here): to carefully put into place

potted meat meat preserved in a can
mayo mayonnaise

to throw s.o. off (here): to divert, to distract

to mound to form a small area of earth that is higher than the surrounding ground – The pitcher in baseball stands on such a raised area (mound).
to duck to lower your body to avoid being seen or hit
to check (here): to stop
streak *Strahl*
impressed *beeindruckt*
trunk *Baumstamm*
to charge to run rapidly
fluid smooth and elegant

to dodder to fly about weakly
orb spider spider with eight eyes that spins a wheel-like web
to pitch to throw the baseball

Silas did, however, like to hear Larry describe the stories. Now he told about the one called "Trucks," where a supernatural force has taken over all the trucks at an interstate exit (and presumably all over the world) and a bunch of people are trapped in a diner surrounded by murderous vehicles. Near the end the trucks start blowing their horns and one of the survivors recognizes that it's Morse code.

Silas was threading a worm onto his treble hook. "What's that?"

Larry had described the dot-and-dash code, then told how the trucks were honking in Morse that somebody needed to fill them up with gas. The story ended with the people serving the trucks, taking turns filling them with gas, the guy telling the story looking up at two airplanes. "I hope to God," he'd said, "that there are people in them."

Silas had been watching the sky.

Larry finished the grass just before noon, and for lunch his mother made him a potted meat and mayo sandwich with saltines on the side. He read a comic book at the table while he ate then drained his glass of Coke and thanked her and got his .33 from the gun cabinet in the hall and two boxes of cartridges and Stephen King's short story collection **Night Shift** and, at the front door, called, "I'm going outside," and let the screen door bang behind him, feeling her coming out behind him, watching him. As always, he headed toward Cindy's house to throw her off, shoulder-strapped the Marlin and walked through the field toward the trees. Once in the woods he doubled back, went east.

Because Silas had started playing baseball at school, Larry worried that he was losing him. He'd invited him to his house once, and they'd played in the barn and Silas had cut the grass, but he knew the black boy wouldn't do that again. Maybe he could take him back through the woods, toward Cindy's house. She'd been his secret, but maybe it was time to share her.

Half an hour later he knelt at the edge of the woods, rifle unshouldered. From across the field he watched Silas standing on a pile of dirt he'd mounded behind the cabin. He looked back over his shoulder toward Larry, who ducked before he realized Silas was just checking an imaginary runner on first. Then he raised both his hands to his chest and kicked up one leg and fired a streak of gray toward the tree sixty feet away. Larry was impressed at the *thwack* the ball made when it bounced off the trunk and rolled back. Silas was already charging to scoop the baseball bare-handed out of the weeds and pretend to throw it back in Larry's direction, as fluid a move as an Atlanta Brave on the television.

His mother's car was nowhere in sight, which meant she was working. Around the cabin the field that had been so dead and gray in winter was now greening, butterflies doddering over the goldenrod and orb spiders centered in their webs like the pupils of eyes.

Back on the mound, Silas checked runners on first and second before he pitched and then he did it all again. Larry sat back against a tree and picked beggar's lice off his socks and pants. He'd hear the thump the ball made then maybe a grunt or hoot from Silas but soon he'd opened **Night Shift** to one of his favorite stories, "The Mangler."

When he looked up, Silas was standing over him, his chest rising and falling. "You spying?"

Larry closed his book. He saw the cat a few feet behind Silas and realized it had probably smelled him and come over, Silas following it.

"No." Larry shrugged and got to his feet and looked down at the rifle. "I just come to see you but you was busy throwing."

Silas watched him. He still held his baseball and Larry wondered did he steal it from school.

Silas looked back toward his mound, the tree. "I bet I can throw seventy, eighty miles a hour," he said.

"Yeah," Larry said. "It looked real fast from here."

"What you reading?"

Larry held the book up. Its cover showed a human hand with eyes in the palm and on the fingers. Some of the hand and fingers were wrapped in gauze like a mummy.

Silas said. "Is it scary?"

Larry told him about "The Mangler," describing in great detail the scene when the detectives go to visit the girl who cuts her finger on the laundry machine. If the detectives' far-fetched theory is accurate, a freakish confluence of events caused the machine nicknamed "the Mangler" to become possessed by a demon. The last piece in the puzzle, Larry told Silas, is the blood of a virgin. So the cops finally ask the girl: "Are you a virgin?" "I'm saving myself for my husband," she tells them. By then it's too late, and the Mangler is coming for them all.

Silas frowned. "What's a virgin?"

"Somebody that hadn't ever had intercourse."

"Intercourse? You mean somebody ain't never been *fucked*?"

"Yeah."

"Tell me another one." Silas said. By now they were walking, the rifle strapped to Larry's back, Silas grinding his baseball into his palm.

He told about "Jerusalem's Lot" and told how it was a precursor to King's novel **Salem's Lot**.

"That's the one I was reading that first day I met you. When we picked yall up. You remember?"

"I don't remember no book."

Larry shrugged.

"Where we going anyway?" Silas asked. "I don't want to go to your house."

They were in the woods a quarter mile from Larry's barn, skirting it and heading toward the Walker place.

"I want to show you something," Larry said. "Somebody."

"Who?"

"You'll see."

"A girl?"

"A real pretty one."

beggar's lice *Kletten*
thump the sound made by s.th. heavy hitting a surface
hoot shout especially when showing scorn (*Verachtung*)
mangler s.th./s.o. that completely destroys s.th./s.o.

cover *Umschlag*
palm inside surface of the hand below the fingers
gauze [gɔːz] light, thin cotton cloth

far-fetched *weit hergeholt*
freakish strange, abnormal
confluence (formal) the combining of events
virgin *Jungfrau*

intercourse *Geschlechtsverkehr*

to grind to rub
precursor (formal) forerunner

to skirt s.th. to avoid coming close to s.th.

Roman candle cylindrical firework that sets off stars of fire
aloof *reserviert*
to goof off (here): to behave in a silly manner
to fizz to make a hissing or sputtering sound
fuse *Zünder*
to quick-draw s.th. to quickly pull s.th. out

to squat to sit on your heels with your knees pulled up to your body

to flick s.th. at s.o. to fling s.th. at s.o.

gunslinger *Revolverheld*
to deafen to make s.o. deaf (*taub*)
blind her one make her blind

to bounce off s.th./s.o. to quickly hit s.th./s.o and then quickly move away

ablaze on fire

"Who is she?"

"Our closest neighbor," Larry said. "Her stepdaddy, Cecil, he's a funny man, always doing crazy things."

"Crazy how?"

Larry stopped, Silas behind him, and began to tell about the New Year's Eve a couple of years before when the Walkers had come over and Carl had brought a bunch of fireworks. Trying to pause when his father did, Larry told how the mothers were in the house talking and cooking a chicken and Larry, Cindy, Carl, and Cecil were outside with the fireworks. Both men were drunk and it was one of the happiest memories Larry had, yellow and red smoke bombs, Roman candles, even Cindy, usually so aloof, laughing as Cecil goofed off and held his fizzing bottle rockets in his hand, one or two exploding before he threw them, which had everybody laughing as he shook his hand, burnt black and smoking. He had a bundle sticking out of his coat pocket, fuse ends up, and he'd quick-draw them and light them and fling them out. Carl wasn't shooting, just watching from the porch steps with his beer and cigarette.

Cecil lit another with a kitchen match and let it sizzle. Cindy was a few feet away, fourteen years old and with pigtails, squatting in blue jeans and a sweater beside her Coke bottle holding a cigarette lighter to a rocket of her own.

"Hey, Cin," Cecil said, and when she looked up he flicked the lit bottle rocket at her.

She shrieked and jumped aside as it zipped past her and blew up in the field.

"Cecil you mean," she said as he quick-drew another and lit it, flicking it at her.

"Dance!" he yelled, like a gunslinger shooting at her feet.

"You gone deafen that girl," Carl called. "Or blind her one."

Larry stepped back, behind Cecil, and watched as he lit another and let it fly at her.

This time it did hit her as she ran away from him, out into the darkness. It exploded against her back and she screamed, Carl starting down off the steps and Larry heading out to see if she was okay. In a panic, glancing back toward the house, Cecil dropped his match. Cindy was crying and the women came out onto the porch just in time to see that she was fine; it had bounced off her and exploded in the grass.

But the match Cecil dropped had landed in his coat pocket where the bottle rockets were, him so drunk he just looked around and said, "Something's burning."

"It's your coat, Cecil," Larry said, pointing.

Cecil raised his arm and looked down as the first bottle rocket hissed out of his pocket into the air, *bang*. Then another. He flung his arm back and yelled as another flew out, and another, his coat ablaze now, the sound Larry heard his father laughing as Cecil began to run, yelling, beating at his coat and more rockets taking off. Then Cindy was laughing and Larry was and even the women, Shelia covering her mouth with both hands as Cecil wrenched off the coat still spraying its fireworks and began to stomp it, laughing himself now, falling, even Larry laughing now, telling it.

But not Silas.

Larry had heard Carl tell the story before and have the men at his shop howling, Cecil hardest of all, in stitches, nodding that yep, it was true, he'd burnt up his own damn coat, plus got in Dutch with the old lady, but Silas never broke a smile.

"Sound more mean than crazy," he said. "I don't know if I want to go see a man like that."

Larry tugged his sleeve. "Come on."

As they got closer to the edge of the woods that bordered the Walker property, Larry put a finger to his lips and knelt and began to creep. Behind, Silas did the same. They were coming up an incline and just before the house came in sight Larry lay flat on his belly. Silas hesitated, as if he didn't want to mess up his clothes, but finally lay alongside Larry and together they peered out of the woods. Fifty yards away, the Walker house was a dirty, uneven rectangle with a series of ill-planned additions covered in black tar paper curling at the edges. Between two of the rooms was a rudimentary deck and here was where Cindy often sunbathed.

Today, though, it was Cecil on the deck, and Carl himself.

"That's your daddy," Silas said. "What's he doing there?"

Larry had no idea.

Carl was smoking a cigarette and talking the way he did at his shop and drinking a bottle of beer, Cecil listening. He had sawyered in the mill until he hurt his back and now he got a small disability, which he used for beer and cigarettes.

"Let's go," Larry whispered. He began to slide back.

"Hang on." Silas grabbed his arm. "We snuck this far. Maybe that girl'll come out."

They waited, huddled on the ground. Larry caught a word now and again as they matched each other beer for beer and seemed fairly drunk when Cindy finally burst out onto the deck.

Larry froze in the leaves.

They watched as Cindy stood on the porch wrapped in a small towel with another one turbaned on her head. She was arguing with Cecil, one arm waving in the air and the other clenching her towel at her chest.

She raised her voice. "Momma said I could go!"

Her mother, Larry knew, worked evenings at the tie factory over in east Fulsom.

"What you say her name was?" Silas whispered. "I seen her at school."

"Cindy."

She was getting madder on the deck, raising her voice.

---

to wrench s.th. off to violently and suddenly pull s.th. off
to spray (here): to shoot off
to stomp s.th. to step on s.th. with heavy steps
to howl (here): to laugh loudly
in stitches (coll.) laughing a lot
to get in Dutch with s.o. to get in trouble with s.o.

to tug to pull hard
sleeve *Ärmel*

incline a piece of sloping land

to mess up to make dirty

to peer *glotzen, spähen*
rectangle *Viereck*
ill poorly
tar *Teer*
to curl to form a curved shape
rudimentary primitive
deck porch

to sawyer to saw logs
disability (here): compensation for an injured bodily part

hang on (coll.) wait a moment
to sneak, snuck, snuck to move along quietly so as not to be noticed
to huddle to gather closely together
matched each beer for beer Each drank the same amount of beer as the other.

to clench to hold tightly

tie *Krawatte*

to nudge to push s.o. gently to get this person's attention
to slap to hit with the open hand
cleavage the space between the top of the breasts
bosom breast

to wink at s.o. jdm zuwinkern
pull (here): drink
to inch up to slowly move up
thigh [θaɪ] Oberschenkel

to stride to walk with long steps

to cinch up to raise and tighten
to slam to close with force

to startle aufschrecken

to sprint to run quickly

to rustle rascheln

to trudge to walk slowly with heavy steps

line Grenze
camouflage Tarnung
to kink to twist
fly Hosenladen
hosed out piss urinated like using a hose (*Schlauch*)
to crackle to cause to make short, sharp sounds
stobbed (dialect) stabbed – to stab: to stick a sharp instrument into s.th./s.o.

stout sturdy, strong
to field (baseball) to catch
return (baseball) a ball thrown back
to wind, wound, wound up (baseball) to swing the ball around several times before throwing it (as done by the pitcher)

gone (dialect) going to

Cecil leaned over and nudged Carl and reached out and tugged at Cindy's towel. She slapped Cecil's hand but he held on and pulled harder, Carl laughing, rising from his seat on the steps to stand leaning against the rail, a better view, more cleavage, half her bosom showing.

"Cecil!" Cindy shrieked. "Let go! I'll tell Momma!"

He murmured something, clinging to the towel. He winked at Carl who was scratching his cheek and taking a long pull from his beer, Cindy's towel inching up her thigh and down her chest as she slapped at Cecil's hand.

Silas was out of the leaves and halfway across the yard, brushing dirt from his knees, before Larry realized he was gone from his side. Striding away, he seemed taller than he had when they'd met.

Still frozen, Larry watched Silas walk up to the two drunk white men on the porch, both speechless at his appearance.

"Yall leave that girl alone," he said.

Cecil let go of Cindy and she cinched up her towel and stood watching the black boy down in their yard, as speechless as everybody else, then she turned and went inside, the door slamming behind her.

The noise startled Cecil. "Who you, boy?"

But Silas was walking, around the deck and house, heading for the road.

"Wait," Carl was saying. "Hey, boy!" He came down the steps with his bottle and circled the house but Silas had sprinted away, gone for good.

Larry began to inch down the land in the rustling leaves like a reptile and lay breathing hard at the bottom. He was about to rise with his rifle and trudge home when, above him, Carl stepped into the tree line. He stood gazing about, maybe looking to see were there more black boys in the woods, and Larry lay flat, thankful for his camouflage. Carl kinked his hip and unzipped his fly and reached into his pants. Larry looked away as his father hosed out piss that crackled in the dry leaves like a fire. When he finished he stood a moment.

"Hey, Carl!"

It was Cecil.

"Any more natives down yonder? Don't get stobbed by no spear."

When Larry opened his eyes his father was gone from the top of the hill.

He found Silas flinging his baseball at a stout magnolia and fielding the returns.

"Thanks for helping her," he said.

Silas wound up and threw into the tree. Instead of fielding, he let the ball die in the weeds. "You always spying on people," he said.

"I don't spy."

"You ever take that girl on a date?"

Larry didn't answer.

"You wasn't gone help her."

"I wanted to."

Silas watched him a moment, then got his ball and began to walk toward home and Larry followed. It was cooler in the woods and they crunched over the leaves and ducked branches. At one point when the brush cleared Silas sprinted ahead and turned, still running, and pivoted and threw the baseball back toward Larry. Larry reached for it but closed his eyes and missed and it bounced behind him and disappeared.

"Shit," Silas said.

He hurried past Larry and began looking for the ball.

Larry knew something was wrong when he walked in the back door, on his way to place the .33 in its green velvet slot in the gun cabinet in the hall.

Carl sidestepped out of the kitchen to face him.

"Come here," he said.

Larry willed himself to walk toward his father, who seized him by his sleeve and dragged him into the living room. He took the rifle from Larry.

"Where's my Marlin?"

Larry looked down at his hands.

"Get it," his father said.

Larry didn't move.

"Boy."

"I ain't got it, Daddy."

" 'Ain't got it, Daddy.' "

"Yes, sir. I mean no, sir."

Larry's mother was behind them now. "Carl," she said.

Carl held up his finger to her and looked at his son. "Where's my dad-blame rifle, boy?"

Larry was kneading his fingers. "I let my friend use it."

"Friend," his father said. "I didn't know you had none."

"Carl – "

"Ina Jean, this boy's subcontracting out my firearms. I want to know who it is. Well?"

Larry didn't answer.

"I ain't asking again."

"That boy we picked up."

"What boy?"

"Silas."

"Silas," his father said. "Silas that nigger boy?"

"Carl."

His father moved his face so close Larry could smell beer and cigarettes, and in that moment he knew that Carl had seen him at the bottom of the hill. "Just a dad-blame minute. You give my gun to your nigger friend?"

"Carl stop it."

He looked at his wife pointing her finger.

ass (vulgar) part of the body you sit on
to squat to live in a building or on land that is not yours without permission

to wedge (normally) to fit s.th. into a small space

to tempt jdn in Versuchung führen

to flap to wave

to struggle (here): sich abmühen

to crow krähen

set my cap for you (fig.) choose you

"Carl Ott, I said stop it right now."

His father let Larry's sleeve go. "Maybe you right. You want to have em over for dinner after church?"

"You're – " she said, "you're just – "

"Tomorrow," Carl told Larry. "Tomorrow first thing you get your ass out there where they're squatting and get my god dang Marlin back. Is that clear, boy?"

"Carl your language."

"Ina Jean, this is not the time."

"Then when is? How long they gone live there, Carl?"

"Shut your mouth."

"It ain't proper."

Larry had wedged himself into the corner behind his father's chair.

"Proper," his father said.

"If they don't leave," his mother said, "then me and Larry are. To-night."

For a moment it seemed his father might laugh, then he just shook his head. "Don't tempt me," he said.

"Carl," she whispered.

He flapped a hand at Larry. "When you able to come out of the corner – "

"Carl."

"Just get the gun back," he said through his teeth. "Whether you're here tomorrow or not."

He went up the hall to the front and banged opened the screen door and went onto the porch and the screen door closed slowly in his wake.

"Carl," she called, following him, peering through the screen. "Where you going?"

From behind the chair, Larry couldn't hear what he said.

That night, as she had every night of his life, his mother came into his room and sat on his bed. He was facing the wall and didn't turn around, even when he felt her hand, its familiar odor of dish soap, rest on his shoulder.

"Larry?"

He didn't answer.

"Son?"

During his attacks of asthma, she'd stayed up with him as he struggled to breathe – nights were worse – rubbing Vicks on his chest, and they'd prayed together for the asthma to go away. When her rooster began to crow he'd know the long nights were nearly over. In first grade he'd told her how he asked Shelly Salter to marry him, sent her a note with two boxes drawn at the bottom, check yes or no. She'd checked no. "Silly girl," his mother had said, rubbing his chest. "Good-looking boy like you? If I wasn't your mother I'd set my cap for you." In second grade, the year he'd begun to stutter, he told her how the kids laughed at him and she'd prayed the stuttering would go away. It hadn't. The asthma either. Both got worse. In the third grade the class read aloud and Larry dreaded reading days. When he stuttered the other boys laughed and his teacher thought he was doing it on purpose and fussed at him. "It's my reading day tomorrow," he'd say as his mother sat on his bed. "Lord," she would pray, "thank you for your grace. Please help Larry read good tomorrow, take that stuttering away, and please help his breathing tonight, and send him a special friend, Lord, one just for him." Eventually the prayers worked, but on a delayed schedule. "God's timing," his mother said, "is His own." The stuttering stopped late in the fourth grade, almost overnight, and only rarely recurred. His asthma subsided gradually, gone entirely by the end of the summer before sixth grade. And then Silas had come. A friend. Silas, who was the first answered prayer he couldn't tell her about, knowing that the chilly mother who'd given Silas and Alice Jones those coats would return, that she would do something to make them leave the cabin in the woods. Now her prayer had become, "Dear Lord, thank you for your grace, and thank you for healing Larry's stuttering and his asthma. Please send him a special friend, one just for him."

Was continuing to pray for something you already had wrong? He'd even begun to worry his stuttering, his asthma, might return.

"Son?"

He was still against the wall and she took her hand from his shoulder.

He didn't answer.

She sat for a while longer. He breathed the smell of his room, the dust behind his bed.

"Larry?"

Finally she sighed and he felt her hand on his shoulder again. "Dear Lord," she prayed, "thank you for your grace. Thank you for healing Larry's stuttering and his asthma. Please," she said, and he heard that she was trying not to cry, "please, God, send him a special friend. One just – one just for him. Amen," she said, and left.

When he woke in the morning his teeth were gritty. He'd gone to sleep without brushing. His mother was in the kitchen cooking breakfast, as if nothing had happened. Through his window he saw Carl's truck gone and wondered if he'd stayed at Cecil's all night.

He slipped outside without eating breakfast and trotted all the way to Silas's with the book in his back pocket. From his spot behind a tree, he saw Silas's mother's car parked in front of the cabin and waited until she came out of the house in her Piggly Wiggly uniform and a hairnet. An old cat that had been sleeping in the sun on the car hood rose and stretched as she scratched behind its ears. Then she shooed it off and got in the car, an old Chevy Nova with rust spots and no hubcaps. She turned its engine over a few times but it finally started and she backed up, the cat sitting in the dirt road watching.

Presently Silas came out and hopped off the porch and began to throw his baseball. He had a glove now, somehow. Larry came out of the woods and walked up to where Silas stood waiting.

"Hey," Larry said.

"Hey."

Larry looked around. Then he thrust out his hand. "I brought you this."

Night Shift.

"I know you don't like to read, but these are all short stories, some just a few pages, so maybe you'd like to try em."

Silas popped his ball into his glove and took the book and looked at it.

"I need the twenty-two back," Larry said.

"How come?"

"I just do. Please, Silas."

"Tell me how come. You got a lot of em. I ain't got but the one."

"I told you. I want it back."

"No. We need it."

"It's my daddy's."

"It's my daddy's," Silas mocked.

Larry had a lockblade knife in the right back pocket of his jeans, and he slipped a finger into that pocket knowing he'd never use the knife, suddenly even having it was a disadvantage.

"You got – " Silas said then stopped. He looked past Larry toward the trees, and Larry followed his eyes, knowing what he would see.

It was Carl with a bottle of bourbon, walking toward them. "Hell," he yelled, "I followed you, boy. Just right behind you, you never seen me. Not once. Drunk I followed you, boy." He stumbled but came on. "You ain't got the slightest idea what's around you, you and your monster books. In the olden days you'd a been dead a long time ago. Some Indian cutting your throat or some gook with a grenade. You got it easy. Momma's boy reading the livelong day. Watch your cartoons, play with your dolls, read your funny books. But you can't unscrew a god dang bolt to save your life, can't charge a dad blame battery. And here when it comes to knuckles, you can't even get your own daddy's gun back from the boy that stole it."

He'd arrived before them and looked down at Silas. "You don't like that do you, boy?"

Silas folded his arms over his chest, the glove in his right hand. He wouldn't look at Carl.

"Answer me, boy."

"Naw."

"Naw, sir."

"Naw, sir."

"Why not?"

Now he looked Carl in the face. "Cause I ain't stole nothing."

"Well, if you ain't stole nothing then don't be offended." He took a long pull from his whiskey and screwed the lid back on and wiped his lips with his fingers. "And if you ain't stole nothing I'll take it all back."

He looked from one boy to the other. "Well now," he said. "Peers like we got us a dispute between the races, here." He looked at Silas. "How old are you, boy?"

"Fourteen."

"Tell me who your daddy is." He waited. "I ain't gone ask you again."

"He dead."

"Dead! Well, ain't that sad. And he didn't leave you no gun? Ain't that one of a daddy's duties? Leave his boy a firearm?"

"Tell you boys what." Carl walked over to the tree and placed his hand on its trunk, scuffed from Silas's baseball, and eased himself down until he sat at its base with his legs crossed.

"So. Yall both want the rifle. You remember in the Bible? Story of King Solomon? Wisest man ever? Two women come before him with a baby both claiming it. Know what he says? Says cut that sum bitch in two, give each woman half." Carl mimed sawing through a baby and giving Larry one side, Silas the other, all the while talking. "The one woman says, 'Good, do it,' and the other says, 'No, don't kill that youngun. She can have it.' And boom, mystery solved. What I'm getting at here, boys, is that yall have put me in the position of Solomon. I got to slice me a baby."

"I'll get the gun," Silas said.

"Don't be so hasty, boy," Carl said, unscrewing the lid. "I just need me one of them lightbulbs to go off over my head. Then we can figure this out. Wait – " He coughed and wiped the back of his hand over his mouth. "I got it. Yall got to fight it out. Man to man. White to colored. Whichever one of yall wins gets the gun."

At first Silas folded his arms and turned away. He turned to go, but Carl said if he did, he'd go tell his mother, that when she came home tired from her two shifts she'd find Carl Ott waiting inside the house, a mite drunker, too.

"Fight," Carl said.

Neither boy spoke.

"Now Larry here's a little older, but on the girly side, so I figure it's even."

Silas said, "You can't make me."

"Oh I can't?"

"Naw."

"Naw, sir. If yall don't fight," Carl said, stripping off his belt, which fell from his fist like a snake unrolling, "I'll whoop you both."

Carl started forward with the belt back and Silas came at Larry and pushed him, not too hard, and Carl stepped away, crouching like a handler at a cockfight. When Larry didn't push back Silas pushed again and Carl yelled, "Fight," and Silas pushed a third time and this time Larry grabbed him in a halfhearted hug around Silas's middle. Silas brought his knee up in Larry's gut and Larry let go and fell, his belly on fire, his breath lost, grateful for that, otherwise he'd be crying.

---

to take s.th. back to admit that s.th. you said was wrong

peers (dialect) appears

duty Pflicht

scuffed scratched or chipped
to ease yourself down to slowly sit down

sum bitch (vulgar) son-of-a-bitch (Hurensohn)
to mime to act a part with mimic gestures

boom i.e. all at once

to slice to cut up

lightbulbs to go off over my head i.e. as used in comics, to indicate that s.o. has suddenly come up with a great idea

mite (old-fashioned) bit

to strip to take off
to whoop (dialect) verprügeln
back (here): behind him
to crouch to bend down
handler a person in charge of an animal
cockfight Hahnenkampf
hug Umarmung
gut stomach

Chapter Five

pansy (slang) effeminate
behind part of the body you sit on
to pop (here): to hit
to swarm (here): to take over
to retreat to step back
to charge to attack
to trip s.o. to cause s.o. to fall
dull not loud
thud sound when heavy objects hit each other
to knee to hit with the knee
nuts (vulgar) *Hoden*
kidney *Niere*
rabbit punch a sharp blow to the back of the neck
check, check Carl is checking off a list of fighting moves. TF
eye gouging putting your finger into s.o.'s eye
to swig to drink a quantity of a liquid
muffled softer because of being covered by s.th.
to quit (here): to stop

to burble to speak in a confused manner

to flash to shine brightly
fierceness aggressiveness

fixing to (coll.) about to

to pop (here): to explode
to blare to make a loud noise

to buckle to collapse

to slur to speak unclearly with words running into each other
to bat away to push away with force

"Get up," Carl said.

He rolled over.

"He down," Silas said.

"Get your pansy behind up, boy," Carl said. He came forward swinging the belt and popped Larry's rump with it.

Larry barely felt it over the shame swarming his cheeks. He saw his hands in the dirt as they pushed up. Silas had retreated a few steps. He crouched, ready, when Larry charged, and sidestepped and tripped him and fell on his back and they were wrestling on the ground, dull thuds in the dust, cloth tearing, grunts. From above he heard Carl telling them to bite if they want to, it's allowed, kneeing in the nuts, allowed, kidney punches, rabbit punches, check, check, eye gouging, go ahead, fight dirty, the whole time swigging from his bottle, until finally Silas had Larry facedown in the dirt. When the dust passed it was over. A matter of seconds.

"Let-let-let go," Larry said, his voice muffled.

"Looks like you won yourself a rifle, boy," Carl said.

"Let me-me-me-me-me uh-uh-up," Larry said again, louder, a note of panic.

Silas tightened his grip.

"La-la-la-la-listen at the little stuttering baby," Carl said.

"Quit it Sssssilas!" he cried. "Ple-ple-ple-please."

Silas held on.

"You," Larry burbled, "you n-n-n-nigger."

Silas let him go and rose. He backed up with his fists open.

Larry got to his knees, brushing dirt from his face, spitting. Tears were falling off his chin now, dripping into the dirt on his shirt. He stood to face Silas and Silas looked different than Larry had ever seen him. His eyes now flashed the same fierceness the other black boys at school had, that the girl Carolyn had. He was already sorry but knew it was too late.

Because here came Silas and Larry saw that Silas was fixing to hit him, now on his own. Was coming around with his left hand and Larry waited for it, closing his eyes, and then Larry's head popped and the world blared with hot white noise and spots of light. When he opened his eyes he was facing another direction. His knees had buckled and he opened and closed his mouth, tasting blood, sorrier yet for what he'd called Silas and seeing, through his flooded vision, **Night Shift** facedown in the dirt. Somewhere behind him he heard their voices and looked back to a world that would never be the same.

Carl had dropped his bottle and begun to fall, hugging Silas for balance, the two dancing weirdly through the bitterweed toward the house, Silas fighting to get away, nearly crying himself as he said, "Let me go, Mr. Ott, please," and Carl slurring something in his ear that made Silas bat his hands away. He broke free and sprinted toward the far woods and Larry was left alone, on the ground, in the weeds, with his father.

Chapter Six

Wednesday morning Silas sat at The Hub's small back table, chewing the last bite of his second sausage biscuit. He'd called Angie the night before to say he wasn't coming but they could have lunch the next day. He'd slept badly and even dreamed about Larry Ott, though the dream was gone by the time he sat up amid his tangled wet sheets to reassemble its strange narrative. On the drive to The Hub he called the hospital, and a nurse said Larry had been moved out of recovery and to intensive care. He'd come through surgery but was yet to wake up.

Silas looked out the window at the mill's smokestacks, relieved again not to have to face Larry. For so long he'd used that stuttered "nigger" as an excuse to avoid him. Coming back home, rare as he did, from Ole Miss, from the navy, Silas had never asked about Larry. Once in a while as he drank and smoked weed with M&M and their pals, Larry's name would come up, Scary Larry they'd begun to call him, should they ride over fuck with him? But Silas would change the subject, put Larry out of his mind. Sure he'd heard Carl Ott had died. Who gave a shit.

"You want another biscuit, sugar?" Marla called. She wore a hairnet over her gray hair and a white T-shirt stained with grease. She was in her early sixties with a potbelly and had been cooking here when he'd been in school. She had leathery hands and a voice like a man. She bore an uncanny family resemblance to Roy French but damn if that woman couldn't make a sausage biscuit.

"No thank you, Miss Marla," he said, dabbing his chin with a napkin from the aluminum dispenser on the table and adjusting his seat on the bench so his handcuffs wouldn't pinch. He wiped his lips and sipped his Pepsi. He loved the food here, especially the hot dogs, which reminded him of Chicago. Marla used kielbasa and grilled them almost black, with a lot of ketchup and mustard and relish and chopped onion. She dabbed hot sauce on top of it and your lips would be burning when you finished.

He got up and put his notebook in his back pocket and took his hat from the chair beside him and walked past an aisle of fishing tackle and cosmetic items and up to the checkout. Facing him a wall of cigarettes, lighters, cheap cigars, aspirin, BC powders, and energy pills.

"I'm bagging you up a couple of hot dogs," Marla said over her shoulder. She had a cigarette in her mouth, the smoke a constant updraft under the hood of her grill.

"Preciate it," he said, passing his hat from hand to hand.

In a moment she came to the counter and handed him one of her greasy bags.

"Thank you, Miss Marla," he said, long past even the pretense of paying her. Instead, as she turned to get something behind her, he slipped a five into the tip jar.

Chapter Six

register *Kasse*

"I saw that," she said, turning back to hand him four ketchup packets and a few salts and peppers. She stubbed out her cigarette in the ashtray by her register. "I heard somebody shot Larry Ott."
"Sure did. I'm headed out there in a bit. Look around."
"Is he all right?"
"He's in the ICU."

grave very serious
to cluck your tongue to make a clicking sound with your tongue to express concern

"Lord, oh Lord Lord Lord," she said, her face grave. "First Tina Rutherford, then M&M, and now this." She clucked her tongue. "Well, they say bad things come in threes, so we got our quota for a while ain't we."
"I'd say we do."
She reached absently behind her for another pack of Marlboros and began to unwrap the cellophane.
"You know, 32, I always felt bad for him. Larry."
"You did?"

rapist *Vergewaltiger*

"Yeah, sugar. Whole county thinks he's a kidnaper or rapist or murderer or all three, but I remember he used to come in here buy comic books. Back when we carried em. The politest thing, that boy. Wouldn't hardly look you in the eye."
"You ever see him now?"

to carry (here): *führen*

to work (here): to operate

She shook her head and slid a cigarette out and lit it with a Bic. "I had me a girl worked the register few years ago. Didn't hear when it happened but she told me later, all proud, how she told that so-and-so he wasn't welcome in this 'family place.' That was about the time I let her go."

to let s.o. go to fire s.o.

Silas nodded and put his hat on.
"You gone see Roy today?" Marla asked.
"Don't know." He opened the bag, still warm, and slipped the condiments in.

condiment sauce that adds flavoring such as relish, ketchup, etc.

"You do, tell him I got in some fresh catfish."
"I will. Thanks." He raised the sack, greasier than when she'd given it to him. "For this, too."
"You welcome, sugar," she said, smoking.

to jiggle to move with quick, short movements
to crumble *zerfallen*
sprig a few blades of grass
to sprout to start to grow

He parked by the gas tanks in front of Ottomotive and got out jiggling Larry's keys. The shop looked the same, its white-painted cement blocks pleasantly crumbling at the edges and sprigs of grass sprouting along the foundation. He turned. Nothing moving out here, the motel across the highway silent, a child's bike parked by the front door. Had Larry caused this section of town to dry up? Fulsom had moved east, sure, but why? Silas tossed the keys in the air and caught them. Then he got back in his Jeep, smell of hot dogs, and pulled past the gas tanks and parked where Larry did each day, over that Ford-shaped rectangle of dead grass, noting the lack of an oil stain. Larry's vehicle must be the most cared-for in the county, a patient with its own full-time doctor, Larry riding along, ear cocked for any rattle, hoping for a knock, a belt to squeal, the brakes to whine.

to toss *werfen, schleudern*

cocked (here): alert
to squeal to make a long, high sound

He selected a key, and when he pushed the office door open a slab of light, punched through with his shadow, fell into the room. He reached in and clicked the light on. Smell of grease and old dust, not unpleasant. The office was small, a desk to the right, a few chairs along the wall under a calendar, an ancient Coke machine and crates of empty bottles, bookshelves.

Of course, he thought. Books. They were everywhere, double-stacked and dog-eared, novels among automotive repair manuals in brown binders. At the other end of the room another door led into the shop. He left it open and fumbled along the wall for a light switch, finding it and splashing the shop into view, a large room, high ceiling with exposed wooden rafters, car bumpers and long pipes and hoses stored up among the beams. The back walls were hung with tools and belts. There was a shelf of Interstate batteries. A metal worktable with a gutter along the back for collecting oil. There were fifty-five-gallon drums stacked in one corner and a large hand jack in another beside a tall red toolbox on casters. He came forward and opened the top drawer, the smoothest bearings he'd ever felt.

He pulled the chain that raised the bay door and stood watching the highway, struck by a memory. When he'd heard about his mother's death several years ago, he'd driven down from Oxford. On the way into Fulsom, he'd gone right past here and from the car window saw Larry standing where Silas stood now, in this spot. Silas had kept his eyes forward, as if Larry could've seen him, as if he'd been standing there all those years, watching for Silas to come back. It had bothered him, and he'd tidied up his mother's affairs quickly, ready to get the hell out of south Mississippi. She'd already paid for her funeral and the little plot out in a country graveyard, already done the work to get ready for her own death; all Silas had to do was sign some papers and collect her few belongings, which included Larry's old rifle. He'd taken it all, the gun in a carrying case, back with him, passing Ottomotive on the way out of town, too, Larry standing there, again, Silas facing forward.

At Larry's house he got out and stood in the sun. He looked at Larry's piece of sky, his view of trees, his house. He breathed Larry's air.

Glancing down, he saw something twinkle among the rocks and dirt of the road. He pushed his hat back on his head and took off his sunglasses, knelt. Glass. Without touching it he lowered his face toward the road, which already gave off heat. Little square pieces, thick. Windshield, or a window. Not many pieces, a few here and there, as if somebody had cleaned most of it up. Now on all fours like a dog, he eased his eyes over the road.

He got a few evidence bags out of the cardboard box of things he'd brought from his Jeep and used tweezers to pick up several pieces.

Next he gave the yard a thorough walk-through, circling the house once, again, finding nothing, not even a cigarette butt, telling himself you couldn't go too slow, that anything might be the piece that solves the puzzle.

---

slab thick slice
punched through with his shadow as if Larry's shadow made a hole in the light

dog-eared with the edges curled
binder ['bʌɪndə] *Ordner*
to fumble (here): to walk along uncertainly because you can't see properly
to splash (here): to completely fill with light
bumper *Stoßstange*
beam *Balken*

gutter long channel that carries off a liquid
drum large container shaped like a cylinder

bearing *Kugellager*

to bother *plagen, quälen*

plot (here): small piece of land in a cemetery
graveyard *Friedhof*

to twinkle to shine with a flickering light

to ease (here): to slowly lower

French came on the radio, asking did he have news. Silas said negative.

"You been to see him? Ott?"

Silas said he hadn't and felt French waiting.

"He ain't awake yet. I'll go when he wakes up."

"If," French said and rogered off.

Far in the distance the growl of a motor. Silas had learned the difference between the chain saws you heard most of the time and four-wheelers you heard the rest of the time. This was the latter. He walked over the field past the barn, firewood stacked neatly along the wall, the larger pieces split with an axe, all of it shielded from the weather by the high barn eave. Out at the edge of the trees he saw a few stumps, trees Larry had cut down to burn, and somehow he knew the only trees Larry would take were those dead or dying, that he would never kill a healthy tree. He turned toward the barn. The ground was soft and he looked down.

Then knelt. Four-wheeler track. He studied its treads. There. Getting up. And there. Walking. There, there, there. In the print of the tire was a perfect circle at regular intervals, probably a nail the four-wheeler had run over. He had one more of French's mold kits, didn't he?

An hour later he was sitting on the porch, sweating, waiting for the mold to dry and eating Marla's hot dogs, when he saw something in the grass. Just a speck he'd missed from his other angles.

Roach end of a joint, dewy, dirty, probably useless, but still. He tweezed it into an evidence bag and realized this alone was worth his morning. If Larry Ott smoked weed Silas would shoot his badge. Somebody else had been here. He laid the bagged roach alongside the twin bags of glass and circled the house again. At the chicken pen the birds all ran over to him.

"Yall hungry, ain't you," he said, taking their clucking and muttering for hell yes, feed us, dipshit.

He noticed the wheels on the back of the cage, frowned as he walked its width and turned and walked, the chickens shadowing him, its length. He toed the trailer hitch. Why would Larry want wheels on his pen? He looked out over the field and saw several brownish spots in the otherwise bright green weeds and wildflowers, each spot the size of the cage beside him. Walking, he imagined Larry tractoring the cage over the land, the chickens fluttering along inside. He paused at the dark spot farthest from the barn, where the weeds and grass were flattened into mud and speckled with shit and feathers, the square where the pen must have sat most recently. Coming back toward the barn, he saw that in the second spot a few sprigs were raising periscopes. In the next, the grass looked better and the shit had begun to smear away in rain and dew. Then more grass still and weeds full throttle, here and there a dot of blue salvia or goldenrod, his elongated shadow falling on the time read in grass. Within five or six days the field had recovered: you couldn't tell the cage had ever been there.

Back at the barn he stepped under the yellow tape and let himself in, taking a moment to gaze at the old tractor he'd sat on so long ago.

He heard the chickens griping so he went along the wall where a scythe hung and other instruments he didn't recognize, one a heavy iron spring coiled around an iron bar. The kind of thing the Rutherfords would hang on their den wall for decoration. He dipped his head into the coop, the chickens scattering out the door. For a moment he stood, puzzling over the twin feed sacks, one full of gray grainy pellets and the other dusty corn. Finally reckoning it was better to overfeed than underfeed, he poured a quarter sack of each onto the ground amid the trident tracks. The chickens, thoughtless, robotic beings, began to peck up the feed, and Silas remembered how he and Larry had overturned logs to catch beetles and cockroaches and pushed them through the chicken wire for the chickens to chase down and eat.

In the barn, he looked in the tack room and saw an old chain saw and Larry's fishing equipment, his rods neatly laid over big nails in the wall, his tackle box in a corner moored to the floor in dusty spiderweb. He knelt and opened it and sifted through the lures and hooks, still clean, some familiar, smaller in his hand than they'd been those years back. He remembered fishing with Larry, the boy always talking, full of information about snakes or catfish or owlets or lawn mowers and dying for somebody to tell it to.

Back at Larry's house he blasted the window unit air conditioner. Wearing gloves, he spent a long time looking at the spines of books, the old titles and plots he remembered so well from Larry's descriptions. In the kitchen he opened the refrigerator and it smelled sour. The case of Pabst. Several bottles of Coke and a few Styrofoam containers from the Piggly Wiggly grocery store. He got a Coke and used a Jesus refrigerator magnet to open its lid and drank it as he opened one kitchen drawer after another. Forks, spoons, knives. He got on a chair and looked in the high cabinets, many of which had become reservoirs for old mail. Catalogs, circulars, newspapers, flyers. Silas took a stack down and blew the dust off its top and looked for the date. June 11, 1988. Another stack was from the early 1980s. One was a stack of monster magazines, *Eerie* and *Creepy* and one about horror movies called *Fangoria*. He remembered reading some of these with Larry. He got down and moved his chair and looked in another cabinet, moving each stack to check behind it. The lower cabinets offered more mail except for one, which held cleaning supplies.

He went into the hall and stood over the gun cabinet. Sighing, he began sifting through the stacks of mail, circulars, and the book club catalogs, *Field & Streams*, *Outdoor Lifes*. A sticker with CARL OTT and his address affixed to each.

Silas had gotten stiff, and when he tilted his neck to uncrink it, he noticed the attic trapdoor.

---

to recover *sich erholen*

to gripe (coll.) to complain
scythe [saið] *Sense*
coiled wound in a series of circles
den small living-room to relax in
to dip to lower
coop cage for chickens

to reckon to conclude
trident tracks i.e. the footprints of the chickens
to peck up to pick up with the beak

cockroach *Kakerlake*

to moor (fig.) to secure with an anchor
to sift through to examine

to blast to turn up full power

spine of a book *Bücherrücken*

case box

Jesus refrigerator magnet a bottle opener with Jesus on it and a magnet that can be attached to the refrigerator door

reservoir a place to store things

affixed attached
to uncrink to loosen the stiffness
attic *Dachboden*
trapdoor *Falltür*

to depend (here): to hang down

land deed *Grundbucheintrag*

parcel small piece of land

lawyer *Rechtsanwalt*

filing cabinet *Aktenschrank*
creak squeaking sound
manila strong paper used for folders
search warrant *Durchsuchungsbefehl*
receipt [rɪˈsiːt] *Quittung*
nursing home *Pflegeheim*
power electricity

drenched (here): full of sweat
AC air conditioner

1-900 a number often used for phone sex for which the caller must pay
to get s.o. off to sexually excite

castoff s.th. thrown away

toad *Kröte*
toddler child who has just learned to walk
lap *Schoß*
maid *Dienstmädchen*

He brought a chair from the kitchen and stood on it and pushed it open. With his flashlight, he climbed into the hot darkness that was a city of boxes. He sneezed. Spiderwebs in the high corners and light through a single window in the front. A string depended from the ceiling, and he pulled the light on. He sneezed and unbuttoned the top of his shirt.

In the boxes he found old land deeds, tax papers, letters yellowed and cracked. He scanned them, amazed how much there was to say about things so long gone, people so dead. He scanned the papers. Carl Ott had once owned over five hundred acres. According to these records, Larry had sold most of them – all but the fifty surrounding this house – in parcels through the last twenty years, to the Rutherford Lumber Company. No surprise there. Larry had no business, no income, and Rutherford was one land-buying son of a bitch.

He began to look for lawyer bills but found none. An hour later he rose in the half-light and stretched his back and noticed a filing cabinet in the corner. He stepped over boxes he'd already searched and found the cabinet unlocked. The top drawer slid out with a creak of protest, showing manila file folders, each labeled. One held five search warrants, from French's visits. Another held receipts for the nursing home where Ina Ott was. Another gas bills, power bills, house payments, recent income tax forms. He slid the one labeled "PHONE" out and set it aside.

The bottom drawer held only a shoe box full of old photographs. He carried this and the phone file back to the trapdoor and lowered himself onto the chair and went to the kitchen and set it all on the table. His clothes were drenched and he went back into the living room and stood in front of the AC for several minutes. He pulled the gloves off, flapping his hands, then went back to the kitchen.

At the table he opened the phone file and studied it. No long-distance calls. Not one. No 1-900 calls to girls who'd get you off. Just the flat local rate. But another set of bills – he frowned – was for a cell phone. French had the cell. The only calls listed were from a single number, which he copied into his notebook. Sometimes a call once a month, some months with no calls at all. He put the file back in order and closed it and pushed back from the table and looked into the living room to where the bloodstain had turned dark on the wood.

The shoe box next, the photographs. Most were from a Polaroid camera, in no order, just piled in. There were a few photo albums in the back bedroom, so these must be castoffs, duplicates. He took them one by one and glanced at them, teenage Larry drawing, reading, holding up fish. Silas went faster, noting how few showed Carl or Ina, and he knew without thinking that Ina had taken the pictures. Larry cutting grass, posing with a rifle, opening a G. I. Joe under a Christmas tree, standing in an Easter suit, holding a toad. Toddler Larry in the tub, on a tricycle, crying, aging in reverse the deeper Silas dug. One photo at the bottom showed baby Larry in a woman's lap. The woman from the chest down, but with black hands. A maid, he thought. He found a few more, her dark arms bathing Larry in the sink, her hand putting in his pacifier, the woman never the point of the shot, in the pictures as a chair would be, or a table.

Only one showed her face. And the thing that stunned Silas, the thing he couldn't believe, was that this woman was his mother.

When Silas was thirteen years old, his mother's boyfriend, the one they'd been living with for almost seven years, had been arrested for assault with a deadly weapon. This was Joliet, south Chicago. Police officers kicked open the door of their duplex and flung themselves in behind shotguns and riot shields and huge square pistols, Oliver, the boyfriend, down the hall and out the back door before Silas could move.

It wasn't a bad neighborhood, and this wasn't normal the way it was for much of Chicago, especially the South Side. The three of them lived on a quiet, all-black street in an all-black neighborhood with Bradford pears planted along the curbs. There was shade, benches, a phone booth. Most everyone had a little backyard with little backyard dogs yapping under the fence bottoms. A lot of families had wading or above-ground pools, and one even had a duck that lived in their pool. It was nothing like Silas's favorite show, *Good Times,* where the Evans family lived in the projects, confined to their apartment. Silas had never even seen the projects, might as well have been Mars to him. But he hadn't seen many white people, either. It wasn't until he and his mother came south that he encountered them.

Oliver, his mother's boyfriend, drove a delivery van. He was gone a lot. When he was home, he ignored Silas.

Now the cops were bringing him back up the hall, handcuffed and scowling at the eight officers searching his house. Silas sat huddled on the sofa with his mother, who was sobbing, but he, Silas, felt no sorrow. His mother's history with Oliver had shown him two things. One, men noticed Alice Jones. And two, when men look for women, the last thing they want in the bargain is a kid. At the time, Silas had no idea that the cops could place Oliver at the scene of a fight two nights before, where a man had been shot and killed, and that they were about to find the weapon that had killed him. Silas only knew that Oliver had made it plain that, if not for his mother, he, Silas, would be in the street.

Now one of the cops said, "Bingo, violation of probation, asshole," and produced a snub-nosed pistol from high in a kitchen cabinet, Alice's face showing she'd had no idea it was there, Oliver's showing disgust. Two of the cops pulled him to his feet and led him from the room yelling "Call a lawyer" to Silas's mother as she covered her mouth with her hands.

Within two days she'd put the house up for bail money. But as soon as he was on the street, not even out of sight of the courthouse, Oliver looked at Alice and said, "Have a yard sale and get whatever you can. It's another warrant on me they didn't find, some reason,

---

pacifier *Schnuller*

to stun to amaze

assault bodily attack
duplex an apartment with two floors
riot shield large shield used by the police for protection

curb *Randstein*

to yap to continuously bark in an annoying manner

confined restricted
projects high rise buildings built to replace the slums
to encounter *begegnen*

delivery van *Lieferwagen*

handcuffed *in Handschellen*
to scowl at s.o. *jdm böse anschauen*
to sob *schluchzen*

in the bargain in addition

plain clear

bingo an expression of success
snub-nosed pistol a pistol with a short barrel
disgust *Entsetzen*

to put s.th. up for bail to offer s.th. as a guarantee that the bail can be financed
yard sale sale of things from your house in your yard
warrant *Haftbefehl*

soons's (coll.) soon as	
to match up to be determined to be for the same person	
to cup s.th. to hold s.th. with your hand in the shape of a cup	

and soon's that one matches up, and it will, I'm back in for good." He kissed Alice on the mouth and cupped her breast, there on the street, in front of Silas. "Good-bye," he said, not even looking in the boy's direction.

And he was gone.

Alice held the yard sale before anybody knew he'd left for good, and they got some cash together. By the time the sheriff's department came with the **outstanding** warrant, Oliver was in Mexico or someplace and Silas and his mother were gone.

outstanding (here): not yet served

On the bus, him leaning against her shoulder as she rocked to the rhythm of the big Greyhound, he'd asked, "Where we going, Momma?"

"Down south," she said.
"How come?"
"Cause I got people down there."
"My daddy?"
"**Hush**, boy. No."
"Who then?"

hush quiet

She elbowed him. "Don't be asking so many questions. Read your magazine."

He opened the *Sports Illustrated* on his lap. But he wasn't in the mood and looked instead out the window. He was glad to be leaving Chicago. If Oliver had spoken to him at all it was to order him to the corner store for cigarettes or to tell him get lost while he and Silas's momma "**he'd and she'd**," Silas going outside onto their tiny porch and looking up the road at a dozen or more tiny porches with people on them, big women with arms **saggy** and loose as pillows, old men smoking cigars and pushing dominoes across a card table at one another, and dogs tied to porch rails. His mother sewed in a shirt factory, and Oliver drove his brown van. It wasn't a bad **spell** of life, Silas would tell himself later. He always had hot food and his own room. TV. Laughing his head off at J.J. on *Good Times*, even Alice smiling, that big whole-face one Oliver could bring out when he imitated Flip Wilson. Silas went to a **decent** school and had friends there. Two streets over was a **vacant lot** where the boys played baseball. Silas had gotten his first glove for Christmas when he was nine; he'd outgrown it and gotten another last year.

"he'd and she'd" They fooled around or had sex. TF
saggy hanging down

spell period

decent (here): good

vacant lot *Baulücke*

Now, south. Getting out of the Greyhound each time the bus **huffed** into another small town, stretching his arms and legs, each station different, the back of an auto mechanic's shop once, a gas station next, then just a **drizzly** corner in **Gladiola**, Illinois, flat, flat Illinois **splayed** along the horizon out the bus window like a still photograph, silos and weird tall houses surrounded by stands of trees but otherwise an ocean of **harvested** wheat or corn, dead and dry and some broken **stalks** in casts of gray snow.

to huff (here): to pull in noisily
drizzly with fine rain
Gladiola fictitious name
to splay to be spread out

to harvest *ernten*
stalk *Stiel*

Then, somehow, he'd slept through both Missouri and Arkansas, waking farther than he'd ever been from home. Next stop **Memphis**, loud clanging Beale Street as his mother **goaded** him along the bright

Memphis city on the Mississippi River in Tennessee
to goad *antreiben*

morning (carrying a suitcase in each hand) and dragging her own two suitcases. The address she'd been given was a boarded-up building, condemned, and they stood looking up at it, wondering what to do as people stepped around them on their way wherever people went.

"Where we going, Momma?" he asked. Back to the bus station, his mother said. It hadn't been too far, had it? They could just walk. She thought she remembered the way.

As they struggled along, it was clear they'd overpacked, so she found a pawnshop on the corner, a tall white man in a bow tie behind the counter. While he flirted and opened the suitcases and removed her dishes and china, each piece wrapped in a bra or slip, as he lifted out the things his mother had spent her lifetime accumulating, Silas stepped away and looked along the shelves and cluttered rows at what people were willing to give up when the chips were down. Fishing rods, rifles, pistols, a dirt bike, television sets, record players. He looked at his mother where she was shaking her head at the low price all her things would bring.

They got out of another bus later that night in Jackson, Mississippi. The driver, a heavy white man, helped Alice lug their last two suitcases to the curb. Downtown Jackson seemed quiet after Chicago and Memphis, quieter without the trains he'd grown up hearing and the sirens and car horns. It was 10:00 p.m., the streets deserted except for a few people lurking in shadows, passing bottles. Against the sky, two or three tall buildings and a silhouetted bridge over some cold river. The bus driver stood there in front of the bricks, sweating despite it being January, his blue uniform shirt untucked at the back. He took off his cap and put it back on.

"Where you folks off to now?" he asked.

"Just find a motel," she said.

He eyed her suitcase, the big one, part of a set taken from Oliver.

"It ain't no motels for a stretch," the driver said. "Just your nicer hotels. The Edison Walthall, half a mile yonder ways."

"Nicer," she said. "You mean won't take black folks?"

The man pulled at his blue Greyhound lapel. "No. I mean their rooms are real expensive. I sure couldn't afford to stay there."

Alice looked up the street.

"Tell you folks what," he said. "I'm about to get off my shift here, and I got my truck parked over yonder. If yall can wait I'll give you a lift."

"You ain't got to do that," Silas heard his mother say.

"Ain't no bother. Just don't go nowhere, and I'll be back directly." He turned before going inside. "Why don't yall wait in the door yonder. It's no loitering after hours, but I'll tell Wanda there."

"We be fine," his mother said.

The driver looked dubious but went on inside.

It was cold, waiting.

"We going with him?" Silas asked.

---

to condemn (here): to declare to be unfit to live in

pawnshop *Pfandhaus*
bow tie *Fliege*
slip women's underwear worn under a skirt
to accumulate to collect
cluttered full of things piled up untidily
when the chips are down when in a crisis situation
dirt bike lightweight motorbike

Jackson capital of Mississippi
to lug to carry s.th. heavy

deserted *verlassen*
to lurk to stand around in a hidden place, possibly to commit a crime
silhouetted with only the outline visible
brick *Backstein*
untucked sticking out

stretch (coll.) long distance

folks (coll.) *Leute, Menschen*
lapel *Revers*

to loiter to stand around with no purpose

dubious doubtful

dry cleaners *Reinigung*
bail bondsman a person or firm that takes over the responsibility for s.o.'s bail (*Kaution*) for a fee

to turn on s.o. to suddenly attack s.o.

to snatch to take s.th. quickly

flashers signal lights

to coax to gently persuade s.o. to do s.th.

She was looking up the deserted street. Across was a dry cleaners, closed, and beside that a bail bondsman. A white man watching them from the steps, smoking a cigarette. No restaurants in sight.

"Momma," he said.

She was leaning, looking. She wore a blue coat and a scarf. A car drove past and the driver, a black man, looked too long at them. Silas glanced back into the bus station where the heavy driver was writing something on a clipboard. He saw Silas and smiled.

"Momma," he said again. "Where we going?"

"Silas," she said, watching the road. "You shhh right now."

"Momma? We going with that white man?"

"I said shhhhh."

"Momma – "

She turned on him so quickly he never saw her hand. She'd hit him before, but not like this, out in the open. First thing he did was look to see if the driver had seen. If he had, he wasn't looking now. Silas's next instinct was to run. He turned to go but she had him by the wrist.

"Don't you dare run," she said, "from the one person in this world who love you."

He snatched his arm away.

"You don't know where we going," he said.

He saw in her eyes that she was nearly crying. He knew he should stop but couldn't. "I'm cold, Momma, I want to go back."

"Back to where?"

"Home."

"Quit it," she said, not looking at him.

Then the bus driver's pickup pulled up and the big man was out, wearing not his uniform jacket but a blue denim coat and a baseball cap with a red bird on it. A Cardinals fan. Bob Gibson. He'd left his flashers on and grunted, lifting her suitcase into the back.

"You transporting rocks?" he asked.

Alice's smile trembled.

"I'm Charles," he said.

Alice said her name and Silas's.

"Good to meet you, Silas." Charles extended his hand.

"Silas," his mother said.

Silas shook the man's beefsteak of a hand while his mother went around and opened the side door and waited for him. Instead, avoiding her eyes, Silas threw his backpack over the truck rail and jumped in behind it.

"Boy, it's too cold to ride back there," Charles said.

"Silas," his mother said, the half-coaxing, half-threatening tone. "Get up front."

The driver clapped his hands. His breath leaked out in a thin white line.

"Boy, do what your momma says."

"Silas."

But he was dug in. "I ain't riding up there," he said. He didn't dare risk a look at his mother and sat enduring her embarrassment as they watched him.

Finally he heard Alice say, fake mirth in her voice, "Well, we from up at Chicago. I reckon this Mississippi cold ain't cold to him."

Before he closed his door, the driver said, "Now if you get too cold, boy, just bang on the window."

He sat against the back of the cab and pulled the suitcase and his backpack against him as Charles drove the truck onto the empty road. He considered jumping out when the white man slowed to turn. His teeth began to clatter and the truck bounced. He stole a look over his shoulder and saw his mother as far over the long bench seat as she could be, against the door. He could tell from the way Charles's hand moved, pointing at things, that he was talking.

Silas knew what the bus driver wanted with his mother, and he thought how he, Silas, was in a way an impediment. Without him here, she could do whatever she needed to, without witness, to get through this cold night, to get wherever she was going. He knew his mother was beautiful.

He thought about jumping out again, the next time they slowed to turn. He'd heard a train whistle a moment before and thought he could ride the rails back north, like the old men who used to gather in the alleys in their neighborhood would tell about, a fifty-five-gallon oil drum with a fire in it and the men speaking fondly of the world seen from a boxcar, drawn by in a never-ending, living mural you tipped your can of malt liquor to.

It was almost ten-thirty now, and Silas noticed they'd passed a string of low-rent motels and he hugged himself tighter. They came to a traffic light and the truck stopped all the way. Silas looked left, past the backpack he'd been using to block the wind, and saw a line of neon signs. Surely a motel in there among them. He looked to the right where streetlights led down a lonely road.

And yet this was the way they were turning. Up ahead the light stopped and the road was dark. He leaned up and looked at his mother's profile as she smiled, listening, to the bus driver who had one hand on the steering wheel and the other flapping, some story his mother was supposed to laugh at. And Silas knew without looking at her that she would, because it was polite and she lived in a world where she had to be polite all the time.

It was a world he wanted no part of. He wanted no part of her. He was already up, backpack in hand, and over the sideboard and gone. He'd catch that northbound and hobo it all the way home. He ran back toward the lights as behind him Charles's brake lights came on. He turned right between two dark buildings and ran down this alley and over a dark street toward another with a few streetlights. He crouched in an alley behind a garbage can as Charles's truck slowly rolled by, then the white man and Silas's mother were out and yelling, his mother's voice so panicked he nearly rose toward it, but instead

---

to endure ertragen

fake not genuine
mirth merriment
to reckon (here): to guess

to clatter to knock together

impediment hindrance
witness Zeuge

alley narrow path between buildings
boxcar Güterwaggon
mural (fig.) painting on a wall
to tip s.th. to s.th. (here): to hold up to s.th. as a sign of approval
malt liquor i.e. beer
string (here): group

northbound i.e. train heading north
to hobo it to travel illegally in a freight car

garbage can Mülleimer

to plug to fill a hole with s.th.

to clamp to hold tightly

decrepit run-down

to stifle to prevent from happening
yawn Gähnen

alcove (here): covered entrance in front of the bus station door
to clutch to hold s.th./s.o. tightly

he turned and plugged his ears with his fingers and ran down the alley.

He didn't know if ten minutes had passed or an hour, had no idea how far he'd gone, and was starting to feel panicky when someone pulled him behind a pair of metal garbage cans, his backpack stripped away and his coat wrenched off, somebody's hand in his pants pockets, taking his pocketknife, his forty cents. He tried to yell but another hand clamped over his mouth and somebody was pulling his Nikes off. He fought and bit the hand and when it sprang away he began to yell. In a moment Charles was there, pulling one thief away while another ran down the alley. The one Charles had by the shirtsleeve was a black boy not much older than Silas.

"Let me go, motherfucker," he said to Charles and snatched his arm so hard the sleeve came off and he was gone down the alley, the bus driver left holding the sleeve like a dead wind sock.

"You okay, baby?" His mother was hugging him. She pushed him away and looked at him. "Did he hurt you?"

Silas shook his head. He was beginning to understand that it was over, he was going to be all right, a few lights coming on in the high decrepit apartment buildings.

His mother and the bus driver pulled him up and helped him back to the pickup, waiting a few blocks away.

"Dammit," Charles said. Someone had stolen his hubcaps.

"I'm so sorry, Charles," his mother said.

She reached and touched his wrist.

They'd stolen Silas's suitcase from the back of the truck, and his mother's from inside. Got her coat, too, where she'd left it on the seat. By some miracle she still had her purse, their money. His mother climbed in the middle and Silas sat by the door, which was cold. Still, he pressed against it, shivering, his feet cold in his socks.

"Lord," his mother said to Charles, "the night we've give you."

"Well," he said, "truth is yall ain't going to find a motel room this late. They all full by now, the decent ones anyway."

"We might have to use one of the other ones, then," his mother said.

"Well," Charles's voice sounded thick, stifling a yawn. "Maybe I could drive you."

Silas heard her protesting, but he was so tired he closed his eyes. When he opened them it was warmer, his socked feet dry under the heater, and he heard Alice talking again, her chatting no longer afraid, she was happy because Charles was driving them all the way to wherever they were going.

Silas closed his eyes.

Sometime later she shook him awake and put him out of the truck, saying to stand in the alcove at the bus station door, she'd be there in a minute. He did as she said, hurrying toward the door, still half-asleep. The concrete was ice to his feet and he clutched himself and shivered awake. He looked in the big window of the bus station, the lights dimmed, the ticket window closed. A large clock said it was almost 6:00 a.m. He looked back toward the truck, where his mother was standing at Charles's window, talking to him.

Something clicked behind him, and the bus station door opened. A white woman with a giant ring of keys looked out. She wore a blue uniform like a police officer and a cigarette hung from her lip.

"Good Lord, child," she said. "Get in here before you freeze to death."

He came in as she flipped a row of light switches that lit the ceiling a section at a time.

"You by yourself?" the woman asked, walking. "Come on." Her name tag said CLARA.

"No," he said, following her over the cold white tile. "My mom'll be here in a minute."

"No, *ma'am*," she corrected. "Where is she?"

"She coming."

Clara smiled at him and stubbed out her cigarette in a standing ashtray.

"You from up north?"

"Yeah."

She raised her eyebrows.

"Yes, ma'am," he said. "Chicago."

"I can tell. You don't talk like the colored boys around here."

By the time Alice came in, a few minutes later, Clara had given Silas some hot chocolate in a Styrofoam cup and even found a pair of unclaimed sneakers from the lost and found. His mother talked to Clara, now behind the ticket counter, then came over to him where he sat in a chair by the radiator.

"Momma – "

"Silas don't talk to me."

He followed her outside into the cold and down a street toward a diner. Inside it was hot and bright with gleaming Formica tables, and for a moment he felt giddy. He smelled coffee and bacon frying. They slid into a corner booth and he wiggled his toes in his roomy new shoes while his mother flapped open a giant laminated menu. Their waitress, a young white girl, arrived with coffee for his mother. She ordered Silas bacon and eggs with grits and toast with jelly and orange juice but said the coffee was fine for her. While they waited she looked out the window and never once spoke. Soon his steaming food arrived, but she didn't watch him eat, continued to stare out the window where clandestine dawn had arrived and figures in coats began to pass the window and cars blare by as his mother held her cup with both hands and sipped.

The waitress brought Silas more jelly and refilled Alice's coffee.

"If yall ain't too busy," his mother asked, "can we just set for a while, till our bus come?"

"Yes, ma'am," the girl said. "Just let me know if yall need anything else."

---

to dim to become less and less bright

name tag small piece of paper or plastic you wear to show your name
tile *Fliese*

to stub out to put out a cigarette by pressing it on a surface

unclaimed *nicht abgeholt*
lost and found *Fundbüro*

radiator *Heizkörper*

to gleam to shine
Formica™ [fɔːrˈmaɪkə] a hard plastic used for the top of work surfaces
giddy dizzy
booth a table in a restaurant with two long seats
to wiggle to move about with small movements
to flap open to noisily open
grits hominy grits (*Maisbrei*)
jelly *Gelee*
dawn *Morgendämmerung*
clandestine (fig.) done secretly

What's missing out of you? (dialect) Why aren't you able to comprehend the situation? What's the matter with you?

to do s.o. a disservice jdm einen schlechten Dienst erweisen

to catch a ride to hitchhike

over easy the top of the fried eggs turned over and just fried for a short time
link sausage small breakfast sausage that is fried
cat-head biscuit large biscuit that is a Southern specialty
to frizz to cause to curl tightly
grump (coll.) bad-tempered person

to do s.o. a favor jdm einen Gefallen tun

job application Bewerbung

to behold, beheld, beheld (old-fashioned) to look at s.th./s.o.

When she left he said, "Momma?"
She didn't look at him.
"Momma?"
"What?"
"Ain't you hungry?"
Now she looked. "What's missing out of you, Silas?" She looked hard. "You ain't seen it that bad. I know. I know cause I have seen it that bad. But you. Up till now you had it easier than I ever did. But now I see what kind of man it's made you, I don't know if maybe I didn't do you a disservice."
He wouldn't look at her.
"I'm done fighting you so I'll tell you what I'm gone do. This here is Fulsom, Mississippi, not far from where I grew up. I'm taking the bus here to a town called Chabot. It ain't far. From there I've got to walk, or catch a ride. To a place I know. It won't be much, at first. But it'll get better, soon as I get me a job. If you want to come, you're going to be a very different boy. Is that clear?"
He didn't answer.
"Silas?"
The waitress appeared with a second plate, two eggs, over easy, four link sausages, grits, and a cat-head biscuit. She moved Silas's plate to set the new one between them.
Alice looked up to the girl's face. "Miss? This ain't ours."
The steam from this and other food had frizzed the girl's hair. "Somebody else sent it back," she said. "That old grump in the corner. He never even touched it. If yall don't want it, I'll have to throw it away."
"Thank you," his mother said.
"Enjoy," the girl said and was gone.
"Silas," his mother said.
"What?"
"Would you do me a favor?"
"What?"
"Would you go find a booth and let me set alone with my breakfast?"
"But, Momma."
"Go, now," she said. "If the place gets busy, you can come back."
He slid out of the booth and found an empty one a few behind her and watched her head move as she ate, slowly. The diner never did fill up, and he looked for the old grump who'd sent his food back and saw no one who wasn't already eating.
He and his mother sat separated the rest of the time until she rose and he followed her and she paid their bill and he stood by the door as she went back to her table and left a dollar tip. Then she asked the girl something and waited as she brought out a paper. A job application.
Hugging himself, Silas followed her out into the morning and up the street to the bus that took them five miles east through more trees than he had ever seen to Chabot where he beheld for the first time the

lumber mill he now saw daily. An old man in an ancient pickup with a cracked dash and a pair of vise grips for a window knob gave them a ride and dropped them off by the store at a bend in the road called Amos. His mother went inside and Silas followed her up and down the aisles as she bought a few things and paid, agreeing with the fat white counterman that yes, it was very cold for this time of year. From there they walked, carrying a paper sack each, without coats and Silas in his overlarge shoes, for two miles along a dirt road. He was shivering by the time they stepped over an old chain and headed down what seemed little more than a path, trees high on both sides and blocking the clouds. When they came to the hunting cabin in the middle of the field surrounded by woods, Alice Jones spoke her first words to her son since the diner.

"Find some wood," she said.

Twenty-five years later, his head full of the past, here in Larry Ott's kitchen, Silas stared at the photograph of his mother. Because they'd lost their things on the trip from Chicago, this was the first picture of her he'd seen in decades, her light skin, hair drawn back in a scarf. The smile she wore was the one she used around white people, not the one he remembered when she was genuinely happy, where every part of her face moved and not just her lips, how her eyes wrinkled, her hairline went back, how you saw every gleaming white tooth, the kind of smile he'd seen fewer and fewer times the older she got. But this plastic smile, the photograph, was better than no picture at all.

His cell buzzed and he jumped.

"You still on for lunch?" Angie asked.

"Yeah."

"What's wrong, baby? Your voice sounds funny."

"Nothing," he said, staring at his mother's face. "I'll see you in a bit."

He closed the phone and, glancing around the kitchen, stuck the picture in his shirt pocket, vaguely aware he was stealing evidence from a crime scene. He stood, covered in sweat, feeling like somebody was watching him. But who would care that he kept one picture? The only ghosts here knew the secrets already.

cracked *rissig*
dash dashboard (*Armaturenbrett*)
vise grip a device with two jaws that are tightened with a handle to hold two pieces of wood together

genuine *echt, authentisch*
to wrinkle (here): to form folds around the eyes

crime scene *Tatort*

Chapter Seven

It was 1982. Larry sat up in bed and rubbed the sleep from his eyes and looked out the window where a fence cut across his view of the cornfield and beyond that the line of trees. His life had changed. He got out of bed and dressed quickly and in the bathroom looked at his face in the mirror. He came down the hall with his hair wet and sat and watched as his mother mashed his eggs with a fork the way he liked them and salted and peppered them and set the plate between his fork and paper napkin.

"Thanks."

"Daddy's already said the blessing."

A paper napkin in his uniform collar, his father sat at the head of the table, leaning back with his head turned so he could see the news. When a commercial came on Carl turned his attention back to his plate of eggs, grits, and bacon. He added salt.

"Where's the mail?" he asked.

Larry hadn't even thought of it. "I forgot," he said.

"Larry," his mother said. "Did you tell Daddy?"

His father paused chewing his bacon but didn't look at Larry. "Tell Daddy what?"

"Larry's asked Cindy on a date."

Now he looked. "I'll be damn."

"Carl."

"Sorry."

His mother sat beside him and blew into her coffee mug. "Tell us how you asked her."

"I just done it," Larry mumbled, though the opposite was true.

The day before, he'd been walking past the Walker place with his rifle, same as a thousand other times. Their car was gone, so he was surprised when Cindy walked out of the house, almost as if she'd been waiting on him. She wore cut-off jeans and a T-shirt and suddenly, as he stood there grateful for the rifle that gave his hands something to do, she was talking to him.

"You like movies?" she asked.

"Yeah," he said. "Movies."

"You ever go?"

"We seen *Star Wars*. And *Smokey and the Bandit*. In Meridian."

"You ever go to that drive-in theater they got?"

He hadn't. It was off on a lonely two-lane, twenty minutes toward Hattiesburg, and only showed movies rated R. He remembered Ken and David talking about it on the playground two years earlier. Now they went each weekend on double dates with their girlfriends, smuggling in beer, marijuana joints, making out with the girls.

"We could go," Cindy said.

"We could?"

"Can you get a car?"

If he had to steal one he could. "Yeah."

And so, standing in the middle of the road, he'd been asked out on a date.

"Friday night?" Cindy had said.

"Friday night," he'd said.

"I'll be dern," said his father.

His mother leaned over and refilled his cup. "Idn't that something, Carl?"

But the news had come back on and his father was watching again, sipping his coffee.

Larry shot his mother a plaintive glance, and she was up and around the table with her coffeepot, blocking his father's view and leaning down eye to eye. "He needs to use my car, Carl," she said. "I told him ask you."

He'd drawn back from her but his face relaxed in a kind way, like after Larry had cut the grass without being told. "If he asks me his self," Carl said, "I reckon he can use it."

His mother leaned back and nodded to Larry.

"Can I?" he asked.

"Can you what?"

"Please borry Momma's car Friday night for a date with Cindy to the drive-in?" He was immediately sorry he'd given that detail.

"To the what?" his mother said. "I don't – "

Carl tried not to grin. "That where they show bosoms?"

"Carl – "

"Not always, Daddy." Larry had begun to blush. "This time it's a western. About the James gang. Name of it's *The Long Riders*."

"*Long Riders*," his father said. "What's it rated?"

Larry looked into his plate. "R."

"Carl – "

"A Jesse James picture, complete with bosoms."

"Carl!"

He was almost smiling and humor kindled his eyes. "They had em back then, too, Ina, I'm pretty sure they did. Yeah, boy," he told Larry, "you can go. Take the Buick. It's got a bigger backseat."

"Carl Ott, you stop!"

"Ina the boy's sixteen ain't he? Hell," he said, "I'll even pay." He produced his wallet and drew a twenty-dollar bill. He flattened it on the table and slid it over to Larry's place mat.

He could have slid a thousand-dollar bill and Larry wouldn't have been more surprised. For a moment he couldn't imagine what to say.

"Larry?" His mother raised her eyebrows.

"Thank you, sir."

"Now go get the mail."

His father still drove him to school, long talkless rides they both endured. Neither had mentioned what had happened at the cabin over a year before, Larry's fight with Silas. Carl had returned home later that evening, no apology, no mention of the rifle, come in the house

---

dern milder form of "damned"
idn't (dialect) isn't

plaintive mournful

his self (dialect) himself

to borry (dialect) to borrow

to grin grinsen

to blush erröten

to kindle (fig.) to cause to glow

wallet Geldbeutel

to slide, slid, slid (here): to move over a surface

apology Entschuldigung

as if he'd been working. Gone to the refrigerator, gotten a beer, and sat in front of the television watching baseball. They'd had supper that night, no one speaking beyond Carl saying the blessing his mother insisted on, "Bless this food, amen," but gradually, the next day, the one after, their life together had resumed, Carl working, his mother cooking and cleaning, out volunteering for the church, Larry going to school.

Riding now, he sat against the passenger door of the red Ford and looked out the window at the landscape of his life, a different landscape today, the trees and vines, the Walker house going by outside the window, its uneven porch, its tar-papered walls, the house in which his date moved, dressed, undressed, her pretty face reflected in the bathroom mirror.

Soon Larry and his father were passing the cluttered houses near Fulsom, then his father's shop, then through downtown, to the school where he said, "Bye, Daddy," and got out, Carl saying, "Have a good one," with his usual glance, Larry with his stack of books going off to homeroom.

He was a junior now, the high school still with more black students than white, but with a better ratio than the Chabot school, and so Larry, one of four white boys in his homeroom, against five black ones, felt safer. The girls were evenly divided.

Slipping into his desk this morning, he couldn't help but say to Ken, who sat behind him, "I'm going to the drive-in this weekend."

"By yourself?"

David, a row over, snickered. "Naw, Kenny, he'll have a date." He made a fist of his hand and mimed masturbating. "Same date he has ever night."

"It's Cindy Walker," Larry said, and turned back to face the front of the room, their teacher coming in, telling the class to pipe down.

"Horse shit," Ken hissed to the back of his head. "She wouldn't go out with *you*."

"Is, too," Larry whispered over his shoulder.

"Mr. Ott," the teacher said, "is there something you want to share with the class?"

All eyes settled on him and Larry said, "No, ma'am."

At break he walked past a classroom building and behind the gym, toward the baseball field. There were two sets of metal bleachers and one had been designated as a smoking area for students. Larry rarely came out here, usually spent his breaks alone in the gym, reading on a bench, but today was different. He knew Cindy smoked and hung out here with her friends in their acid-washed jeans and T-shirts. On the field the baseball team was practicing, and Larry saw Silas in the shortstop position, fielding hard-hit balls and flipping them effortlessly to the second baseman, Morton Morrisette. The double-play combo was locally famous, 32 Jones and M&M, two youngsters, the newspaper had said, you couldn't get a ball between if you shot it out of a gun.

Larry watched awhile, then spotted Cindy smoking in a cluster of white girls. He stepped out of the bleacher's shadow and waved to her. She said something to her friends and walked over to him.

"Hey," he said.

"Hey." She sucked on her cigarette and dropped it between them. "What's up?"

"Just thought I'd tell you," he said, "that *The Amityville Horror* is the movie at the drive-in."

"The what?"

"*Amityville Horror*. It's about a haunted house. I read all about it in a magazine. My momma, she would never let me see a horror show," he said, "so you know what I told her?"

Cindy was looking toward the baseball field. "What."

"That we were going to see *The Long Riders*. It's about Jesse James."

"Who?"

"He was an outlaw, in the old west?"

"Oh."

They stood a moment.

"Listen," she said. "I gotta go."

"Wait. What time you want me to pick you up?"

"Seven, I guess. The movie don't start till dark."

"Okay," he said, but she was walking off.

Then she turned. "Larry?"

"Yeah?"

"Can you get some beer?"

"I guess so."

He stood a moment watching her go, then looked back toward the field, where Silas had been staring at the two of them. Larry lifted his hand to wave, hoping the black boy had seen him talking to Cindy, but then M&M said something behind his glove and Silas turned back just in time to short-hop a grounder.

It was the slowest week of his life, clocks his enemy, their hands mocking him with their frozen minutes. Classes that took forever anyway somehow seemed longer now, and he'd lost all interest in reading. In the afternoons his mother picked him up and asked about his day. Fine, he would say. Did he talk to Cindy? No, ma'am. Why not?

"Momma, stop asking me," he said on Wednesday.

"I just thought you'd talk about what yall were gonna do."

"We did Monday. I told you. We going to the movie."

"Is she excited?"

She didn't seem to be. He'd wave to her in the cafeteria and she'd nod or raise her chin, acting embarrassed.

"I guess so."

"I remember my first date," she said.

"With Daddy?"

to spot to notice

haunted house Haus, in dem es spukt

outlaw Gesetzloser

to short-hop a grounder (baseball) to catch a ball that has bounced

hands (here): Zeiger

embarrassed verschämt, verlegen

She glanced at him. "No. It was with another man." She talked about going fishing with him, how he baited her hook and nearly fell in the water he was so nervous. As his mother kept talking, Larry wondered if he should take Cindy fishing on their second date.

Thursday at lunch he brought his orange tray with its fish sticks, green beans, and corn to the white boys' table and sat a few feet down from the cluster that included Ken and David. Each table had a teacher at its end, to keep order, Mr. Robertson, the vocational agriculture teacher down at the far end with a fat boy named Fred whose father raised cattle. Larry sat where he could see Cindy across the heads of black boys and girls bent over their food, watched her eat, her hair pushed back by a band. Silas sat, as ever, with the baseball team and Coach Hytower.

"Ott," Ken called.

Larry looked up and Ken motioned him over. Surprised and worried, he slid his tray down the table.

"You got a rubber yet?" David asked.

Larry shook his head.

"Best place to get em," David said, "is Chapman's Drugs. Old man Chapman'll sell em to you. He'll sell you a *Playboy,* too."

"He will?" Larry asked.

"What's he need a rubber for?" another boy, Philip, asked.

"Ott here's got him a date Friday. Ain't that right?"

Larry nodded.

"With who?"

"Jackie," somebody said, and the table laughed.

Blushing, Larry was about to answer when Ken said, "Cindy Walker."

The boys' heads all turned toward him.

"She's a slut," one boy said.

"How you know?" asked Ken.

"How you think?"

"I heard she likes niggers," Philip said.

"Yo momma likes niggers," Larry said quietly. Before he'd thought.

For a moment their table became the incredulous calm eye of the cafeteria's hurricane, the boys looking from Larry to Philip, Larry aware of the lockblade knife in his back pocket. Then Ken laughed and held his palm out and Larry slapped it.

"You a badass now?" Philip asked.

"He got you," somebody said.

"What's the movie?" Ken asked Larry, breaking the tension, and when he told them they began talking about it, how it was supposed to be bloody, even Philip talking, wanting, Larry imagined, to put being bested behind him.

Larry looked at the corn on his tray, too happy to eat, a date the next day and friends to tell about it. Across the cafeteria, Cindy got up with two of her pals and made their way through the crowded tables to the window where their trays were taken by thick black hands, then headed out to the smoking area.

Outside, he found himself walking along a sidewalk with Ken and David, who took out his wallet.

"Here," he said, handing Larry a flat cellophane wrapper. It said TROJAN.

Larry, who'd never seen a condom but knew what it was, took it, slippery inside the foil. "You don't need it?"

"Hell no, he don't," Ken said, and the three of them laughed, Larry removing his own wallet and putting it beside the twenty-dollar bill.

He hovered in the kitchen, his father in the next room watching the news and drinking beer, his mother making cornbread behind him. He went down the hall past the gun cabinet and looked at himself in the bathroom mirror and came back out, his father in his chair, and went back into the kitchen. He opened the refrigerator and counted nine Budweisers. His mother, humming at the counter, glanced at him and smiled.

"Be a gentleman," she said.

"Okay."

"Do you know what that means?"

"Be nice?"

"Well yes, but also stand up when she enters a room. Open doors for her. Hold her chair if yall go eat somewhere."

"We're going to the movie," he said.

"Then pay for the movie. With that money Daddy gave you. Ask her if she wants popcorn and go get it for her. It's romantic to share a bucket, but if she wants her own, that's okay, too."

He slipped a can of beer into his pocket, nodding, keeping that side away from her as he edged out of the kitchen. His father sat sipping his beer in his socks – his work shoes on the porch by the door. In his room he hid the cold can under his bed then went past his father and back into the kitchen and opened the refrigerator.

She was buttering a pan. "What's that movie yall are seeing?"

He told her *The Long Riders* again and when she asked what it was about he told her again, keeping the impatience out of his voice and slipping another beer in his pocket.

"Boy," his father's voice called.

He stopped, cold in the door. "Sir?"

"Bring me a beer."

"Yes, sir," he said, slipping the can from his pocket. When he came back out of the kitchen Carl was squatting in front of the console changing the channel. He set the can on the coffee table near his chair and turned.

"Hey," he said and Larry stopped.

"Sir?"

Carl was watching him. "Don't give Cecil none of that money."

"I won't, Daddy."

Trojan name of a firm that makes condoms

foil thin piece of metal or plastic

to hover (here): to stand around

bucket small, round container

impatience Ungeduld

to sneak, snuck, snuck (here): to secretly steal

"You got any change, bring it back."

"Yes, sir."

He snuck one more beer, knowing that was all he dare take, his thigh cold and a wet smear on his pocket.

At supper Carl cut his roast into bites and Larry's mother talked about their first dates, Larry barely chewing his rice and gravy.

"Slow down," she said. "You don't want to be early. A girl hates that."

"Yes, ma'am."

Carl asked for the potatoes and she passed them.

"You remember that old tree, Carl?" she asked.

"Tree?"

"Oh you remember. It was before we got married. Over at the bluff?"

bluff steep cliff near a river or ocean

stew dish of meat and vegetables cooked slowly in a liquid

"Yeah." He was mixing his roast into his rice and gravy, adding in the carrots and potatoes, making a big stew of it all. "Old Man Collins's land."

"That was his name. There was this tree," his mother told Larry, "growing off the side of a bluff. What kind of tree was it, Carl?"

live oak a shade tree (*Quercus viginiana*)

"Live oak."

"Yes. You could see the roots all down the side of the bank, and below there was just this awful mess of briars, you remember, Carl?"

mess disorderly mass
briar *Dornbusch*

"Yeah," he said, "would've took a dern bulldozer to move it."

bonfire large fire built in the open

"That's where Daddy and me used to go meet our friends, didn't we, Carl? We'd build a bonfire and the boys would climb that old tree and swing off a rope they had up there, like Tarzan of the Apes, and we'd watch, all us girls."

"Your momma never would do it," Carl said.

decent *anständig*

"Well, it wouldn't have been decent," she said. "In a dress."

They ate for a while, his mother filling his tea glass even though it was nearly full.

"You remember that time," Carl said, "that I paid Cecil to swing off it, him drunk?"

She said no.

Larry watched his father.

to wink at s.o. *jdm zuwinken*
gal (coll.) girl

"Oh, maybe you wasn't there then," winking at Larry, "maybe I had me some other gal."

"Carl Ott."

Larry said, "What happened?"

to pop to open with a small, explosive sound
tab *Lasche*
to scale to climb up s.th. high

Carl pushed his plate away and stood up. He went to the refrigerator and got another beer, Larry nervous he would notice there were only five left. But Carl sat down and pulled his plate back and popped the tab.

"What you did," he said, "was scale that tree. It was two big old limbs up there, the one you'd stand on and the other one, higher, where we'd tied that rope. We had a big old knot in it that you held

loop *Schleife*

on to and a loop for your foot, and you'd stand on the one branch and catch your breath, and then bail off over that gully. Best time was night, you'd be out there flying around in the dark like a dang bat."

Larry imagined it, sailing out over the world, leaving your stomach back at the tree, weightless as you turned and turned, nearly stopping at the rope's apex and swinging back where you grabbed the limb waiting like a hand.

"Now your momma's right bout that briar patch down there," Carl said. "Black-tipped thorns big as a catfish fin. You'd be better off jumping in a pit of treble hooks. Poison ivy, too. Like something out of one of your funny books.

"Now Cecil, he's scared of heights, right, don't even like going up the steps on the school bus, and wouldn't be caught dead in that tree. But the day I remember, it was six or eight of us boys out there and we'd been drinking beer and riding him all afternoon, calling him chicken, sissy, and finally bout dark I say, 'Hey Cecil. I'll give you a dollar if you go do it.'

"Cecil, he looks up that big old tree trunk and says, 'That ain't worth no so-and-so dollar.'

" 'Okay then,' another fellow says, 'make it two.'

"Cecil, he's drinking his beer, says, 'Boys, it's some things can't be bought. I'll do it for three.' "

His father smiling telling it. "He makes us take the money out so he can see it. Ain't wearing nothing but cut-off blue jeans, no shirt, no shoes, his whole family poor as niggers. Ever summer when school let out his momma'd cut off his long britches for short ones and save his shoes for one of his brothers. Went barefoot in summer, we all did, back then, feet so tough you could saw on em for a while with your knife before you felt it.

"Anyway, Cecil, he takes him another swig, he's already drunk as Cooter Brown, pops his knuckles, looks like a demented Tarzan shinnying up the tree and straddling that lower limb, not looking down, bout ten feet off the ground but the bluff out there was probably twenty, twenty-five feet down, a good long fall."

Carl paused and took a swallow of his beer. "Now I sidle up to one of the other fellows by the fire there and say, 'Watch this,' just about the time Cecil gets the rope in his hand. We can barely see him it's so dark. Trying to stab his foot in that loop. You knew he was drunk otherwise he'd a never scaled that tree much less jump. But about then he lets out a whoop and bails right off that limb. He's yelling his Tarzan yell but about halfway into it we hear it change and sort of trail off, all of us down there at the edge, looking out, trying to see. And what we see? The dang rope comes a-flapping back empty, without Cecil. We hear this scream out there in the dark then a crash, way the heck down in them briars. We all looking at each other with our mouths hanging open, thinking, we done killed Cecil.

"But about then the cussing starts, way down in the bottom, sounds like it's about a half mile off. Son-of-a-blank and mother blanker and G. D. this and G. D. that – "

to bail off to jump off
gully small valley formed by running water
dang milder form of "damn"
bat *Fledermaus*

apex highest point

patch small area of ground

treble hook fish hook with three hooks
poison ivy *Giftsumach*

to ride s.o. (coll.) to tease s.o.
chicken (coll.) a coward
sissy effeminate boy

trunk *Stamm*

it's (dialect) there are

britches trousers

swig (coll.) quick drink
to pop (here): to cause to make a cracking sound
demented (here): crazy
to shinny up to climb up using your hands and legs
to straddle to walk on s.th. with the legs wide apart
swallow *Schluck*
to sidle up to s.o. to move up to s.o. in a quiet way so as not to be noticed
to stab (here): to place into a narrow space with an aggressive movement
whoop [hu:p] loud cry

to trail off to become gradually quieter

heck milder form of "hell"

cussing *Fluchen*
blank (here): bitch
mother blanker (here): motherfucker
G.D. goddamned

to absorb s.th. (here): to reduce the effect of s.th.

welt raised mark on the skin because of being injured
ever where (dialect) everywhere
knot (here): swelling
to choke (here): to become unable to breathe properly

mill i.e. the lumber mill

to flick to move with a sudden movement
ner ever (dialect) never ever

yard *Hof*

to mess with s.o. (here): to treat s.o. roughly in a way not meant to be serious

"Carl – " his mother said, trying not to smile.

"Well, by now we was all falling down on the ground we was laughing so hard, poor old Cecil, he didn't even have him a layer of clothes to absorb the briar and thorns.

"And when he finally come climbing back up the bank bout twenty minutes later he looked like he'd been in a cage with a bobcat, welts ever where, cut all to pieces, bleeding, got a big ole knot on his head. We'd long since stopped making noise we's laughing so hard, I couldn't even catch my breath, red in the face, bout to choke, Cecil standing there in the firelight with briars sticking out of his hair, but then when he seen us laughing that fool starts to laugh himself, holding out his bloody palm for his money."

His father was shaking his head and smiling, his mother laughing and Larry, too.

"Where's that tree?" Larry said, thinking he might take Cindy. "Is the rope still there?"

Glancing at him, his father said, "Naw."

"What happened to it?"

"They cut it down. Mill did." He pushed his plate aside and rose from the table. "Enjoyed it," he said, got another beer from the refrigerator, and went into the den.

Larry and his mother sat a moment, the television clicking on in the living room.

"You best go," she said. "Don't keep her waiting."

He got out of the Buick at the Walker house, their car gone, which meant Cindy's mother was at work. Cecil was waiting on the porch, smoking. He wore his usual greasy baseball cap and cut-off jeans and a dirty white T-shirt and no shoes.

"Hey, Cecil," he said, crossing their yard, smiling thinking of him all tore up and bloody.

Cecil flicked his cigarette toward him. "Boy it ain't Cecil today ner ever again. It's Mr. Walker now, got it?"

Larry stopped.

"I said you got it?"

"Yeah."

"Yeah what?"

"Yes, sir."

"Get over here," Cecil said.

Larry crossed the yard, glancing at the windows of the little house, hoping Cindy might come out.

"Is it something wrong, Ce – " he said, nearing the porch, " - I mean, Mr. Walker?"

He stopped at the bottom step, hoping Cecil was joking, that any second that ignorant smile with its missing bottom tooth might break open, that he would elbow Larry and say, "I'm messing with you, Larry boy. You something else."

But the fist that grabbed his shirtfront and pulled him up the stairs was as hard as a sledgehammer, this man no lacerated winking fool. Cecil spun him and pushed him face-first into the coarse wall, its ancient gray boards and their faintly sweet tickle in his nose. Something, a tear, blood, ran down his cheek. Cecil had one hand behind Larry's neck and the other in the small of his back, his whiskers prickling his cheeks as he ground his face so close Larry could smell beer and cigarettes and the old meat in his teeth.

"If you so much as get a finger in her," Cecil hissed, "I'll cut your little pecker off myself." And now the grip at his neck was gone, but before Larry could move the hand had grabbed his testicles.

Larry's knees gave way but the hand was back at his neck, pressing him into the wall.

"You get me, sissy boy?"

Larry thought he might vomit. When Cecil moved his hand Larry collapsed. He heard shoes on the porch boards and tried to move.

"I said you get me? And if you say one word to your daddy – "

"Cecil!" It was Cindy, between them, pushing at her stepfather. He laughed, stepped over Larry on his way to the door. "Go on out with that one," he said. "He ain't gone do you no good tonight, you little whore."

The screen door slammed.

Cindy tried to help him up but he shook his head and lay breathing.

"I'll be right back," she said.

His eyes were closed but he felt water – not even tears, just water – spilling over his cheekbones, dripping off his jaw and chin. He burped several times, the hot roast, it was everything he could do not to throw up. He heard them yelling inside.

Then the screen door screaked and slammed and she was back, pulling him to his feet. He was aware of her against him, her sweaty perfume and cigarettes.

"Can you walk?"

"Yeah."

They went toward the car.

"He's a son of a bitch," Cindy said. "I hate his guts."

He opened the door for her. She slipped in without saying thanks and he closed it and limped around the back of the car watching the house. He got in. She was looking out the window, across the road.

"It's half a hour," he said. "fore it gets dark."

She didn't answer.

"What you want to do first?"

"This," Cindy said. "Scootch over."

He slid toward her on the seat, surprised they'd kiss here and not at the drive-in, but instead she opened her door, got out, and ran around the car and climbed in the driver's side.

Cecil came back out, lighting a cigarette.

"You get the beer?"

---

fist *Faust*
sledgehammer heavy hammer with a long handle
lacerated with skin wounds made by a sharp object
to spin, spun, spun s.o. to cause s.o. to rotate quickly
coarse rough
tickle *Kitzel*
small of the back (here): lower part of the back
whiskers short, unshaven hairs on the face
to grind, ground, ground to rub a surface
pecker (vulgar) penis
testicles *Hoden*
to give way to collapse

to vomit *sich erbrechen*

whore *Hure*

to burp *rülpsen*

to hate s.o.'s guts (coll.) to thoroughly hate s.o.
to limp to walk unsteadily

to scootch over (coll.) to move over

"Just two."
"Shit. Well?"
He reached under the seat and handed her the first.
She took it and glanced at him. "It's warm."
"Sorry."
When she popped the tab it spewed foam on her. "Shit," she said, flinging beer off her fingers.
She cranked up the Buick and spun off, flipping out her middle finger to her stepfather, and Larry looked back to where Cecil had left his porch and was walking quickly toward them, even as they peeled away throwing gravel.
Cindy sipped the beer and grimaced. She clicked on the radio and began turning the dial, settling on a station playing the Bee Gees' "Stayin' Alive." She lowered all the power windows and had trouble lighting her cigarette and then raised them all and lit it and lowered them again, accelerating over the dirt road, holding the beer in one hand and the cigarette in the other. She had on a short skirt that lifted in the wind and he could see far up her legs, her thighs slightly apart and brown from all her lying out. If Carl found out somebody else drove the car, Larry would be in trouble. Would Cecil tell? Was he right now walking over to their house?
"I better drive," Larry said. "Do you even have your license?"
"Listen," she said, "you got to do me a favor."
"Okay," he said.
She drove without looking at him, sipping the beer. "I need to get someplace else tonight," she said. "Other than the movie."
"What you mean? Where?"
She glanced at him, smoke from her lips pulled out the window. "That bastard'll only let me out of the house with you."
"Me?"
"Yeah. He thinks I'm safe with you."
"You are," Larry said.
"I know. That's why I need to go to Fulsom. I got to go see him."
"Who?"
"My boyfriend."
He moved his legs carefully, his balls still tender. "But – "
"Listen," she said. "You have to help me. Nobody else will. That Cecil's after me, and if I can't go see my boyfriend, I'll never get away from him."
"But," he said.
She slowed as they approached the highway and turned without looking or using her blinker. She was going the opposite way from the drive-in.
He didn't know what to say. The nausea was subsiding but another thing was taking its place.
"Cindy," he said. "Can't we just have our date?"
"I'm gonna tell you something," she said. "Something nobody else knows."

"Okay."

"Something you got to swear to God you won't ever tell nobody. Okay?"

"Swear."

"I swear."

"To God."

"To God."

She threw her cigarette out the window.

"I'm gonna have a baby," she said, drinking more beer.

He didn't know what to say. "A what?"

"Baby. An itty-bitty baby. And if Cecil finds out, he'll kill me."

itty-bitty (coll.) tiny

"Who's the, you know, daddy?" he asked. "Your boyfriend?"

She looked at him. "I can't say. If Cecil finds that out, he'll kill him, too."

"What you need me to do?"

"I'm going to meet him so we can talk. We got to make us a plan. You just ride around a while, but don't let nobody see you. Go on to the movie, but not till the second one starts. They stop taking admission then and you can drive on in and won't nobody see I ain't in the car with you. Park in the back.

second one i.e. second film
to take admission to sell tickets before the movie begins

My boyfriend'll drop me off at the road to my house. You can pick me up there at eleven and drive me home. That way Cecil won't never know."

He'd imagined their date dozens of times. Pulling into the drive-in, paying five dollars for the car, rolling over the grounds, past the other people in their cars and trucks, past the posts where the speakers hung. David had told him you drove to the back two rows where you had the most privacy and detached your speaker and hung it on your window and climbed over the seat with your girl and got under a blanket – his brother had one, hidden under the seat with the beer – and you began to make out. When the time was right, when the girl was hot, her legs opening, you put your rubber on and . . .

to detach to remove

Now that was all flying away, passing him by at sixty miles an hour on the highway toward Fulsom. She threw her empty can out the window and said, "You got the other one?"

"Cindy," he said, giving her the beer. "I don't want to do this. Can't we just go to the movie?"

"Didn't you hear me? Shit – " The beer exploded when she opened it.

"Didn't you hear what I said?"

"Yeah."

Wiping her hand on the car seat. "Fuck a movie. You the only person in the world who can help me, Larry. God damn it. Please?"

fuck (vulgar) (here): forget

"Can you find your way back?" she asked, out of the car, bent to see him through the passenger window.

She'd driven past Fulsom, the four-lane back to a two, then turned down an unmarked county road and then onto a dirt road.

to veer to suddenly change direction

A blacksnake had been crossing the gravel and she veered to run over it. He didn't even try to stop her. She'd parked by another dirt road, no houses in sight. The trees high and green and filled with birds.

"I said, 'Can you find your way back?'"

"Yeah." Not looking at her.

"Just be at the road to my house at eleven o'clock, okay?"

"Okay."

"Will you come?"

He nodded.

"Swear?"

"Yeah."

"Swear to God, Larry."

The steering wheel was still warm from her hands and the car stank of cigarette smoke and the seat was wet with beer. He'd have to leave the windows down so his mother wouldn't smell it.

"I swear to God," he said.

to pull a car up to stop and park

He pulled the car up and she stepped out of the way as he backed into the dirt road and turned around. She waved at him but he didn't wave back, just clenched the steering wheel and nudged the gas pedal, the Buick bumping over the road, passing the blacksnake where it lay, leaving her in the woods in the gathering dark, watching her in the mirror as he drove away, watching her turn and begin to run – *run* – toward her boyfriend, waiting somewhere down that road.

to nudge to touch lightly
to bump to move up and down
to gather (here): to increase

feature main film

intermission *Pause*

Later he would do as she told him. Ride around alone. Take the Buick to the drive-in, park out of sight and watch as the first feature ended, the movie family fleeing the house in Amityville and its devils, wait through the intermission, food advertisements, coming attractions, the radio playing songs he didn't hear and describing weather he didn't feel. He waited until the second feature began and then pulled with his lights off past the ticket booth, which, as she'd said, was empty. With the screen flickering over him, he eased the Buick past cars and trucks filled with men and women and boys and girls and past the metal poles with their speakers blaring and squawking, past popcorn boxes pushed by the wind, empty Coke cups rolling in his wake. He parked on the row second from the back, near the corner, shadowed from the moon by trees, lowered his window and unhooked his speaker and watched the people move on the screen.

to blare to make a loud sound
to squawk to make a loud, sharp sound

slot (here): place for a car to park

The movie was half an hour in when a car backed out a row up and several slots down. In the light from the movie, he watched it become Ken's father's Ford Fairmont and realized they must have seen him drive in. Its parking lights on, the car rode to the end of the row and turned and began coming back toward him. As it neared the Buick, it slowed, then stopped and backed into the spot behind Larry. Its parking lights snapped off. From there, Ken and David, or Ken and his date, would be able to see that Larry was alone.

He reached beneath the seat for the blanket he'd brought. Quickly, he covered his open hand with it and held it up beside his shoulder as if it were a girl's head, Cindy sitting very close. He watched his rearview mirror, unable to see the Ford's interior. Maybe it wasn't even them. But he knew it was. He sat, hoping they wouldn't get out, even bent his arm as if she were leaning to whisper something in his ear. Maybe kiss him. When his biceps began to tire a few minutes later, he reached and pulled the armrest from the seat and rested his elbow there, barely aware of the movement on the screen.

In his mirror the Ford's interior lit Ken and David's faces as Ken opened the driver's side door. He got out and stood. Maybe he was just going for popcorn. Still, Larry reached around, under the steering column, his wrist at a painful angle, and started the car. Ken was coming forward now, getting close, angling his head to see. Larry pulled the shifter down to drive and lurched away, steering with his left hand, straining to keep his right up, the blanket steady, as if he and Cindy had decided they'd had enough of the movie, leaving Ken standing in his empty spot.

He arrived at the road fifteen minutes before eleven, hoping to see the boyfriend. Maybe recognize his car. He had an idea it was an older fellow. Her mother worked a late shift in the tie factory on Fridays and wouldn't be home until midnight, but, in case Miss Shelia got off early, he rode past their mailboxes and parked farther on, out of sight. He sat with the windows down, hoping the cigarette and beer smell had dissipated, watching for lights.

At eleven, he sat straight in his seat. They'd be along any minute now.

But at eleven-fifteen, no car. The half moon blackened the trees in front of it and rose yellow and cocked in the sky. No car at eleven-thirty. Maybe the boyfriend had dropped her off early. But wouldn't Cindy want to sustain the illusion of her date with Larry? He cranked the car and, lights on low, drove slowly by the turnoff, expecting to see her standing by the mailboxes with her purse.

She wasn't there. He drove by again and parked in his same spot, growing more worried.

At ten to midnight he got out of the car and stood at the edge of the highway and listened, trying to hear over the crickets and frogs. Looked one direction, the other. Overhead, an airplane winked across the sky, the moon's high cratered cheek centered in its spackling of stars. He stepped into the road to better see. Maybe they'd had an accident. How would he explain that to Cecil? To his father? Maybe, a dreadful thought, they already knew, the police having called.

At ten past twelve he began to hope he'd missed them somehow. Maybe the boyfriend had snuck in with his lights off, afraid Cecil might be lurking about. Larry cranked the Buick and clicked the headlights on low beam again and eased onto the pavement and turned off at the familiar dirt road that snaked past the Walker house and ended up, a mile farther, at Larry's house. He drove, hoping Cindy might pop out of the trees, angry at him, *Where the hell you been?*

---

biceps muscle in the upper arm

angle Winkel
to angle to tilt
shifter Gangschaltung für einen Automatik
to lurch away to abruptly drive away
to strain to do s.th. to make a great effort to do s.th.

to dissipate to gradually become less

cocked raised up
to sustain to maintain

turnoff a place where a road leads off from a larger road

to wink (here): to fly with blinking lights
spackling having many little spots

dreadful awful

to pop out to suddenly appear

diorama three dimensional scenic representation	
slashed with leaves (fig.) with leaves seemingly cutting through the trees	
to case off to enclose	
ditch long channel dug along a road or field	
strained tense	
to crunch to make a crushing sound	
passed out unconscious	
to alert to warn	
to work yourself up for nothing to unnecessarily worry about s.th.	
commotion (here): crisis	
torch Fackel	
to ignite to make s.th. start to burn	
boozy (coll.) characterized by alcohol	
to lurch forward to suddenly move forward	
to slam to move with force	
gear gearshift	
park the position of the gearshift of an automatic transmission when a car is parked, to prevent the car from rolling	
belt loop strip of leather you put the end of the belt through	
to snap off to break off with a sudden noise	
to sling, slung, slung to throw with force	
to scrabble away to move away hastily on all fours	
to growl to speak in a low, angry voice	
to strangle s.o. jdn erwürgen	
threadbare shabby, worn	

I said eleven! Cecil's gone kick my ass and yours, too. But no mad girl in his lights. Just the dusty diorama of trees hung with vines and slashed with leaves and the bobwire fence casing off the woods from the ditch.

He sat for five more minutes, fingers drumming the steering wheel. His own parents would likely be worried, too. He was more than an hour late. Because he'd never had a date, he didn't know if they'd sit up and wait or what. He imagined his mother's strained face. How had the date been? He turned the lights off and began to crunch over the gravel, the crickets as he passed silencing and then starting up after he'd gone. Maybe Cindy was someplace between the road and house. Maybe drunk and passed out. He slowed again, barely moving now, afraid of running her over if she lay on her back.

Afraid of alerting Cecil, too. Maybe he'd have already passed out. Likely they were both there, him and Cindy, and Larry was working himself up for nothing. Certainly there was an explanation. Why did he have to make such a commotion out of this? He eased, lights off, closer to the house.

Finally, the last turn before the yard would open out. Fingers still drumming. He knew what he had to do. He had to go up and see if she was home safe.

When he rounded the curve the house was dark. He slowed, thinking about that. Were they all asleep? Wouldn't they leave a light on for Cindy's mother? She wasn't home yet because he didn't see her car. He touched the brakes and reached for the gear, about to shift into reverse, when Cecil appeared from the darkness like a torch ignited, filling his window with hot boozy breath and anger and sweaty arms.

"Where you been, you little fuck?"

His hands grabbing Larry's neck, his shirt collar, Larry fighting the arms, the car lurching forward, his feet stabbing at the brakes. Cecil held on to him and he slammed the gear up into park just as he felt himself pulled out the window, the door lock caught in his belt loop, snapping off. Cecil had him by the shirtfront, against the car.

"Where is she?"

"I don't know," Larry said, "I thought she was home."

"Thought she was home?" He slung Larry around, into the dirt. "Why the fuck would she be home?"

"I let her out," Larry said, scrabbling away.

But here Cecil came, straddling him now, both on the ground, Cecil growling, "Dropped her off where?" and Larry trying to speak but the man's hands were around his neck and he might, he thought later, have been strangled if car lights – Miss Shelia, home from work – hadn't suddenly found them there, wrestling in the dirt.

Half an hour later the sheriff arrived.

Before that, before Larry's parents drove up in Carl's truck, Miss Shelia, her hands shaking, had put on coffee. Larry sat centered on their threadbare sofa, his first time, some part of him realized, inside this house. It was low and dark, uneven floors. A small television with a rabbit ear antenna and the channel knob missing. Ashtrays with mounds of cigarette butts and a few framed class photos of Cindy on the wall. He tried not to look at them. Waiting for the Otts, Miss Shelia had busied herself sweeping the floor and collecting empty beer cans while Cecil sat across from Larry in a kitchen chair, glaring at him and smoking one cigarette after another. He'd switched from beer to coffee, Miss Shelia hissing, "You don't want to be drunk when the law gets here."

The sheriff, with an air of getting to the bottom of things, out of uniform and wearing no socks under his house shoes, sat by Larry, ignoring the parents, asking him, patiently, *exactly* what had happened. Said don't leave nothing out. Larry told how she'd wanted to be dropped off in the woods, aware of the adults watching him. When he got to the part about the drive-in, he skipped using the blanket as her head and said he'd decided to leave during the second movie. Because he'd sworn not to, he didn't mention her being pregnant. The sheriff put his hands on his knees and sat back. Teenagers, he said. Wasn't no point in getting all worked up. She was probably out with some boy and would show up later that night. Was such behavior beyond the girl? No, her mother admitted, it wasn't. Teenagers, the sheriff repeated. Well, why didn't everybody just go on home. If she hadn't come back by morning, give him a call, he'd look into it.

That seemed to satisfy everyone but Cecil, who stormed outside cursing, but when Larry stood to go the sheriff said, "What a minute, buddy."

Larry stopped and felt the man reach into his back pocket and pull out his lockblade knife.

"All boys carry em," Larry said.

"Well," said the sheriff. "Let's see what tomorrow brings." He put the knife in his pocket.

Tomorrow did not bring Cindy home. Nor the next day or the one after that. Word got out that she had disappeared on a date with Larry, and then, Monday at school, Ken and David told about seeing Larry and Cindy screeching off. The sheriff was notified. Because Larry hadn't told that part, his story seemed flawed, revised, and on Tuesday he found himself, along with his father, riding to the sheriff's department for the first of many "talks." Here, the sheriff growing stern, Carl angry, Larry confessed to how she said she'd been pregnant. Why hadn't he said this the other night, the sheriff wanted to know. Because I swore I wouldn't, he said.

The three rode in the sheriff's car, Larry in the backseat, caged off from the front, no handles on the doors, to the spot in the woods where he'd dropped her off, the sheriff asking Larry did he see any tracks that would verify a car had been waiting. Did he see a cigarette butt? A rubber? Anything to help prove Larry wasn't lying? No, no, no, no. Well, the sheriff said, hadn't Larry worried about leaving a

---

rabbit ear antenna small TV antenna placed on the TV
channel *Program*
mound pile

the law a police officer
to get to the bottom of s.th. to find out the facts to explain s.th.

to skip to leave out

beyond the girl not typical of the girl

to storm to go somewhere in an angry, noisy manner

to curse *fluchen*
buddy an informal manner of addressing s.o.

to screech off to noisily drive off
flawed (here): having parts that do not seem to logically fit in with the narrative
revised (here): changed to hide certain facts
stern very serious, severe
to confess *gestehen*

to verify to confirm

deputy assistant sheriff
hound hunting dog
to wade to step through shallow water
to drag (here): to thoroughly search between the surface and the bottom of a body of water
bulletin public notice
fervent ardent, intense

to dwindle to become steadily less
to trickle in (here): to occasionally appear
disheveled untidy, unkempt

period (here): completely
to mind (here): to take care of s.th /s.o.

crack sharp sound when being hit
clink sharp, ringing sound

to rape vergewaltigen
to recede to move gradually away
duffle bag large soft, cloth or leather bag for traveling
crew cut a very short haircut
army recruiter person who tries to convince young people to join the army
to stand trial to appear in court because of being accused of a crime

bland not having much taste
assignment time (here): the time to decide what special training one would should have

young girl alone in the woods? What kind of a gentleman would do that? Out of answers, Larry was led back to the car.

Cindy's friends were asked to volunteer information about her, who she might've left with, where she could've gone, but nobody knew anything, everyone swearing she wasn't seeing *anybody*. Meanwhile, deputies looked for Cindy in Carl's woods, pulled by hounds, kicking through leaves, wading the creek, searching other parts of the county as well, dragging lakes, interviewing Larry over and over, sending out bulletins, nailing up posters. Larry never returned to school, the weeks stretching into months, and when even the most fervent optimists were beginning to doubt she'd run away, after Silas had left for Oxford, Larry spent his hours in his room, reading. His father switched from beer to whiskey and drank more and more, starting earlier in the day as his business dwindled, fewer and fewer customers each month until the cars that trickled in were the cars of strangers, strangers who found a disheveled drunk sitting in the office smoking cigarettes, a man who'd stopped talking to his son period and quit telling stories. Larry's mother stopped going to church and stayed home, minding her chickens, often standing in the pen gazing into space or at the kitchen sink in her yellow gloves, hands sunk in gray dishwater, looking out the window. Their lives had stopped, frozen, as if in a picture, and the days were nothing more than empty squares on a calendar. In the evening the three of them would find themselves at the table over a quiet meal no one tasted, or before the television as if painted there, the baseball game the only light in the room, its commentators' voices and the cracks of bats and cheers the only sound, that and the clink of Carl's ice.

Larry wouldn't remember, almost a year later, whose idea it was, his going to the army. But because Cindy's body had never been recovered, because no trace had been found, not a hair, a spot of blood, a thread from her short skirt, and despite most of the county's belief that he'd raped and killed her, Larry had been allowed to board the bus in Fulsom, his mother receding in the window as he sat with his duffle bag and crew cut and rode across the bottom of the state away from Fulsom then north to Hattiesburg for basic training. The army recruiter had informed his commander of his situation and all agreed, should evidence occur, that he would be returned to stand trial. They'd keep their eye on him.

In the bus he saw his face reflected in the window and reached up, took off his glasses. He looked thinner without them and left them on the seat when he arrived at Camp Shelby.

There, he found that the anonymity of army life fit him, basic training where he lost twenty pounds, the bland food, the busy hours. When assignment time came, a sergeant asked him what his talents were and Larry said he didn't have any. The man asked, well, what did his daddy do. Larry said, "He's a mechanic." The sergeant wrote something on a form and mumbled, "If it's good enough for him, son, it's good enough for you." Which was how Larry found himself in the motor pool among engine blocks hanging from chains and upraised hoods and good-natured city boys with cigarettes in their uniform pockets. Larry smiled at their jokes but kept to himself, in his bunk, in the mess hall, alone over his clean work station handling wrenches, ratchets, screwdrivers, and pliers that felt and weighed the same as his father's had, that smelled and gleamed the same, his year-long apprenticeship as a mechanic in this army barracks where Jeeps and trucks came in an endless line, Private First Class Larry Ott, Serial Number US 53241315, not so disinclined as his father had claimed, emerging a certified mechanic. With his duffle bag and a shopping bag filled with paperbacks, thinner in his uniform, he was transferred to Jackson, Mississippi, this new part of his life seeming not so much like another chapter in a novel as a different dream in the same night's sleep.

Each time he went home on furlough – Christmas, Thanksgiving – he found his parents both older and stranger, his mother forgetful of where the dustpan was, how the gas stove worked. Larry was somehow taller than the father who couldn't seem to look at him, always out of the house, working, though his shop was as empty those days as it would be after Larry took it over, after Carl, who passed out every night in his chair by the television, finally ran his truck off the road into a field on his way home one summer's evening and went through the windshield and broke his neck, the overturned truck barely damaged, still running perfectly when it was found. Larry was called in to his captain's office near the end of his third year of service to hear the news. Honorably discharged, he was moved shortly thereafter back home where all agreed – the new sheriff, the chief investigator, and the lieutenant in charge of Larry's unit – that he should care for his mother.

In Chabot, Silas was still gone. And still no Cindy. She hadn't returned, and no hunter, no lumberjack, had stumbled upon her bones, no hound had nosed them up. Cecil and Shelia Walker had moved, he didn't know where, and the old house without them seemed to have given up, ended a brave stand, sagging with the relief of vacancy, weeds sprouting through the steps, privet over the windows and kudzu vines slithering around the porch posts. The NO TRESPASSING sign someone had nailed on the door had begun to fade.

For years, after Larry had signed his mother into River Acres, he would wake each morning to the faraway growl of power saws cutting down trees on the acres he'd been forced to sell, the shriek of back-up alarms, the grumble of log trucks trundling the muddy ruts to deliver their quivering wet hardwood to the mill's teeth. Soon the land he had walked as a boy, the trees he'd climbed, had been winnowed to three hundred acres, the land surrounding it clear-cut, replanted with loblolly pines that rose quickly toward the sky and would, he knew, be ready for harvest in another fifteen years. Days, he waited for customers, his shop more a tradition than a business. Evenings, on his porch or by his fire, he read. Nights he spent alone,

---

bunk Stockbett
mess hall (AE) where soldiers eat their meals
wrench Schraubenschlüssel
pliers Zange
apprenticeship Lehre

to emerge (here): to end up as s.th.
certified official

on furlough [ˈfɜːrloʊ] on holiday that is officially granted a soldier

honorably discharged ehrenhaft entlassen

lieutenant [lüˈtenənt]

lumberjack Holzfäller
to stumble upon s.th. to accidentally discover s.th.
stand (here): defense
to sag to hang down
relief Erleichterung
vacancy i.e. no-one living in the house any more
to slither to glide
to fade (here): to lose the bright colors of the letters
growl deep, loud sound
shriek high, unpleasant sound
grumble long, low sound
to trundle to move along slowly and noisily on s.th.
to winnow (fig.) to reduce in size

seldom thinking of his mother's old prayer, the one where she asked God to send him a special friend.

Until it was answered.

Chapter Eight

Silas just beat the lunch rush and got a corner booth. He put his hat off to the side and waited, gazing out the window at the high crumbling courthouse across the street, its arched windows and columns, at the white lawyers in suits walking down one side of the long concrete steps and the families of the black folks they would convict or acquit walking down the other. The diner door opened and a group of white ladies came in, all taking at once. Silas usually avoided this place – his mother had waited these tables for more than twenty years, bringing his supper from here so often he'd grown to hate the food. But today the diner held a comfort. Maybe it was the closest he could get to Alice Jones, dead so long with her secrets. And his.

A young waitress with enormous breasts and blue eyeliner arrived with pitchers of iced tea in each hand. "What's up, 32 Jones? Sweet or un."

"Sweet, please, ma'am," he said, turning one of the glasses on the table upright so she could fill it, trying to remember her name.

"I seen you was in the paper," she said. "That article about M&M."

"You did, huh?" He'd forgotten the *Beacon Light* came out today. No mention of the rattlesnake in the mailbox, then. With dead bodies and missing girls, must not be news enough. Because it was a weekly paper, the news about Larry being shot wouldn't be printed for a while.

"Um hm," she said. "You ready to order yet?"

He said he was waiting for Angie and, still trying to remember the waitress's name, afraid to stare at her chest, where her name tag was, he opened his phone. The girl was gone by then, her next table. Nobody had called. Silas shut the phone and sipped at his tea until the door opened and Angie came in. Even in her light blue uniform shirt and navy pants she looked good, her mouth to the side, her hair braided. He liked that she never wore makeup or did her nails. He got up and they kissed briefly, then slid into the booth, facing each other.

"You been busy?"

"Not long as you don't call," she said, taking one of the giant plastic menus from its rack. "What you hungry for?"

"Just this tea."

She looked at him over the menu. "You ain't still green from yesterday, are you?"

"Naw," he said. "I eat two of Marla's hot dogs earlier."

"Lord, 32. You want me to call Tab and get him to bring our defibrillator?"

The waitress came and topped off his glass.

"Hey, Shaniqua," Angie said.

"Hey, girl. How you manage to finally get this man come eat in here?"

"You know he do everything I tell him."

Silas, who'd been staring out the window, glanced at them and smiled.

"Thanks, Shaniqua."

Angie ordered a hamburger with everything. Oh, and fries – mustard on the side – and a Diet Coke.

"What you so glum for?" she asked when the waitress left. "Paper ain't call you 31 again did it?"

"Naw."

"Then what?"

"Just thinking about Larry Ott."

"You been to see him?"

"Naw."

"He ever wake up?"

"Not last I heard. I been over at his place all morning. Roy wants me to handle this one while he works on that missing girl."

"Tab thinks he shot himself," she said.

"Roy thinks so, too. Else he wouldn't a put it off on me."

"Them two ought to know."

"Why now, though?" he asked. "After all this time, why shoot his self now?"

"Maybe he did take that girl."

Silas was shaking his head. "Naw, I can't see it."

"Think about it," she said. "If he kidnapped that first girl way back when, then maybe he got a taste for it. Maybe he's been nabbing girls all along and getting away with it. Or else been holding off long as he can. But either way, he sees cute Tina Rutherford and goes all Hannibal Lecter on her. Then it's all over the news and he realizes who it was, big rich family, and gets worried." She made her hand a pistol and pointed it at her own chest. "Bang."

"What if he didn't take that first girl? In high school."

"Maybe everybody thinking he did's finally added up for him. All those years of nobody talking to him. You think he ever gets laid? Man with his rep? Maybe he finally snapped and said to himself, 'All right, if they gone treat me this way then where's the nearest girl?'"

Shaking his head. "I just don't think he's got it in him."

"How you know?"

Silas took a breath. Then he said it. "Cause I used to be friends with him."

Shaniqua appeared with the food but Angie didn't seem to notice.

"You welcome," Shaniqua said, leaving.

"What you mean, friends?"

"A long time ago. When I was fourteen years old . . ." He hesitated, looked out the window again, people and cars passing in front of the big white building devoted to the law, three floors of it.

"32?"

"When I was fourteen years old, me and my momma came to Amos from Chicago. On a bus." From there he started to talk, things he'd never said out loud, how they'd ridden down from Joliet, how they moved into Carl Ott's cabin, no water, no electricity, walking two miles to the nearest road, how Carl and Larry picked them up until Ina got wind of it and gave them those old coats, how the next day Silas's mother came home in a Nova and never did say where she got it. He was still talking when Shaniqua passed by again and said, "If you ain't gone eat that, Angie, somebody else will."

Angie ignored her but started on the food, opening the mustard packets and squeezing them onto her plate for her French fries, chewing her hamburger slowly, sipping her Diet Coke through a straw as Silas told how, at first, he'd been shocked how quiet the woods seemed compared to Chicago, no crowds, car horns, sirens, no el train clacking by. But in the woods, if you stopped, if you grew still, you'd hear a whole new set of sounds, wind rasping through silhouetted leaves and the cries and chatter of blue jays and brown thrashers and redbirds and sparrows, the calling of crows and hawks, squirrels barking, frogs burping, the far baying of dogs, armadillos snorkeling through dead leaves and dozens of other noises he slowly learned to identify. He found he'd never seen real darkness, not in the city, but how, if you stood on the cabin porch on a moonless night, or took a walk through the woods where the treetops stitched out the stars, you could almost forget you were there, you felt invisible. Country dark, his mother called it.

"I didn't like it at first," he said, "being down here. But after a while, after I'd got me that rifle from Larry, and after I started playing baseball, I felt like I belonged here. It's part of why I came back, after all that time. I'd never forgot this place."

Shaniqua came and stood over them with her pitchers. "More sweet?" she asked Silas. He nodded and she filled it. "You want another DC?" she asked Angie.

"No, thanks."

Silas was looking back out the window, rubbing the brim of his hat. He told her about Carl and the fight with Larry as she slowly stopped eating. "After that," he said, "me and Momma moved. To Fulsom. She'd done saved enough money for a house trailer. I went to Fulsom Middle and didn't see Larry again till high school. By then I was playing baseball. Everybody calling me 32. Name in the paper all the time. And Larry Ott, he was just a hick that nobody liked."

"How come?"

"He was weird. Lived so far out in the country he didn't have any friends. Never came to ball games, didn't go to the junior prom. Always reading his books. He used to bring stuff to school, snakes he'd catch, trying to make people notice him. I remember one time, Halloween, must've been junior year. He come to school with this monster mask."

Silas hadn't thought of this in years. It was a zombie mask with fake hair and rotting skin, made of heavy plastic and red with gore, as realistic as anything anybody had ever seen, like a real severed head. "I can see it plain as day right now," he said. When Larry had

to get wind of s.th. to find out about s.th. secret
Nova Chevy Nova – type of car

to clack by to ride by on rails that cause short, loud sounds
to rasp to produce a rubbing sound
hawk *Habicht*
to bay to bark with long tones

DC diet Coke

she'd done saved (dialect) she had saved
Middle Middle School: school grades five to eight
hick (coll., AE) stupid person from the country

junior prom formal high school dance for the junior class

zombie a walking dead person
rotting *verrottet*
gore blood
severed cut off
plain clear

Chapter Eight

to flock s.o. to gather around s.o. in large numbers

dumbstruck so surprised as to be unable to speak

haunted house *Spukhaus*

abandoned (here): deserted
to beam (fig.) *strahlen*
awkward clumsy, lacking grace

dizzy causing a spinning sensation
to litter to cover in a disorderly manner
bale large bundle
aloof distant

plastered sticking closely
skull *Schädel*

floodlight *Flutlicht*
to deflate to become smaller because of losing air
to pave *pflastern*
to whip (here): to flatter violently
senior (AE) a student in the last year of high school

to linger to continue to wait somewhere for a while
to purr (here): to run (an engine) quietly
brights high beam of the headlights

shown up in homeroom wearing it, kids flocked him. Silas saw him by the gym, as pretty girls, cheerleaders, passed it head to head trying it on. When dumbstruck Larry got it back and pulled it over his own face again, it must've smelled like Love's Baby Soft Perfume and Suave shampoo and Certs. Then another group of girls was calling Larry over. Could they see his mask, try it on? Would he bring it to the Fulsom First Baptist Church Haunted House that night? Wear it in one of the rooms?

Of course, he would.

Silas had practice that afternoon, and afterward, he and M&M and other teammates rode in the back of somebody's pickup truck over to the abandoned house on Highway 5. Larry was already there, wearing a white sheet with a hole scissored for his head, beaming. When he gave Silas an awkward wave, Silas turned his back. For the next three hours Larry had his own room in the haunted house, a room dizzy with strobe lights and littered with fake body parts, shrieks from speakers hidden among bales of hay. People streamed through all night, groups of teenagers, boys pushing at one another, couples, some with terrified children. Silas, aloof, watching it while sneaking beers from the back of the truck, keeping an eye on Larry, thinking that tonight Larry must've felt almost normal.

At midnight, the end, Larry came out of the house, pulling off his mask, his face red from heat, his hair plastered to his skull. He stood, waiting to be noticed, congratulated on his performance, maybe, welcomed by the group, given a beer. Cindy Walker was there, too –

"Who?" Angie broke in.

"The girl," he said, annoyed he'd brought her up, "who went missing."

She watched him.

"Anyway," he went on, "when Larry come out of the haunted house, we all just kind of pretended not to see him. All of us."

He told her how Larry stood in the floodlight for a long time. Figuring it out. The mask deflated under his arm. Finally he turned and walked down the dirt road toward the paved one. He paused at the road in his whipping sheet and waited, as if a car was coming though none was, waited a long time, and still no car came. Some of the seniors had forgotten him and were passing cigarettes and beers, but Silas watched as Larry finally crossed the road and walked into the parking lot. He stopped there, too, and took off his sheet and looked over the cars, as if selecting one to buy. He'd forgotten where he'd parked his mother's Buick, that's what he was doing now. In case anybody glanced over and happened to notice him and yell, "Hey, look! It's Larry! Come back! Join the party!"

No one did, including Silas, including Cindy. And after Larry got in the car and lingered in the parking lot, its engine purring, Silas didn't run after Larry as he slowly, slowly crackled through the parking lot, didn't signal him over as he sat with his brights on, shining down the dirt driveway to where everybody looked away and kept talking, and

Silas didn't wave to him as Larry drove past them slowly, and they all watched his brake lights as they lingered through the trees, and lingered still, as if he might come back. When he was finally gone, Silas remembered, Cindy and everyone else, himself included, began to laugh.

Angie's lips were over to the side and he knew she was thinking. "How long was it, from that night, till that girl, Cindy, went missing?"

"Couple months?"

couple (of) (coll.) about two

He paused as Shaniqua appeared and cleared away Angie's dishes.

"You want more sweet?" she asked Silas.

"Naw, I'm good."

"Thanks, girl," Angie said. Then to Silas: "Did you ever go out with her?"

"Cindy?" Not meeting her eyes, turning his hat over on the table. Thinking *Just tell her* but instead shaking his head nope, saying, "Her stepdaddy was one of them white men any smart black boy would avoid, especially in Mississippi."

nope (coll.) no

Still watching him. "Who ever accused you of being smart?"

to accuse beschuldigen

He smiled.

"But Larry took her out?"

"Yeah."

"Why'd she go? If he was such a loser?"

Her radio squawked and Tab came on, wreck over on 201.

"Shit." She rose with her drink. "Sorry, baby. I hate to leave cause this is the most you have *ever* talked."

She leaned to kiss his head. "We gone finish this conversation," she said and hurried out, the ambulance pulling to the curb, lights flashing.

Shaniqua came to the table. "Yall talking about Scary Larry?"

He looked up. "Yeah."

She began collecting dishes. "My momma went to school with him? She say that boy used to always have snakes in his pocket."

Silas took off his hat as he passed through the hospital's electric doors and stopped at the information desk and asked where he could find Larry Ott. The red-vested volunteer, an old white man with eyebrows thick as mustaches, put on a pair of glasses and frowned at his computer screen.

"Are you family?" he asked, then gave a half smile to let Silas know he didn't have to answer, it was a joke. "I'm Jon Davidson," he said, offering Silas his hand. "Jon," he said, "without an *h*."

"Nice to meet you."

"You're Constable Jones, right?"

"Yeah."

"Read about you in the paper here." He handed Silas a copy of the *Beacon Light,* folded to the story. Silas glanced at it. "Body Found" the title read. The story was brief, just the facts, burning car, etc. Silas

to give s.o. the credit for s.th. to recognize s.o. for having achieved s.th. important

exception *Ausnahme*

on duty *im Dienst*

You got it. I shall do as you say.
to scrawl to quickly write in an untidy manner

to tap (here): to push down the keys of the keyboard with the tip of your fingers
labored breathing slow breathing that requires a lot of effort

to tap to strike lightly
to appraise s.o. to examine s.o. closely to form an opinion about this person

unconscious *bewusstlos*

IV rack a rack that holds bottles of fluids that are introduced into the body intravenously
drainage tube tube inserted into a wound that allows blood to run out

to pull through to survive

given credit as the officer who found the body but all the quotes were, as usual, from French.

"Ah, here we go," Davidson said, scrolling down on his computer. "He's still in the intensive care unit. Second floor, left out of the elevator. Visiting hours for there are three to five, but they'll make an exception for you." He winked. "Just tell the nurse on duty you're famous."

Silas thanked him and went past the gift shop to the elevator, then turned around and came back.

"Has anybody else been to see him?"

The volunteer took off his glasses and frowned. "Let's see. I'm on duty noon to six, five days a week. But no. Nobody else I know of. You want me to ask the other volunteers?"

"If you don't mind," he said. "And if anybody does come by, could you get their names? Let me know?"

"You got it."

He scrawled his phone number on a corner of the newspaper – business cards weren't in the budget, he'd been told – and rode the elevator to the next floor. He pushed through a glass door that said INTENSIVE CARE. The nurses' station was quiet, one black lady in green scrubs tapping at her computer. Behind her he heard, on a monitor, labored breathing. The walls were glass, and through them he could see several beds, most empty.

"Hello," he said, approaching the desk.

She glanced up. "Good afternoon. Can I help you?"

He tapped his hat on his thigh. "I'm here to see about Larry Ott."

She took off a pair of eyeglasses and appraised him.

"How is he?" he asked.

"Well, he made it through surgery last night but he's still unconscious.

The doctor should be back at four to check him, but he's stable right now."

"Can I see him?"

She rose. "Just for a minute."

He followed her and saw she'd been playing solitaire on her computer.

Larry was alone in the unit, several other dark beds around, him in the center, connected to the heart monitor and ventilator and an IV rack. He was shirtless and pale, his chest bandaged with drainage tubes down both sides. He had more tubes going into his nose and mouth, taped over his skin.

"It's amazing he's still alive," the nurse said. "When he came in there hadn't been time to get him over to Hattiesburg, where they're better equipped to deal with gunshot wounds. The doctors did the best they could, but . . ." She didn't finish the thought.

"You think he'll pull through?"

"I couldn't say," she said. "But he was clinically dead twice during his operations."

"Operations?"

"Yes. The surgeon removed the bullet, and we gave him six units of blood. The bullet missed his heart by the breadth of a hair, Dr. Milton said. But then, not long after we got him back here, he suffered a minor heart attack from the stress and went back into the O.R."

This close, Silas saw lines of gray in Larry's hair. The stubble on his chin around the tape was gray, too. There were wet tracks out of his eyes, down the dry skin of his face.

"Is he in a coma?"

"We can't tell yet," she said. "We're sedating him with Diprivan."

"When you think you might know more?"

"You'll have to ask the doctor," she said.

Jurisdiction, he knew, meant more than geography. It meant responsibility. Somebody had to tell Mrs. Ott about Larry's being shot, and, since French had pawned this case off on him, he got out of the Jeep and stood in the parking lot of River Acres, a nursing home he'd thus far only seen in passing, on his way somewhere else. Such places depressed him as they did, he supposed, everyone. He squared his hat on and took a breath. The building was a single-story brick structure with seedling pine trees growing out of the drainage gutters along the edge of the roof, which needed new shingles. There was a row of windows down the side of the home, many cracked and some opened and others with air conditioners hanging out, chugging, dripping to puddles beneath, propped with boards.

The front door was opened and a black man of Silas's build sat inside smoking a cigarette and reading a NASCAR magazine. He wore a white uniform with yellow stains on the front. Silas recognized him – DUI arrest, a year ago – and nodded, wondering why the dude didn't sit his chair outside, as it seemed hotter inside.

"Morning," Silas said and removed his hat. "Where I go to see Mrs. Ott?"

Without looking up the man nodded down the hall and Silas thanked him and followed it to where he found a sliding glass window with nobody behind it. The odor of disinfectant didn't cover the faint smell of urine. He leaned in the window, a desk with a crossword puzzle book and Oprah on a muted thirteen-inch television. He rang the buzzer and in a moment a heavy woman with big glasses came, in no hurry, from an adjacent door.

"Morning," Silas said. "I'm Officer Jones from over at Chabot."

The woman sat in the chair and looked up at him with amusement in her eyes. "I know who you are," she said. Her nails were long and decorated with stars and he wondered how she punched the buttons on her phone. Her name tag said BRENDA. "You was up ahead of me in school," she said. "I used to watch you play baseball."

He smiled. "Long time ago."

"You calling me old?"

His smiled widened. "I wouldn't do that."

"What you need up in here? Clyde done broke his probation again?"

stroke *Schlaganfall*

"Not that I know of. I'm here to speak to a Mrs. Ott, if she's able."

The woman raised her eyebrows. "You can try if you want to. She had some strokes a few years ago, plus she got Alzheimer's."

"How bad?"

"Bad enough. Most times she ain't know anybody. Can't move her whole left half. Just be laying there. What you want to see her for? Her son in trouble?"

"Why you ask that?"

"Cause she tried to call him yesterday. She get her a good day once in a while. But he never came."

"He come see her a lot?"

ax (Southern dialect) asked

"Several times a week. Crazy man ax would I call him ever time she have a good day you know what I told him?"

"Told him no?"

"Told him hell no. I ain't no answering service. She can call him her own self whenever she wants to."

"Well, you might not have to worry about him again. Somebody shot him. That's why I'm here," he said.

recliner chair with an adjustable back and footrest
bedpan pan used as a toilet for people who can't leave their bed

Her room was a double, two hospital beds with recliners beside each, TV on a rack high on the wall. In the far bed, by the window, an ancient black woman lay gazing outside. The room smelled like somebody had forgotten to change the bedpans. Mrs. Ott sat in her recliner watching him like he was a lamppost that had just walked in. Overhead, on the wall, a television played *Wheel of Fortune*.

From behind him Brenda said loudly, "Miss Ina? This Officer Jones. He want to talk to you about your son."

She looked at him vacantly.

"Call me if you need," Brenda said, touching his arm. "I'll be right out here."

"Thanks."

vacantly in a manner showing no sign of thought

"Who are you?" Mrs. Ott asked, mild alarm in her voice, the left half of her face frozen, her mouth in a permanent frown. She looked past him where Brenda was examining her nails in the hall. The sight of her seemed to relieve Mrs. Ott.

to relieve *erleichtern*

robe bathrobe
gown nightgown
rolling stool a stool with small wheels
to slump to sink down
suspicion *Misstrauen, Argwohn*

Silas barely recognized her as the woman who'd given him and his mother coats so long ago. She wore a robe untied down the front and a gown beneath. She had no breasts to speak of and a neck thin as his wrist. He pulled a rolling stool over to her chair and sat, holding his hat, trying to slump so he wouldn't seem so big. She'd watched him the whole time with something like suspicion in her eyes.

"Clyde," she said. "Tell them others to stop."

"I'm not Clyde, Miss Ina," he said. "My name is 32. I used to know your boy, Larry."

"Who?"

"Your son," he said gently. "We were friends together, a long time ago. You give me a coat one time."

"Clyde?" she said.

"No, ma'am. 32. My name is 32."

"32?" She looked alarmed. "I'm much older than that."

"No, ma'am. My real name is Silas."

"How's Eleanor Roosevelt?"

He frowned and glanced out at Brenda. "That's one of her chickens," she said.

"Oh." Turning back to the old woman. "She's fine, Mrs. Ott. All the chickens are fine. I fed em yesterday."

"Rosalynn Carter's the best layer."

"I speck so."

"But Ladybird Johnson's prettiest."

"Yes, ma'am."

"Who are you?" she asked.

He told her again.

"Clyde?" she said.

He sat a while longer, unable to convince her he wasn't Clyde, then he said good-bye and rose. In the hall, he offered a card and asked would Brenda call him if Mrs. Ott had a good day. She said of course she would.

In the parking lot, shaded by a big pecan tree, he sat in the Jeep, elbow out the window, his hat on the seat beside him. The day he'd spent at the Ott house, so long ago, kept coming back to him. Catching lizards with Larry. That giant snake. Those chickens in the barn. At one point, as they'd assembled what Larry had called their herpetarium, a row of Mason jars full of wary reptiles, Silas had spotted a lawn mower, pushed under a low wooden rack.

"You get to cut the grass?" he'd asked.

"Get to?" Larry said. He set his jar down, the lizard inside watching him. "You mean have to."

"I ain't never cut none," Silas said.

"You want to?"

They rolled the push mower out of the barn and into the sunlight and Larry showed him how to check the oil and gas and how to prime the pump, how to pull the cord to crank it. Then, yelling over the noise, Larry showed him how to adjust the motor speed and push the mower in rows, narrowing toward a center. Silas snatched the handle and said okay, his turn. He loved it, the buzz of the motor, hot fresh cut grass in the air, between his bare toes, wild onions sizzling on the frame, the bar vibrating in his fists and the occasional mangled stick flung from the vent. When he was a kid one time, Larry yelled, walking alongside Silas, Larry's daddy was cutting grass and Larry watching and his daddy ran over a rock that shot like a bullet and bounced off Larry's bare stomach and left a red imprint of itself. Larry's daddy had laughed real hard. Even took a Polaroid and laughed every time he looked at it. You had to be careful of where you let the vent aim, was Larry's point. You didn't want to spray any rocks out toward any cars or toward people, see? Silas turned and left Larry standing and mowed rows and rows and kept mowing, loving the progress through

---

layer (here): producer of eggs
speck (dialect) expect

to convince überzeugen

pecan tree Hickorybaum
to assemble to put together
herpetarium a space for exhibiting reptiles
Mason jar widemouthed jar with a lid that can be sealed – It is used for canning food.
wary cautious, watchful
lawn mower Rasenmäher
to get to do s.th. to be allowed to do s.th.

to prime the pump to put into working order by filling it with gas
to crank s.th. (here): to start s.th.

bar safety bar that has to be held down
vent opening on the side to eject the cut grass

imprint mark made by pressing s.th. on a surface

the grass, the design he was making. It felt good, like combing his hair. Larry wandered to the front porch steps and picked up a book. He watched for a while, not even pretending to read, then abruptly dropped the book and ran into the yard and pushed Silas away and turned the mower off.

Silas shoved him back as the motor sputtered to a stop. "Don't be pushing me."

"Sorry," Larry said as they looked at each other, Silas's palms still vibrating.

"I don't like nobody pushing me."

"It's just," Larry said, "we ain't got much time left."

"I don't care." Silas cranked the mower again and began to push it. Larry watched for a while then went back to the porch and sat, his hands on his knees.

A moment later he was jumping and pointing. It was getting dark now, lightning bugs floating over the fields, and Silas had nearly finished. He saw headlights coming through the woods. He left the mower running and darted across the lawn kicking up grass. He leapt the fence and was gone into the woods. Behind him Larry ran to the mower, still puttering, and began to push it. The lights were Carl Ott's, and he got out of his truck with a bag of ice and a brown sack. He was greasy from his day's work but he looked over the yard and began to nod.

"Good work, boy," he called to Larry.

Silas knew this because he'd crept back through the cornfield. Mr. Ott said something else now, something Silas couldn't hear, and then walked inside. Larry turned and pulled the mower toward the barn, looking over to where Silas had run, staring, it seemed, directly at him.

Good work, boy.

Silas remembered it. He had felt, at that moment, most acutely in his life, the absence of a father. He'd walked home that night, through the darkening woods, aware that all this land – over five hundred acres, Larry had said – was theirs, which meant it was Larry's, or would be. And Silas, who had nothing, looked up to where the sky had been, now he couldn't even see the tops of trees as night peeled down along the vines. He started to run, afraid, not of the darkness coming, but at the anger scratching in his ribs.

When he got home, his mother's car was there. Inside, his Styrofoam box from the diner sat on the small wooden table between their beds where they ate each night, a carton of chocolate milk beside it. His mother still wore her uniform, her hairnet. Her cat was on her lap as she sat on the end of her bed.

"Boy, where you been?"

"Out in the woods."

"Out in the woods, Silas? After dark?"

"Sorry, Momma," he said, the lie coming easily. "I got lost."

For a moment, rubbing that cat's neck, she'd watched him, wondering perhaps whether to believe his lie or not, maybe too tired not to believe it, because what she'd said, finally, was, "Eat your supper. It's already cold. And the milk's done got warm."

Now he cranked the Jeep. He backed out of his parking space. So he'd had a father all along, and not some deadbeat black man who'd knocked up Alice Jones and left, but a white man who'd slept with his maid and then sent her off to Chicago when she got with child.

His windows down, he cruised the highway among the log trucks and SUVs, heading back toward the Ott property. He wondered, leaving the city limits, traffic more sparse, if that old cabin was still there.

When he turned onto Campground Cemetery, he saw a four-wheeler riding in the center of the road. He came up behind it, the thing going about forty miles an hour, and flicked on his headlights. The boy on it, white, skinny, looked behind him and tossed a bottle into the weeds and waved him around, but Silas stuck his arm out the window and pointed him off the road.

The kid was sitting on it with his leg over the gas tank lighting a cigarette when Silas got out and walked up. When he saw Silas's uniform and gun belt he straightened on the seat. "Hidy there," he said.

Silas said, "You ain't supposed to have that thing on the road."

The kid looked up at him.

"You got a driver's license?"

"You a game warden?"

"Chabot constable. Where's your license?"

"Must've left it home. You're 32 Jones. I heard of you. What's a constable?"

"Police officer. What's your name?"

"Wallace Stringfellow."

"You live out here, Wallace?"

He cocked a thumb behind him. "Few miles yonder ways."

"You hadn't been drinking, have you?"

"No, sir, Officer."

"You didn't throw a beer in the weeds back there?"

He shook his head.

"You mean if I went back there I wouldn't find a bottle with your fingerprints on it?"

"You might would. I probably threw lots of bottles out, always been a litterbug, but never when I was riding."

Silas noticed a dirty pillowcase stuffed back in the cage behind the seat and wondered should he look inside it. Wondered for a moment would it have eye holes, though in truth today's racism seemed less organized than when he'd been a boy. He said, "You carrying a gun?"

"No, sir."

"You ride out here a lot?"

"Sometimes."

"This is Rutherford land, most of it, and if you're on it you're trespassing."

---

deadbeat (AE) person who continuously refuses to pay his/her debts and expenses
to knock s.o. up (coll.) to get a woman pregnant
to get with child (coll.) to become pregnant
to cruise to drive at a steady speed
traffic more sparse with fewer vehicles

hidy (coll.) how do you do

game warden Jagdaufseher

to cock to raise

litterbug person who throws litter around in public places

to trespass to enter a piece of property or building without permission

posted with signs indicating the land is private property

ticket Strafzettel

preciate (dialect) appreciate
to kick-start to start the engine by pushing down on a pedal
to rev to suddenly increase the revolutions of the engine

to stoop to bend the body downward
fence row a fence with uncultivated land on each side
bobwire Stacheldraht
to relish to anticipate with great desire
red bug mite: small insect that sucks blood
tick Zecke
barb Stachel
lodged stuck
limp not stiff, not firm
to dote over s.o. to treat s.o. with excessive affection

despite trotz

to squirm away (here): to manage to get away

ivy Efeu
briar Gestrüpp
ragged irregular in shape
scarred vernarbt
deadfall mass of fallen trees and branches
knot Ast

"You mean it's against the law just to ride?"
"If the land's posted, it is. And fenced off."
"Well, you learn something ever day. I appreciate you telling me."
"Where you going?"
"Nowheres in particular. Just enjoying the weather."
Silas watched him but he was thinking of the hunting cabin. "Well," he said, "I'll let you off with a warning this time. But you ride that thing on the side of the road all the way home, hear, and if I see you on the highway again, drinking or not, I'm gone write you a ticket. Or worse."
"Yes, sir. Preciate the warning."
He watched the kid kick-start it and rev the engine. He gave a little salute and motored off, bumping along the side of the road, the pillowcase flapping. Silas stood shaking his head.

The Jeep ticking in front of Larry's house, Silas slipped off the lanyard with his badge and, to cool down, removed his uniform shirt, hung the lanyard back over his neck, and tied the shirt around his waist. He fanned his face with his hat walking over the field toward the trees, stooped under an old fence row, careful not to snag his T-shirt on the bobwire. He didn't relish the thought of red bugs, ticks, mosquitoes, or snakes and kept a careful eye out as beggar's lice stuck to his pants legs and briar barbs lodged in his shirt.

What's missing out of you, Silas?

His mother had had to work two jobs plus clean houses to pay for the trailer home she'd bought in Fulsom. Back then he'd told himself she just wanted him out of the way. That was why she'd sent him off. Lying to himself even as he opened the letters she mailed him in Oxford, unfolding the limp five-and ten-dollar bills she sent each week so he could go to his classes and play baseball without having to get a job. He knew now she'd loved him despite his never writing her back, despite the trouble and fear he caused her, despite the thing missing out of him. He'd returned her love by rarely coming home, and when he did she'd doted over him, as if every meal was his last, or hers, straightened his paper napkin and lain another chicken leg on his plate and filled his milk glass or his iced tea so much he could barely stand it. He'd refused to see the truth, that she was starving from loneliness. In fact, he could barely look at her. All he could do was eat quickly and squirm away and go out into the night (driving her car) and find M&M and his other high school friends while she sat waiting for him to come home.

Now, as he walked, slipping through leaves and vines and ivy and spiderwebs and arcs of briar, he noticed how different the land was, how quickly it could change, such a ragged jungle now, scarred with white deadfall, no longer the brief paradise two boys had had those years ago. He topped a hill and descended to the bottom of a hollow, stopped to rest by an old magnolia tree, black trunk so big it would be hard to reach his arms around, something familiar about its knots and whorls, good places for feet, hands. He looked up and saw two boys in the branches, one white, one black. He hurried on, ducking a fierce shuck of briar, soon saw another familiar magnolia, this one buffeted smooth at waist level by a boy's old baseball. Using his hat to rake down the briars, he was breathing hard and nearly bumped into the wall of the cabin before he saw it.

Smaller somehow, darker wood, more weathered. Vines and kudzu had nearly overtaken the place, it seemed the heart of some struggle, as if the vegetation were trying to claim the structure back into itself, pull it down, the earth suddenly an organic breathing mass underneath Silas, he could almost feel the friction, hear the viscous grumble of digestion. In front he eased up the steps, soft as moss, the porch like a cave, vegetation on all sides and bees boiling out of white blooms, live vines constricting dead ones, hanging from the roof. An enormous gray moth cupped to the wall. Gently, he moved coils of ivy aside and peered through the snakehead kudzu leaves to where the front door was secured with a rusty padlock.

He stepped backward and hooked his hat on a limb and pushed around the side of the cabin, a layer of wet leaves under his feet, the walls mummied in kudzu and constricted by hundreds of vines thick as chicken snakes. At the first window he angled his light through the dusty glass, probing the shapes of the headless single bed he'd slept on and the bed his mother had used, the table between them, the rusting iron hulk of a stove in the corner where they'd huddled for warmth in those first coatless days and nights.

He tried the window and found it locked from inside. Looked like it hadn't been opened in years. He wormed his way through the foliage along the side of the house and turned the corner to the back wall, that window locked, too, leaves tickling the top of his neck, spiderwebs with bug husks and the skeletons of leaves and twigs snagged in their cross-stitching. On the third wall he stopped and looked closely. Someone had raised this window. He could see where it had been forced up, the wooden runners lighter and splintered, one of the four panes of glass broken, pieces on the floor inside. An arm through, turning the rusty lock. He resisted lifting it, shone his light through the broken pane instead, a much clearer view without glass to reflect his light, the side of his once-bed, its mattress sagging in the middle, coils of rusty spring through the filthy cloth. On those first nights, his mother had slept with him, crossing the dirt floor in the darkness, her breath visible in the dim stove light, saying, "Slide over, son, fore we both freeze."

Somebody had been inside, he saw now. There was a long smear over the floor. He imagined the intruder dragging his feet to erase his tracks. His pulse quickened as he fixed his beam beneath the bed. There it was, a shadow image of the bed cast in rumpled dirt, a place where someone had dug, he realized, a grave.

---

whorl small spirals
fierce sharp
shuck mass
to buffet to strike repeatedly
to rake (here): to push aside
to bump into s.th. to hit s.th. by accident

friction the action of one surface rubbing on another
viscous thick and sticky
grumble long, deep sound
digestion Verdauung
to constrict to press together
coil tight circle
padlock Vorhängeschloss

chicken snake rat snake
to angle to move up and down
to probe s.th. to search and explore s.th.
to huddle to draw yourself together to keep warm

foliage a cluster of leaves and branches

husk hard outer shell
to snag to cause to be caught
cross-stitching the crossed threads of the spiderweb
runner channel along the inside of the frame of a window along which a window can slide
lighter (here): easier to slide on
splintered with thin pieces of wood broken off
pane Fensterscheibe
dim not bright

intruder person who enters a property illegally

rumpled not smooth, not tidy

Chapter Nine

When he was thirty-one years old, not long after he'd taken his mother to River Acres and ten years before Tina Rutherford would vanish, Larry began to notice things amiss in the barn. Those were days when Ina Ott was more alert, her Alzheimer's in its earlier stages, Larry visiting her each night on his way home from work, longer on weekends, a silent black lady in the other bed snoring gently or gazing out the window. His mother would always ask if he'd had any customers and he'd say, "Oh, one or two." Then she'd ask about her ladies and he'd tell her about Eleanor Roosevelt. "Laid a big speckled egg this morning."

When he noticed that somebody had been sneaking in the barn while he was at work, he told her this, too, how one evening he found the back door ajar, and another the pitchfork down from its nail. She was alarmed and said he should lock the doors; it was probably some boy out for adventure. "A barn is a wondrous place to children," she said, and he agreed, remembering the boy he'd been there, the boy he'd been then.

The benefit – she would have said *blessing* – of her Alzheimer's was that the first swath of history gone from her memory was the incident with Cindy Walker and its long-reaching aftermath. To Larry's mother, reclining in her chair by her bed, none of this had happened and bore no connection to the mischief Larry described, the barn's woodbox left open in the tack room, the bags of chicken feed overturned, the chain saw moved, Carl's tackle box a jumbled mess where Larry always kept it neat, lures and sinkers missing, the rods hung askew. To avoid alarming her, he didn't tell his mother how the rooster was missing when he came home one evening, his old bicycle another time. Instead, he described the small, bare footprints in the dirt around the back of the barn. On another visit he told her how, that morning, in place of driving to work, he'd parked his truck in the barn, hidden from outside, and waited in the hayloft, reading a novel, leaving out how odd if felt, being someplace not the shop, worrying that today might be the day a car stopped by, and then, at about ten o'clock, how he heard someone tromping over the dry dead leaves behind the barn. Larry descended the ladder and hid in a stall in the room near the back door. He had his old zombie mask and pulled it on. Presently the door screaked open and a ruff of blond hair eased in. He was filthy and brown as an egg and Larry smiled in the mask. He let the boy get fully in – cut-off blue jeans and no shirt or shoes, carrying a bent stick – waited to allow his small eyes to adjust to the darkness, before he stepped out from behind the stall with his arms raised and his fingers claws and yelled, "Argh!"

The boy rose from the ground as if ejected and yelped and turned in midair and landed and ran slap into the door and got up almost before he fell and was gone. Still smiling, Larry pulled the hot mask off and tossed the stick out and opened the barn's big bay doors and drove through them and closed them behind him and left the mask in its spot in his closet and went to work.

"That should fix him," his mother said, smiling, coleslaw on her chin. "Did you hear that, Doris," Ina told the tiny, palsied black woman in the next bed, but the woman continued to gaze out the window.

"Poor thing," his mother whispered. "She's forgotten her name."

Because of Larry's past the women who shared her room were forever the furthest gone, those who wouldn't be aware that a perhaps-murderer visited, those with no family, no one to complain.

And as the years passed so would the black women. To Larry's count four had died in their sleep as Ina lived on, waiting for him to come, losing an hour at a time the days and weeks and months of her memory, until she, too, had forgotten her name and Larry's as well, the chickens last to go, and then even they were gone and now the ever-thinner woman he visited on Saturdays lay waiting to die without knowing it, alongside yet another black woman who also lay waiting, without knowing it, to die.

Ten years after Larry had frightened him from the barn, the boy came back. It was a Friday after work, November, Larry reading on his porch still in his uniform, sweaty but not dirty, the shirt untucked, his shoes beside the front door, another habit left over from his mother, who'd never allowed work shoes in her house.

He'd already eaten, his usual KFC meal of two breasts, no wing, double mashed potatoes with gravy and a biscuit, and was on his second Coke, which he brought home from the shop in the yellow plastic crates that used to be wood. The night had been set to unreel like any other in his life: read, watch TV, take a shower, go to bed, read more until he fell asleep. Get up in the morning, shave, dress in a clean uniform shirt but, because it would be Saturday, blue jeans instead of his regular pants, then go back to work. In the evening he'd ride out and see his mother, bring fresh flowers and the photo album, hope she remembered him, if not just sit there with her, him staring into the same space she did, wondering what she saw. He had his cell phone in his pocket now, as always, in case she called, but the calls had been so rare lately he knew that any one might be the last, that she might slip off into that space where she stared, go for good to whatever she kept watching.

When he heard the vehicle out on the highway a little over half a mile away, he paused in his reading, his finger marking the page, its nail surely the cleanest of any mechanic in Mississippi. The vehicle grew closer and soon he heard tires crunch over gravel and saw flashes of white through the trees bordering the right side of his yard. He looked down at his feet and wondered should he put on shoes – greeting a visitor in your bare feet seemed rude – but didn't. Even though he was the only person on this road, someone coming to see *him* was

coleslaw salad made with raw cabbage
palsied with no control of the body

furthest gone (here): in the last stages of Alzheimer
to complain sich beklagen
to pass (two different meanings): to go by or to die

untucked (here): outside the trousers

mashed potatoes Kartoffelbrei
set to unreel (*abspulen*) about to continue in the usual manner

to crunch to make the sound of s.th. being crushed
bordering along the edge of

Chapter Nine

unlikely unwahrscheinlich
bandolier belt for carrying bullets and worn over the shoulder
firecracker small firework
UPS United Parcel Service, a private delivery firm
to trim to decorate the edges

goatee a beard on the chin
scruff dirt
wrinkled not ironed
ratty worn and shabby

clammy sticky and cold

dish parabolic antenna
to jut to stick out

old-timey (coll.) outdated
channel Kanal, Sender
to appreciate zu schätzen wissen

boom (coll.) suddenly

devoted gewidmet

hundred 100 dollars

spell short period of time
Been a long one. i.e. It's been a long day.

---

unlikely. Maybe somebody lost. Or somebody with a few beer bottles or a bandolier of firecrackers. He set his Coke down on the concrete and put the book in his chair and stood up to wait.

It was a late-model van of the style UPS used, but trimmed in blue and labeled DIRECTV. The driver didn't seem lost; in fact he waved, and rolled to a stop beside the road behind Larry's Ford and turned the key off. For a moment the driver, sunglasses, dirty blond hair, sat behind the wheel, collecting things from the passenger seat as the engine began to tick itself cool. The driver opened the door and got out and slammed it and waved again as he walked up the hill toward Larry.

"Hidy there," he said. "My name's Wallace Stringfellow." He was early twenties, Larry saw now, a bit under six feet, a goatee and scruff on his cheeks, bony, his untucked, wrinkled DIRECTV shirt a size or two large on him and long khaki shorts under it, ratty sneakers. There were a few Stringfellows in Fulsom but Larry didn't know them.

"Good evening," he replied. "What can I do for you?"

Wallace stuck out his hand, which was dirtier than Larry's and small. For a moment Larry looked at it before he took it and found Wallace's palm clammy. He could smell that he'd been drinking.

"Well," he said, putting the clipboard under his arm to get a package of Marlboros out of the DIRECTV shirt pocket, "we on what us dish technicians call a installation drive? I was just out riding around, bout lost, and happened to see you ain't got one. A dish." He shook a smoke out and lit it and jutted his chin toward Larry's roof. "That old-timey antenna? What you get, like three channels?"

"I appreciate your riding all the way out here," Larry said, "but I don't reckon I need it. Three channels are more than enough."

"You can't watch but one at a time, right," Wallace said. "But look, you don't know what's out there. Something for every taste. Get you a dish, boom, your evenings are as full as you want em to be." He pointed again. "I can screw her in right up there, they always look like a ear, I think, listening at the sky. You like cooking shows, boom, we got you covered. Murder shows? Crime investigation? Wrestling? It's a whole channel devoted to that."

"I appreciate you coming all the way out here," Larry said, "but – "

"Here," Wallace said, passing him one of the brochures.

Larry took it and unfolded it, a long list of channels. "There sure are a lot," he said.

"You don't know the half," Wallace said. "I can get you a hundred twenty-something channels, won't be a hundred a month. ESPN, HBO, Skinemax."

Larry was shaking his head.

"What if I just set a spell, then?" Wallace asked. "Been a long one. I ain't gone bite."

"Yeah," Larry said. "I'm sorry. I just don't get that many visitors."

Wallace followed him up the steps to the screen door and almost bumped him when Larry stopped.

"Why don't we sit out here," he said. "It's cooler."

"You the boss, hoss."

Larry said, "I'll be right back."

He went in and looked at the clock. News would be on soon. Through the screen, Wallace was peering inside. "Nice place," he said. "You get somebody to clean it for you?"

"No."

Larry laid the brochure on the kitchen table and pulled a chair from beneath it and when he came back out Wallace had set the other brochures on the porch and used the clipboard to weigh them down. He put the cigarette in his lips and took the chair Larry offered, turned it around and sat with his elbows over the back.

Larry stood by the door. "Can I get you something to drink?"

"Now we talking. You got a seven and seven?"

"No, sorry."

"Bourbon?"

"I got a Coke."

"What you got to go with it?" Wallace smiled.

Larry looked inside, behind him. "I don't have anything like that," he said. "I don't drink alcohol."

"Not even a beer?"

"Sorry."

"Just brang me a Co-Cola then."

He nodded and went inside, got one from the refrigerator and unstuck a magnet-opener from the fridge door and pried its lid off and restuck the magnet and came back out. Wallace had turned his chair the right way and sat propped against the wall, his legs dangling.

"Thank you," he said and drank most of the Coke in the first swallow.

"What's your name?"

"Larry."

"Larry what?"

He hesitated. "Larry Ott."

The name didn't seem to register, Wallace polishing off his Coke and clinking the bottle back down.

"Well, Mr. Ott – "

"Just Larry."

"Well, just Larry, where'd you go to high school?"

"Fulsom."

"Same as me. When'd you graduate?"

Larry shrugged. He didn't want to say it but Wallace waited. "Never did."

"How come?"

"I quit."

"Me, too." Wallace laughed. "How come you did?"

"Just did."

"Me, too. Couple a dropouts ain't we. Momma keeps saying get my GED and I reckon I might, one of these days."

---

boss, hoss a rhymed joke – hoss (Southern dialect): horse

seven and seven a drink with whisky and a soft drink, 7 Up

Bourbon a type of American whisky

to brang (dialect) to bring

to pry to open with force

to hesitate zögern
to polish s.th. off (coll.) to finish drinking s.th.

dropout person who doesn't finish school

to toe s.th. out to move s.th. out with your toe
to peck (here): to pick s.th. out

infamous [ˈɪnfəməs] notorious
to fidget to keep moving about in a nervous manner

sure as clockwork (fig.) absolutely certain

to trot to run taking short steps
to grind the gears to not properly change gears so the gears make a grinding sound
to stall to stop because the engine no longer functions
to shift umschalten
to weave to move forward moving to the right and left

scruffy rough, untidy, dirty

Larry stood a moment, not asking if his boss minded he drank when he drove a company van. Then went to his chair and moved the book and sat down.

"What you reading?" Wallace asked, finishing his cigarette.

He held the book up. Wallace dropped his Marlboro on the porch and toed it out. "I seen that movie. You get you a dish? You ain't got to worry about reading." He pecked another from the package and lit it and grinned through his smoke. "Say your name's Larry Ott? Ain't I heard of you?"

Larry glanced at him. "Not many folks around here that ain't."

"Wait." Wallace grinning now. "You the one they say did away with that girl. Back in high school."

Larry looked down at his feet, wished he'd put his shoes on.

"That's how come you quit school, huh. Shit, boy," Wallace said. "You famous." He eased his chair down. "Or *in*famous."

Larry stopped himself from correcting Wallace and fidgeted in his seat.

He said, "You still want to sell me a dish?"

"Hell, hoss, I don't care what you done. I'll still sell you a dish, you want one. Sell you two or three, you want. All I gotta do is get on your roof there, find the clearest spot to the sky, screw her in, and then run your cable down. But all that can wait to Monday."

"Monday?"

He dug his cell phone out of his pocket. "It's after five-thirty in the p.m. and it's Friday. My weekend has officially begun."

"How bout that." Larry stood up with him. "Have a good weekend, Wallace. I'll see you Monday?"

"Sure as clockwork."

He gathered his clipboard and brochures and hopped down off the porch and trotted across the yard. In the van, he waved again and Larry waved back, standing with one hand on the porch post and watched him crank the van and grind its gears looking for reverse. When he got it turned around he tooted the horn and it nearly stalled as he shifted and Larry watched him weave over the road and then picked up the chair and turned and went back inside, Wallace's engine still growling through the trees.

That night as he lay in bed he thought of Wallace and smiled in the dark. That he'd been lied to didn't bother him. He'd placed him as the boy who'd snuck into his barn those years before. Same face, just longer and scruffier. Same small eyes. Larry remembered how he'd jumped and he smiled again. Wallace didn't seem dangerous, just curious. Larry hoped he hadn't stolen the van, though, remembering the stolen lures, the missing rooster.

He rolled over.

As he did each night before sleep, Larry prayed for his mother, that the following day might be a good one for her, that his cell phone might ring or that, if it was time, the Lord take her quietly.

In her sleep. And that God would forgive him his sins and send him customers.

After work the following Monday Larry sat on his porch not reading but waiting in his usual company of bats and birds and insects, the tinkling of his mother's chime each time the earth breathed its wind. He was disappointed but not surprised when night stole the far trees and the fence across the road and then the road itself and finally the sky, Larry's truck gone too in the dark and stars beginning to wink in the sky like nail holes in the roof of a barn.

He'd given up on him by the time Wallace came back, two months later. Larry was reading when he raised his head at a buzzing over his land, the motor gnawing closer and closer and then the four-wheeler emerging where the trees broke, its bareheaded rider bouncing in the seat. He cut the engine as he approached Larry's house and coasted to a stop, a cigarette dangling from his lips, a crumpled brown bag between his thighs.

"Hidy, just Larry," Wallace called, sitting astride the four-wheeler like a horse.

Larry stood, one hand on the porch post, the other holding his book. "Hidy, Wallace."

The young man rolled a leg over the gas tank and dismounted as if he were a cowboy, wearing a baggy T-shirt and shorts that looked like they might be the same pair he'd worn for his last visit. He hiked them up and brought the paper bag with him, holding it by its bottom.

"You surprised to see me?" he asked.

"Little bit."

Wallace came onto the porch and set the bag by the post. He took a Pabst in a can from the bag and offered it to Larry.

"No thank you."

"Well cheers then," Wallace said, popping the tab and drinking.

"So I don't get me a dish after all?"

"Would you believe," Wallace said, his face contorted from the beer, "them DIRECTV bastards fired me?" Wallace sat on the top step and leaned back against the post where he could look up at Larry, who moved his book and sat back down.

Larry said, "So you been at the unemployment?"

"Naw, painting houses. I do that sometime. What you reading now?"

Larry told him.

"Shit, that's a movie, too. You ever seen it?"

"Yeah," Larry said. "Book's better."

They sat for a while.

"Larry," Wallace said. "You don't like me much, do you."

It surprised him. When he looked at Wallace he saw how acutely the boy was watching at him.

customer *Kunde, Kundin*

to gnaw (fig.) to make a loud chewing sound
to emerge to appear
to coast to move along without the engine running
crumpled crushed into folds

to dismount to get off a horse, bike, or motorbike
to hike s.th. up to pull up

contorted twisted

unemployment i.e. unemployment office

acutely keenly

to make fun of s.o. *sich über jdn lustig machen*	
to rock *schaukeln*	

"It's okay," Wallace said. "Not many folks do. All thank I'm weird. Why I quit school, got tired of em making fun of me."

Larry had begun to rock again. "It ain't that I don't like you, I just don't know you." Then he added, "I don't get many visitors, neither."

"Why not? You a hell of a conversationalist. I figure you'd have folks over here day and night, telling em jokes, making em laugh. Serving em beers and seven and sevens and getting high and tight as Dick's hatband."

high *drunk*	
tight as Dick's hatband (Southern idiom) *rather drunk*	

For the first time in longer than he cared to remember, Larry smiled in the presence of another person, and then his hand came up, the old habit, covering his mouth. He said, "Last visitor I had, apart from this DIRECTV fellow, was . . . well, a bunch of teenagers come through a few months ago, drunk. Bout one a.m. Drove by in a Ford Explorer, stopped out there" – pointing at the road – "started throwing beer bottles on my roof, yelling for me to come out."

"Did you?"

to part *to move apart*	
drapes *long, thick curtains*	
to cross your mind *to come into your mind*	

He shook his head. Remembered how he'd stood looking through the parted drapes, chickens noisy behind the house, glad his mother didn't have to be here for this. It had crossed his mind he wouldn't use the telephone, even if they tried to come in.

"It was one of em," he said, "got out with a baseball bat."

"Shit."

"Stood there a while. Big fellow."

"What'd he do?"

"His friends was yelling for me to come out." Calling him *murderer, rapist, faggot, chickenshit*. Nothing he hadn't heard before, wouldn't hear again.

faggot (vulgar) *homosexual*	
chickenshit (vulgar) *coward*	

"Finally," Larry said, "he took that bat and busted out my headlights."

to bust (coll.) *to break*	

"Fuck."

"Then my windshield."

"Ain't you got a gun?"

Larry shook his head and Wallace sat there with his mouth open, as if he were unable to fathom gunlessness. "You ought to ride out to Wal-Mart, get you one of them single-shot twelve gauges they got on sale. Bout a buck eighty-nine. I could go with you." He sipped his beer. "What they do then? Them fellows?"

to fathom *to comprehend*	
buck eighty-nine (slang) *$ 189 TF*	
single-shot *a bolt-action rifle or shotgun with which a cartridge has to be inserted manually before shooting*	
twelve gauge *shotgun with a barrel having a large diameter*	

"Nothing. Left."

He didn't tell Wallace the rest, that he hadn't even minded, once they'd gone. Fixing the light? The windshield? It gave him something to do the next day. When he drove up to the parts house, the windshield like a net hanging in, Johnson behind the counter took his order and said, "Ain't that your model Ford?" and Larry said it was and Johnson raised his eyebrows and went to the back, helped him carry the windshield wrapped in its brown paper to the bed of Larry's truck without a word, just stared at the truck that looked like, well, somebody had taken a baseball bat to it.

parts house *store that sells auto parts*	
bed *platform behind the cab*	

"Shit," Wallace said, "bunch of rednecks tried that with me? I'd go out there with my aught six. Hey."

"What?"

"How come you ain't got a dog?"

"I'm allergic."

"I got me a good one. Part pit bull, part Chow? Name John Wayne Gacy? You ain't never seen a better watchdog. Hates niggers worse than anything."

"How come?"

"Just smart I guess. One ever comes up in the yard, he bout goes crazy. You ever want to borry him, say the word. We can stake him out here and I dare anybody to come messing with you."

"That's all right. It ain't the black folks that messes with me."

Wallace finished his beer and crinkled the can and put it in the bag and got another. He sat awhile, drinking, smoking, then started talking about the dogs he'd had before John Wayne Gacy. "One was a little old white bitch named Trixie that got heartworms? Used to walk over the floor and just stop and stiffen up and fall over and lay there on her side awhile with her feet poking out." He said it was funny as hell until the time she didn't get back up. Another dog, big brown shaggy one called Pal, some collie somewhere back in his family tree, he was a car chaser, got flattened to a smear by a log truck. Well, Wallace had had, let's see, five or six dogs killed on the road. Three shot, one by himself (biter), one caught in a trap, one that drunk antifreeze, another one bit by a cottonmouth. "Neck swoll up like a damn goiter."

"Where'd they all come from?"

"Strays, most of em." Wallace opened another beer. "Plus I had a slutty ole bitch named Georgia Pineapple? She had puppies bout twice a year so we had a endless stream. Till she died."

Larry didn't want to ask.

"Train hit her," Wallace said. "Anyhow, she had this one litter up under the house one time? We had a busted gas line and didn't know it, and that dog, she'd lay down there by that leak when it got hot and them damn pups was born by the pipe. Come out all deformed." He was laughing. "One didn't have no eyes. Nother one missing its tail. One had its paws all fucked up."

Larry was shaking his head. "What'd you do with em?"

"Momma said get rid of em so I thew em in a pond. After that I got John Wayne Gacy off a Mexican used to fight him. Come he had such a temper. He used to go out at night and catch armadillos and brang em in the yard, sometimes be two, three dead ones laying there in the morning. Just tore all to hell and back, look like old leather purses strung out over the dirt. Come Momma makes me keep him tied up. That's something else we got in common, me and John Wayne Gacy."

"What?"

"I can't stand a damn armadillo. One of Momma's boyfriends, pipefitter, he used to call em armored dildos. When I was a boy we used to catch em. Get em by the tail and swing em around. Punt em

aught six hunting rifle using the .30-06 Springfield cartridge

pit bull a breed of dog for fighting
Chow chow chow: a muscular dog of Chinese origin

to stake (here): to tie to a stake
to mess with s.o. to deal aggressively with s.o.
to crinkle (here): to crush

bitch female dog
heartworms an infestation of the heart by a parasitic worm
to poke out to stick out

shaggy with long hair
pal Kumpel

trap Falle

swoll (dialect) swollen
goiter Kropf

stray (here): a dog without an owner
slutty having many sexual partners

litter puppies born at the same time

paw Pfote
thew (southern dialect) threw
off (slang) from
Come he had such a temper. (dialect) He came with such a temper.
armadillo Gürteltier
to string, strung, strung out (here): to spread out
pipefitter Rohrleger
armored gepanzert
dildo object shaped like a penis for sexual pleasure
to punt (football) to kick a football which is dropped from the hands before it falls to the ground

leprosy *Lepra*	
to incriminate yourself to show that you are involved in a crime	
to drain (here): to drink what is left	
track (here): *Rennbahn*	
greyhound *Windhund*	
to bury *beerdigen*	
tight fist a gesture to emulate masturbation	

like footballs. Drown em. Now they say a armored dildo'll give you leprosy."

"Wallace." Larry ready to change the subject. "Tell me the truth."

"Long as I don't incriminate myself."

"You never worked for DIRECTV, did you?"

He grinned and drained the last of his last beer. "Okay, you got me. Truth is, I borrowed that van from Momma's boyfriend. He's the one installs them dishes. Give us ours for free. All the pay-per-view channels and ever thing."

"Did he know you borrowed it?"

"Hell no. Him and Momma went over to the dog track. He ever finds out I took it, be hell to pay, plus interest. Now speaking of dogs, that's a badass one there," Wallace said. "A damn greyhound? Fast as hell. You can get one after they retire it from racing? Keep em for pets? But you better be careful. You got a toddler around and it goes running by? That goddamn greyhound'll chase it down like it's that little electric rabbit and tear it apart."

"How come you took the van? Why not just ride your four-wheeler?"

"Hell, man with your rep? I didn't know if you might not cut me up and bury me out in the woods." He was smiling. "Naw, I just figured it'd be a good way to, you know . . ."

"Test the water?"

"Yeah."

They sat a while longer. Wallace crinkled his can and put it in the bag with the others. "You sure you ain't got nothing to drank?"

"Just a Coke."

"Well. I best get going, then. Once I start dranking, I don't like to stop."

He stood, leaning on the post. "You know, Larry, if you want one, I can probably get my momma's boyfriend to run out here, put you a dish up. Long as you promise not to say I was in his truck."

"That's all right."

"Or I could bring John Wayne Gacy by. Tie him to your post here."

"Preciate it, no."

"You ever been married?" Wallace asked, his next visit.

He said he hadn't.

"Got you a girl?"

"No."

"What you do when the ole pecker gets ready?" He made a tight fist and held it up. "You ain't one of them forty-year-old virgins, are you?"

"No," Larry said. "I'm forty-one."

Wallace laughed like it was the funniest thing he'd ever heard, smoke shooting from his nose and mouth.

"Hell," he said, once he'd caught his breath. "I'm single, too. But it's a ole gal over in Fulsom? I see her once in a while. Evelyn. One a them on-again, off-again situations.

"But I go up to Dentonville and paint houses with my uncle sometimes. It's a nigger girl over there I'll visit now and then. She's a crackhead and she'll suck you dry for twenty bucks, fuck your eyes crossed for thirty. Name's Wanda something another. You drive, we can go over yonder, bust your cherry."

"Preciate it, no."

"That's where I been."

"Painting houses?"

"Yeah. Getting in trouble."

"What kind of trouble?"

"Fighting in a bar."

He'd brought a case of beer this time, bungee-corded to the back of his four-wheeler, and had gone through much of it, getting so drunk Larry had begun to worry. It was cooler, leaves in the air and scratching over the road, geese formations overhead pointing south. Larry sat wearing his uniform jacket and a cap, Wallace a sweatshirt with a hood he kept pulling on and then pushing back off. Long pants, frayed at the bottom. He had pictures of John Wayne Gacy the pit bull on his phone and showed them to Larry.

"He's mean-looking, all right."

"Boy you know it. My momma's boyfriend? He keeps saying I ought to shoot him, but I always say, 'Jonas? You shoot that damn dog it's libel to just make him mad.' " He sipped his beer.

"Wallace," Larry said. "You was the boy I surprised that time, wasn't you? In the barn?"

He looked over his shoulder and grinned. "Yep. Guilty as charged. You bout scared me to death in that damn mask."

"I just didn't want you getting hurt in that old barn."

"Well, it kept me away, that's for sure. For about a week."

"You came back?"

"To that barn? Hell no. But it'd take more than that to stop me from fishing in that creek over yonder. Even found your spot, Larry, that old five-gallon bucket you set on, seen a beat-up cork stuck out in the tree over yonder where you couldn't get it back. I'd brang my rod and reel, pull me a purple worm through the same water you did, but I never did catch nothing, figured you'd done fished it dry."

"Naw, I didn't fish it dry. It's downstream from all the lumbering and it's so full of silt there ain't been nothing in it for years."

"I used to pull off my clothes and swim in it," Wallace said. "Nekkid. You wanna know the first time I ever heard of you? It was at school. Fourth grade. All the kids talking about it, that creepy fellow that went there same as us, that sat in some of them very desks we was in, how you abducted that girl and done away with her."

"That's what the kids said?"

to bother *belästigen*

Dentonville fictitious name

machinist *Maschinenschlosser*
sumbitch (dialect) son of a bitch
to haul s.o.'s ass (vulgar) to force s.o. to go along

in a pinch if necessary

thank (dialect) think

shore (dialect) sure

to cuss (coll.) *fluchen*

fixing (dialect) about

to launch into s.th. to begin with s.th.

to tap to strike lightly

"Some of em. The teachers, they'd all say, 'Yall just forget about him. Just let him alone, he might be dangerous. Don't go bothering him.' " Wallace grinned. "So here I am, bothering you, right?"

"You ain't bothering me."

"Well, I never was much good at doing what they tell you at school, anyway. It was one teacher, though, liked you. Mrs. McIntyre? Taught English and art. She used to tell us what a good drawer you was. She'd show us your pictures. One of a little truck, which she said was a perfect example of prespective."

"*Per*spective," Larry said.

"But the first time I ever *seen* you?" Wallace went on. "Was at church. Bout eleven years ago? Up at Dentonville? The Second Baptist? My momma's boyfriend lived over there."

"The DIRECTV fellow?"

"Hell no. This one was a machinist. He'd come fetch us for the weekends. That fat sumbitch – I can't even remember his name now – he didn't go to church but Momma always did, no matter where the man she's seeing lived she'd haul my sleepy ass off the couch and borry his car and drag me to whichever church it was, Baptist she could find it but we'd try a Methodist, too, in a pinch. Anything but a nigger church. Or the Catholics. I always liked the Methodists best, though, cause you'd get out quicker.

"Anyway," he said, "I's out front fore the preaching, talking to some boys my age, little younger, and one of em goes, 'You thank he'll come back?'

" 'He better not,' another one says.

" 'Thank who will?' I asked em.

" 'Scary Larry,' first boy said. 'You know who that is?'

"I said I shore did; we went to the same school, me and him. In Chabot, Mississippi.

" 'No you ain't,' he said.

" 'How the fuck you know?' I said and they was all impressed I cussed right there on the church porch.

"Bout then one of their mommas stuck her head out the door and said we better get on in, the singing was fixing to start. So we all went in and they sat with their mommas and daddies but I took me a seat right there in the back. My momma, she didn't care I sat with her or not, long as I was quiet.

"And sure enough, they'd just launched into the first song, and I hear the door open real quiet-like and shut and look over and there you are. I knowed it was you right off even though I hadn't ever seen you. Way you come in. Way you wouldn't look at nobody looking back at you. You's wearing a suit and a tie. Sat across the aisle, in the back row like me. Other folks recognized you, too, turning their heads and whispering, and I could tell they didn't like you being there and I thought you was smart, coming in late like that." He paused to tap his ash onto the porch and said, "I watched you the whole time, way you stood up and sung the songs, knew all the words, sat down and listened to the preacher, following his Bible verses in your Bible, closing your eyes in the prayer. And I knew you'd leave fore anybody else did, and sure enough, right after the last amen you was up and out.

"I was right behind you. Went out the door and seen you walking off real fast holding your Bible and I yelled, 'Hey!' at you but you never even looked back. Just about run to that red pickup, same one setting right yonder." Wallace leaned forward. "You remember that?"

He did. He remembered Wallace, saw in his face now that same boy's face. The boy who'd followed him out, called "Hey" in a way he'd not heard before, not angry but curious, a boy with small eyes and stringy hair and ears that stuck out, a scruffy kid in clothes not quite nice enough for church, who'd been sitting alone during the service, opposite him in the back, fidgeting, sneaking looks at him. Because of that boy, more than anything else, he hadn't returned.

"Well," Wallace said, "it was a long time ago. We went back to that church next week? But you didn't come. Them boys said if you had? Somebody was gone write you a letter saying you wasn't welcome in their 'fine Methodist church.'"

"I guess not," Larry said. "You can't blame em."

"Naw," Wallace said. "But fuck em anyway."

Then he said, "Trouble with beer? You can drank it all night and it don't do nothing but make you piss. But I got something else," he said, patting the zippered pocket of his short pants, "that'll get my head right." He unzipped the pocket and pulled a Sucrets tin out and laid it reverently across his knees, pressed together, opened the tin and removed a plastic Baggie and a bent pad of rolling papers.

Larry hesitated. "I wish you'd wait till you got home to do that." He looked at his feet.

Folding one of the papers in half, Wallace began to dribble in crushed green bud. "How come?" Without looking up.

"I just don't need any trouble. With the law."

"Man with your rep? Scared of a little Mary J. Wanna? Shit. Fuck the law, Larry. You see em anywhere? Nothing out here but us dropouts and them buzzards. But we can go inside, it makes you more comfortable."

Rolling the paper between his fingers, he glanced at Larry and winked, then licked the edge of the paper and then put the whole thing in his mouth and brought out a bent white joint. The first one Larry had ever seen. The boy dropped his half-smoked cigarette and toed it out and with his Bic lit the joint and took a deep toke, holding it, and extended it toward Larry.

"No thanks."

"You sure, hoss?" Breath still held, smoke in his teeth. "It's good shit from that nigger over in Chabot. Call him M&M. You know him?"

"No," he said, but he did, from school. One of Silas's teammates.

Wallace blew a line of smoke into the air. "I always say, 'M&M? You plain or peanut?'" He toked again then offered it to Larry. "You sure you sure?"

to coil to circle

to chirp zwitschern
monkey grass Liriope, a low, grass-like, flowering plant
tender sanft

to scald to burn

BB gun an air gun for children

eggnog drink with eggs, cream, sugar, and often alcohol
hearth [hɑːrθ] fireplace

rug Teppich

ribbon Band
checkering a pattern of squares cut into the wooden handle
blueing protective coat on the metal parts of firearms
grip part of a firearm you hold in your hand
sight small, thin metal part on top of the barrel to aim with

"Yeah."

Wallace sat there, the smoke coiled around him. He looked out across the field. He seemed to have forgotten where he was, and for a while Larry rocked, bats fluttering over his view and crickets chirping in the monkey grass along the edge of the porch and his mother's wind chime jingling, delicate notes too tender to be metal, more like soft bone on wire, he'd always thought the chime sounded like a skeleton playing a guitar, and for a time they sat together on the porch and watched the sun scald the sky red and the trees black.

December 24, Wednesday, after work. He hadn't seen Wallace in a few weeks. In the morning – Christmas one of only four holidays he took each year – he planned to ride over to River Acres and give his mother the presents he'd gotten her at Wal-Mart, a new nightgown, a chicken-shaped pot with flowers in it, and a pair of slippers. He'd got a pair of slippers for the woman beside his mother, too, in all spending nearly an hour at the giant store, this one of his favorite evenings of the year.

At home he built a fire in the fireplace and sat looking at the picture of his parents. Then he made a chicken-fried steak TV dinner and turned on the television and, eating, watched the Grinch steal Christmas again and bring it back. Then he watched his favorite holiday movie, *A Christmas Story*, and felt his eyes water when Ralphie's father got him the BB gun. He drank the eggnog he'd bought at Wal-Mart and read a while and fell asleep in his chair by the hearth.

Something woke him around midnight, somebody on his porch. He sat up in the chair and the book fell off his chest and landed on the rug. Nobody had ever messed with him on this night, and he went to the window but saw no one. Quietly, not turning on the light, he opened the door and peered out through the screen into the cold night, the smoke of his breath sucked away by the wind, the chime playing fast, the rocking chair rocking by itself.

Nothing.

He was about to close the door, thinking it must have been a stick blown over the porch. But then he saw something in the chair. He pushed the screen door open and went over to where a shoe box sat in the wicker seat, tied shut with a frayed red ribbon.

He looked around. Then took it inside and lowered himself into his chair by the fireplace and held the box. He shook it, put his ear to it. He untied the ribbon and lifted the lid and saw an old pistol, a .22 revolver, its checkering worn off and most of the blueing gone as well. Its wood grips were tight, though, and its sight intact. He picked it up and held it and saw oil on his hand. Somebody had cleaned it. Beneath it was a box of cartridges, .22 longs. Off to the side was a piece of white notebook paper folded in half. He opened it and read, "Merry Xmas, Larry, from Santa."

On New Year's Eve Wallace brought a bagful of bottle rockets and they were shooting them over the field.

"Had me a visitor," Larry said, watching the sky pop.

"Oh you did?"

"Left me something."

"What's that?"

"Pistol. A nice .22."

"Well, I'm glad to hear it. Next time them fuckers comes messing with you, you shoot a few times in the air I bet that'll scare em off."

"Thanks," Larry said.

"For what?"

Larry had brought out two Coke bottles for the rockets, but Wallace would hold them by their sticks and light them, wait a moment as the fuse burned, and throw them, watch them lag and then take off and explode against the night. It reminded Larry of the New Year's Eve the Walkers had come over with bottle rockets, and as he began to tell Wallace the story he remembered telling it to Silas, who hadn't laughed, but now as Larry told it Wallace began to laugh as Larry imitated Cecil running and pounding his pocket.

Later they sat on the porch in their coats, Larry rocking, Wallace on the steps drinking beer. He'd smoked tonight's joint to a nub and reached down and smushed its end gently on the porch and put it in the Sucrets box and closed it and zipped it back up in his pocket. Once in a while he lit a firecracker and flicked it into the yard, the night grown so dark and starless Larry only saw him in these moments of fire, the ember of his cigarette, the joint, the night becoming its sounds as each night did, their voices, the squeak of Larry's chair, the pop of Wallace's beers opening, crickets, the skeleton playing guitar. Near midnight, Larry yawning, Wallace lit another firecracker with his cigarette and threw it into the yard and they sat waiting as the fuse hissed but that was all.

"Dud," he said.

"Larry?"

Larry yawned, stretched. It was a month later, Wallace coming once or twice a week, drinking his beer, smoking his cigarettes and marijuana as the nights deepened.

He said, "Tell me about that girl."

"Girl?"

"You know. The one . . . ?"

"Oh."

"Did you do it?"

"No," Larry said.

"You mind talking about it?"

"Well, nobody's asked me in a long time."

"If you had done it, would you tell me?"

"I took her on a date is all."

"Oh. What happened? On the date? You get in her pants?"

to lag to not function immediately

to imitate nachmachen

nub (here): just a small piece
to smush (dialect) to crush

ember Glut

dud a firecracker, missile, bomb, etc. that fails to explode

queer (slang) homosexual

faggot (vulgar) homosexual

"Naw."
"How come?"
"I just didn't," Larry said.
"You ain't queer, are you?"
"No," Larry said. "Not the way you mean, anyway."
"That's good," Wallace said. "I can't stand a damn faggot."
Wallace said, "You know what we ought to do sometime?"
"What?"
"Go out to that cabin you got."
"You found that, too?"
"Yeah."
"I expect it's about to fall in."
"Yeah. You know what I used to do?"
"What?"
"Play in it."
"It's locked, ain't it?"

to prize open to force open with a lever (*Hebel*)
possum opossum: *Beutelratte*

"Yeah. But it was a window you could prize open. Back window. Climbing in there with all the dust and spiderwebs. Seen a possum one time? Like to shit my pants and didn't go back there for a month. I'd be scared to death, you know, sneaking in like that, thinking you in Scary Larry's hunting cabin. Thinking is you crazy? But I was wondering, too, what if this is where he, you know, hid that girl.

"I tried to find some place you might've hid her, but I never did find nothing, not even a dirty magazine or a old rubber.

high (here): high because of marijuana

"I ought not to be telling you this," he said, "but I'm bout as high as a buzzard on laughing gas now and you know what? I used to imagine you'd find me playing in there and tie me up and keep me prisoner. But instead of killing me you'd just keep me out there and we'd get to be friends."

hit (here): a puff from the marijuana cigarette

It was dark and Larry heard him creak open his Sucrets box and knew he was plucking out a roach, as he called it, saw the flash as he lit it with his Bic and took two more hits before he said, "Shit," and flung it from his fingers into the yard where it pulsed a moment like a dying firefly.

"You know what else?" he said. "I don't care if you done it or not, took that girl. We'd still be friends if you did."
"I didn't."

to gag to put a piece of cloth over or in a person's mouth
to smack to hit with an open hand
to strangle *erwürgen*
doggie-style (vulgar) from the back
to do s.o. up the bunghole (vulgar) to have anal sex

"Sometimes they like it, getting raped. They want you to do it. Carry em out to that cabin and thow em on the floor. Gag em. Start tearing off their clothes and hitting em a little bit, smacking em on they little white ass. Using a belt to strangle em, get on doggie-style and do em up the bunghole, show em who daddy is."
"Wallace, I don't like that talk."
"You don't ever thank about it? I used to listen to Momma and them fellows she was with. She liked em to smack her on the ass."

Larry stood up and his knees popped. "I think it's about time for me to get to bed. You've done got pretty drunk. And high, too, sounds like."

"Wait – "

Larry passed him where he sat and moved along the porch in the familiar darkness and opened the door and reached inside and clicked on the switch and flooded the night with light, Wallace blinking, covering his eyes with one hand and his crotch with the other. But not before Larry saw the lump in his pants.

"Good night," Larry said, looking away.

He went inside and closed the screen and fastened its hasp and shut the door. Locked it.

Outside, bright in the window, Wallace was up, adjusting his crotch, cupping his hands against the window to see inside.

"Larry," he yelled. "Wait."

"Go on home," Larry called. "Drive careful and come back when you're sober."

"Just wait!"

"Good night."

For a moment Wallace looked like he might cry, and then he slammed his forehead against the window. "Fuck you!" he said, then said it again, louder. "I know what you done. Know you raped that girl and killed her. Ever body's right about you" – yelling now – "you crazy!"

He banged his head on the window again and kicked the wall. "You fucking freak," he yelled, "I'm gone go tell the law on you right now, how you said you done it, killed that girl, told me ever thing – "

Larry unlocked the door and opened it and came onto the porch where Wallace was backing up. He fell pinwheeling off the porch and landed in the yard, still yelling. "You crazy!"

"I ain't never hurt nobody in my life," Larry said, "so you can just go on home!"

Wallace, still yelling, was running for his four-wheeler. He climbed on yelling all the while, illuminated in the porch light, kicking the starter until the motor sputtered to life. Then he got back off and crossed the yard to Larry's pickup and kick at the headlights, missing once, kicking again, shattering the left one, the right, then clambering onto the truck's hood and jumping on it, stomping in the windshield, yelling, "Fuck you! Fuck you, Scary Larry!"

Larry turned, went inside, where he watched until Wallace tired himself out and climbed down off the truck and got on the sputtering four-wheeler and flicked its headlamp on and gunned the engine, turning donuts in Larry's grass, then sped away.

For a while Larry stood at the window, looking out at the night. Tomorrow he'd have to replace the windshield again. And the headlights. Pop out the dents in the hood.

And he did, another windshield from the parts house, headlights, more lifted eyebrows from Johnson. Using a bathroom plunger to undent the hood, epoxying the rearview mirror back.

newscaster (AE) person who reads the news on TV or the radio

freak abnormal person

to sic the law on s.o. (fig.) to call the police in order to arrest s.o.
caller ID a small window on a phone that shows the number and sometimes the name of the person calling as well

suspicion Argwohn, Misstrauen

to endure (here): ertragen

plumbing [plʌmɪŋ] **salesman** a person who sells pipes that supply and carry away water in a building
radiator Kühler
charged geladen
to smirk to smile because you are satisfied with yourself

on the straight and narrow (path) (fig.) living an honest life

Wallace didn't return after a week. A month. Larry grew worried and even got the phone book from its drawer and looked up Stringfellow. This was late February, the warmest winter in lower Mississippi in years, global warming, the newscaster thought. There were nine Stringfellows listed, but when he called the first a woman's voice said, "Larry Ott?" before he'd told who he was. Alarmed, he hung up.

The phone rang again a moment later and a man said, "Why you calling us, you fucking freak?"

Larry said, "I'm sorry, it was a mistake."

"You goddamn right it was. If you ever call this number again I'll sic the law on you."

He'd forgotten that people had caller ID and put the phone book away.

He waited during the day in his shop and at night on his porch. He'd pause while reading, lift his chin to listen for cars. When he visited his mother he wanted to tell her about Wallace, how God did work in His own time, healing Larry's stuttering, his asthma, even sending him, at last, this friend. But his mother had forgotten the old prayer along with everything else, and so he just talked about her chickens.

When she was awake, the senile, skeletal black lady in the bed beside Ina would watch him with eyes narrowed by suspicion, but not because of Larry's past, he figured, but his skin color, a woman close to ninety whose family had left her here, and Larry would wonder how many wrongs she'd endured from white people in her almost-century of living. Sometimes he thought of Alice Jones, of Silas, how Larry's mother had given them coats but not a ride in her car. How what seemed like kindness could be the opposite.

In May in Wal-Mart on his grocery run he bought a case of Pabst Blue Ribbon beer. A few nights later he opened one of the cans and tasted it, then poured it down the sink. Some evenings he took the pistol Wallace had given him from its box in its hiding place in his closet and loaded it and aimed at buzzards floating overhead, but he never fired it.

In June two customers stopped by the shop, one a plumbing salesman from Mobile on his way north with an overheated radiator and the other a black woman from Memphis with a battery that wouldn't stay charged. He smirked at himself in the bathroom mirror the night he'd replaced the battery and thought that with all this business he should hire some help. If Wallace ever came back, he'd offer him a job on the condition the boy stop drinking and smoking so much and never on the job, train him to be a mechanic, start simple, oil changes, tire rotations, work up to brake jobs, tune-ups, rebuilding carburetors. Larry wouldn't live forever, and the shop had to go to somebody, maybe it would keep Wallace on the straight and narrow.

Sitting on his porch one late July evening he remembered the church his mother would visit occasionally after the Chabot Baptist had become "uncomfortable" for her. The First Century Church, a group of Holy Rollers north of Fulsom, spoke in tongues and had faith healing services and asked its members to fast for three-day periods at certain times of the year. Larry never accompanied her to the fabricated metal building they used, understanding it was easier for a congregation to accept the mother of an accused killer than the killer himself, but, hungry for God, he would abstain from food when she did. He found the first skipped meals the hardest, the hunger a hollow ache. The longer he went without eating, though, the second day, the third, the pain would subside from an ache to the memory of an ache and finally to only the memory of a memory. Until you ate you didn't know how hungry you were, how empty you'd become. Wallace's visits had shown him that being lonesome was its own fast, that after going unnourished for so long, even the foulest bite could remind your body how much it needed to eat. That you could be starving and not even know it.

"Dear God," he prayed at night. "Please forgive my sins, and send me some business. Give Momma a good day tomorrow or take her if it's time. And help Wallace, God. Please."

to fast *fasten*

fabricated constructed from standardized parts
congregation *Kirchengemeinde*
to abstain from s.th. *auf etwas verzichten*
to skip to not do what you usually do
hollow having an empty space inside
to subside to become less and less

unnourished without food
foulest most awful
to starve *hungern*

Chapter Ten

Was it Monday yet? He'd barely slept the week before, and now Silas couldn't stop yawning even though the mill roared and drummed behind him like an angry city. Each passing face in its tinted glass regarded the constable with ire, this tall black man standing shadowed in his hat in the road with a whistle in his teeth, pickup trucks bumping over the railroad tracks and away from the mill while impatient cars and SUVs inched forward.

A week ago he'd found Tina Rutherford's body under Larry Ott's cabin and been in all the local papers and a few national ones, his picture this time, snapped by the police reporter as Silas stood by the cabin, watching agents from the Criminal Investigation Bureau in Jackson carry the body bag out. The article said that he'd been investigating Larry's Ott's shooting, a possible suicide attempt, and happened across the old cabin.

He'd have been a hero if he'd found her alive.

"You what?" French had asked, on the radio.

Panting, "I think it's her, Roy."

"Don't touch a thing," French had ordered, "and don't tell a soul. Just set up your perimeter and wait."

He and the sheriff had arrived sharing a four-wheeler not long after, search warrant in hand, prying the lock off the cabin door and moving the bed aside, French saying he'd walked this land himself, twice, both times missing the cabin, camouflaged as it was by kudzu. How in the world had Silas found it?

"Just lucky," he'd lied.

The cabin was illuminated that night by harsh floodlights on tripods, heavy orange extension cords leading outside to where portable generators had been trailered in by four-wheelers. French filmed the two forensics experts from the C.I.B., wearing Tyvek suits and respirators, as they descended into the floor using entrenching tools to move the soft dirt. Half an hour later one raised his head and gave French a thumbs-up.

Standing in the corner by the stove, Silas had no way to catalog his emotions as what he'd been smelling for a while bubbled up out of his throat and he fled the house, out the door through the vines and ivy spot-lit and drawn back like curtains. The coroner and two deputies and the sheriff stood outside smoking and talking quietly. Silas gave them a weak nod as he lurched into the night, past where the lights could find him, and retched until his eyes burned and his gut hurt.

Later he went back in. Hand over his nose and mouth, he forced himself to look down at what they were discussing, photographing. She'd been thrown in naked on her stomach, he could tell, he could see part of her spine but not, thank God, what would have been her face. What he saw was not even a girl anymore, instead something from one of Larry's horror books, black and melted-looking and dissolved. What drove Silas back out of the house the second time was not her spine with dirt in its intricate lines or her shoulder blades bound in strands of flesh or the matted green hair where skin from her skull had loosened, but the wrist one of the C.I.B. agents lifted in his heavy rubber glove, her small bony hand with its fingers cupped, showing French's camera the nails that still bore chipped red polish, and, loose on one of the fingers, her class ring.

Now, his arms up to halt the trucks, Silas's cell phone began to ring. It always did during traffic duty. Anything official came over his radio, phone calls were personal.

Fuck it, he thought. He dug out his cell.

"Officer Jones?"

"You got him."

"This Brenda."

"Who?"

"Up at River Acres? Nursing home?"

It was hard to hear for the traffic and he stuck a finger in his opposite ear.

"Hey," he said. "I can't talk now."

"You wanted to know when Mrs. Ott was having a good day?"

"Yeah?"

"She having one now."

"Thanks," he said. "I'll get over there soon as I can."

"You best hurry," she was saying as he hung up.

The mill had shut down for Tina Rutherford's funeral. Hell, Chabot had. Black ribbons on the office and store doors, a long line of cars from the Baptist church following the hearse over the highway, Silas directing traffic for that, too, his post at the crossroads of 102 and 11, the four-way stop in his jurisdiction where the procession might get broken up by log trucks, shadows of birds flickering over the road, his uniform pressed and his hat over his heart as cars trolled by with their lights on, him standing, as he had not in years, at navy attention. The windows of the Rutherford limousine were tinted and he couldn't see the girl's parents, just a pair of white hands on the steering wheel. And after what must've been a hundred vehicles had rolled by, he'd driven to the church and sat in his Jeep, unable to go inside. Later he caboosed the procession to a graveyard miles out in the country, whites only buried there, lovely landscaped grounds shaded by live oaks with Spanish moss slanted in the wind like beards of dead generals. Nothing like the wooded cemetery where Alice Jones lay under her little rock on the side of a hill eaten up with kudzu, the plastic flowers blown over and strewn by the wind. During the Rutherford girl's burial, a high bright sun and two tiny airplanes crossing the sky, he'd stood at the edge of trees, away from the grief – French had been the one to tell Rutherford his daughter was dead, and for that Silas had been grateful – while the white people near the open grave and the black ones surrounding them

---

intricate complex
shoulder blade Schulterblatt
strand strip
matted forming a wet and dirty mass

bore (here): trug
chipped with small pieces broken off
class ring ring to show your class and year of graduation

to hang, hung, hung up auflegen

hearse [hɜːrs] Leichenwagen

pressed ironed
to troll by (here): to slowly move by

to caboose (fig.) (here): to drive behind the procession

slanted leaning to the side

to strew, strew, strewn to scatter

grief Trauer, Leid

bagpipe Dudelsack

to crave to have a strong desire for s.th.
limelight Rampenlicht
in the loop (coll.) part of a group dealing with s.th. important

cruiser squad car, police car

to sling, slung, slung to throw s.th. somewhere in a careless manner
to go over the edge (idiom) to become crazy
to fire up (here): to start up

gone (dialect) are going to

thermos thermos bottle

gawker s.o. who stares at s.th./s.o. in a stupid way
shuffler person walking slowly without lifting the feet
robe bathrobe

at a distance sang "Amazing Grace" accompanied by bagpipes and while Larry Ott lay in his coma, belted to his hospital bed, a deputy posted by the door.

Silas had asked that French let him have the midnight-to-six shift there.

He wasn't a deputy but it was in French's power to use him. "Fine by me," the CI had said. "Long as you can stay awake. Nobody else wants it, and we short-handed as it is. But I'm curious."

"I need the money," Silas said. Just one damn lie after another.

"Yeah right."

Silas figured French thought he just craved more limelight, didn't want to give up the case, wanted to stay in the loop. Which was partially true, and which also helped explain why Silas had gone by Larry's house every day since he'd found the girl. The first day the deputy stationed there was sitting on the porch in Larry's rocking chair with his feet crossed reading one of Larry's books. Silas parked behind his cruiser and got out and nodded.

"What you up to, 32?"

"Feed the man's chickens."

The deputy followed him back and into the barn and watched Silas sling corn into the pen, the chickens pecking it up, Silas wondering if they'd think he'd gone over the edge if he fired up Larry's tractor and pulled the cage to a fresh square of grass.

"I could do that," the deputy said. "Save you running all the way out here."

"I don't mind."

"You ought to collect the eggs, too. With no rooster in there they just gone rot."

"You want em?"

"God almighty no. I bring home eggs from Scary Larry? My wife'd thow em at me."

"You could probably sell em on eBay," Silas said. "Or one of them serial killer Web sites."

The deputy toed the lawn mower wheels. "What's these here for?"

Silas explained as he filled the water tire and shooed the setting hens aside and collected half a dozen dry, brown, shit-speckled eggs, and carried them back to his Jeep. He began taking them to Marla at The Hub, who said she was glad to have them, eggs was eggs.

Nights he sat in a folding chair outside Larry's door, a tall thermos of coffee and one of Marla's greasy sacks by his feet, the overhead lights dim, Silas squeaking around on the chair and trying to convince himself of why he was here. He'd brought **Night Shift** from his office, and because his ass hurt walked the hospital hall reading the stories he never had as a kid.

They'd put Larry in a room at the end of a hall to keep gawkers away, Silas having to stand up a few times each shift to warn off shufflers, old men in robes clinging to their portable IV racks, or nurses from other floors and, once, a hugely pregnant woman in a robe and hospital flip-flops who told him she was in labor.

Silas said, "You a long way from the delivery room."

Trying to look past him, Larry's door cracked. "They said walk around." She pushed her hands into the small of her back. "Try to get this little bastard kick-started."

Larry was now a suspect – *the* suspect – in Tina Rutherford's murder, and Silas had given French his tire molds and the evidence bags with the broken glass and roach in them. Larry's keys, too. The newspapers and television stations following the story had dug up the scant facts on the Cindy Walker case, as well, how a quarter of a century earlier Larry had picked her up for a date and, hours later, come home without her. A new road had been slashed into Larry's land and the cabin dismantled, the earth beneath it excavated, French hoping that the Walker girl's bones might be recovered as well, closing that case. But despite the fact that no more bones had been found, reporters and newscasters were speculating that Larry Ott had attempted suicide because of what he'd done to Tina Rutherford and possibly Cindy Walker and, who knew, maybe other girls. There'd been one from Mobile missing for eleven years. Another from Memphis. Maybe these two – and, who knew, others – were buried somewhere on the last acres Larry Ott had refused to sell to the lumber mill.

Under orders not to talk to reporters, Silas didn't tell Voncille about moonlighting as Larry's guard, knowing she'd peer at him over her glasses, worry he might fall asleep at the wheel and ram his Jeep into a log truck. He imagined her saying he couldn't burn his candle at both ends, or, for his own good, telling Mayor Mo.

But Angie was Silas's main problem. Aside from being worried about him herself, she said she'd gotten so used to him staying over she had trouble sleeping without his long arms and legs all up in her space, not to mention his other long thing. They slept on their left sides, spooning, his left arm under her neck and reaching around so he could cup her right breast, his right arm over her side, cupping her left breast. He loved feeling her heart beat through it. He hadn't seen her since their lunch at the diner, and knew he was using his guard duty as an excuse to avoid finishing their conversation. She called on his cell each night as she lay in bed and talked in his ear, detailing her day of wrecks and heart attacks, of Tab, an old hippie, ranting against the war in Iraq. She had one sister over there in a base east of Baghdad, working in the pharmacy. Oh, and her other sister was pregnant again, by a different man. She told him the movies she'd watched, how much she liked the pastor at her church. She was on nights Saturday and Sunday, so Silas promised to take Monday night off and knew he'd have to tell her something and worried it might be the truth. The rest of it. He'd avoided it so long himself it sometimes didn't even seem real, what had happened in 1982. He wondered how it would feel to tell her everything, say who he really was, and he worried that if he did, she might start to see him differently.

to nod off to fall asleep for a short time
to pace to walk up and down in a small space
twined wrapped
restraint (here): a strap that keeps you tied to s.th.
catheter [ˈkæθɪtər] a tube to carry away urine
fluids i.e. IV feeding

initial first

lot parking lot
to fade (here): to slowly become less interesting
to regain to get back
consciousness *Bewusstsein*

cocksucker (vulgar) bastard

When he nodded off in his chair he'd get up and pace the hospital hall. Sometimes go into Larry's room, stare at him where he lay twined in among his machines and wires and tubes and cords. And the leather restraints on his wrists. He looked helpless and weak but was, Silas had been told, stable. His chest wound clear of infection, healing accordingly. Draining well but Larry still using a catheter, still on fluids.

But he was big news.

After the initial reports, before and after the funeral, the vans from Jackson, Meridian, Mobile, and even Memphis had camped out in the hospital lot, their satellites aimed at the sky, but now they were gone, this news fading as Larry slept and the world continued to supply new horrors, crashing planes, suicide bombers, kids shooting other kids. He supposed when – if – Larry ever regained consciousness, the parking lot would fill up again.

Each evening when he arrived, already yawning, he asked Ray, the deputy on evenings, if anybody had been by. French, the deputy reported. Old Lolly, the sheriff, once in a while. Doctors and nurses. Patients. Now and then a reporter.

"They feeding him through a tube," Ray said. "You ask me, they ought to just let the cocksucker starve."

Silas had unfastened Larry's leather restraints the first night, like undoing a belt, but Ray told him the next evening that one of the shift nurses had complained and that the restraints were to remain on.

Sometimes when the nurses were gone Silas would stand over Larry and watch him, his IV machine flashing its faint lights and the heart monitor beeping or whistling, the ventilator inhaling, exhaling. He wondered how broken Larry was by the events of his life, how damaged. What would Silas tell him if he ever woke up? Sometimes he couldn't help but wish he wouldn't.

"Larry?" he would say.

No response.

"Larry?"

The second night as rain fell outside the window he glanced at the door. Then whispered, "I don't know if you can hear me, Larry, but when you wake up it's gone be bad." He came around the bed and rolled up a stool and put his face near Larry's and spoke directly in his ear. "Don't tell em nothing, Larry, you hear? Hear? They gone try to get you to confess, but don't say nothing, Larry. Hear? Nothing."

On his way out of the hospital, somebody called, "Hey, Constable Jones?"

The information desk.

"Jon without an *h*." Silas veered over and the old man handed him a Styrofoam cup of coffee.

"Thanks. I thought you was afternoons."

"I fill in when they let me. Take my word for it, son. Don't ever retire. You're young, it ain't enough hours in the day and you sleep through most of em anyways. But once you get to be my age, sleep's a memory and you beg just to get to work for free."

"I'll remember that."

"No, you won't. Or when you do it'll be too late."

Silas yawned, checked his watch.

"You asked about anybody else coming to see Mr. Ott, didn't you? Well, one of the other volunteers, he remembered it was somebody came by, not long after you did that first day. Before all this brouhaha. Reason he didn't tell me sooner is that some of us are a tad on the senile side. If I could remember his name I'd tell you."

He waited for Silas to smile. "Reporter?"

"Naw, it's been plenty of them, but that wasn't what you wanted, was it?"

"No."

"This fellow, didn't say who he was. Just asked if Larry – used his first name – had ever woke up."

"What'd he look like?"

"Marlon, that was the other guy, he said he was early twenties, skinny, white. Said he was, what was the word he used? Oh, he said he was 'kinda stringy-looking.' "

"Thanks," Silas said. He glanced behind him. "Yall got cameras in here? Maybe a video of him?"

"Supposed to. But it's been broke awhile. They tell me it's in the budget to get it fixed, but you know how budgets work. Get money for one thing, takes it from another."

"Got that right," Silas said.

When he went by Larry's that afternoon, a new deputy and a plainclothes officer from the C.I.B. were in the house going through Larry's papers. Both men came out and watched him feed the chickens as if it were an exhibition.

Each day was different at Larry's, different lawmen, French there the next afternoon, shaking his head at the farmer constable.

"What's going on?" he asked.

Flinging in the feed. "What you mean?"

"You know what I mean."

Silas just shrugged and went to get the eggs. He looked out at French, regarding him from the other side of the wire, and told him about the stringy-looking man. French said without more than that, the tape, say, or an ID, it sounded like a dead end. "Stringy-looking?" he said. "Hell, that's practically a goddamn demographic in southeast Mississippi."

The next day, when Silas drove out, he found the house and barn deserted, Sheriff's Department seals on all doors, including the barn's, warning intruders that this was a crime scene.

"How am I supposed to feed yall?" Silas asked out loud. "Or get them eggs?"

---

to beg to ask earnestly

brouhaha [ˈbruːhɑːhɑː] (coll.) excitement
tad (coll.) a bit

stringy thin with muscles showing

plainclothes wearing ordinary clothes

ID some kind of identification
demographic (study) a study that gathers statistics about certain groups of people

seal *Siegel*

to tell apart *auseinander halten*

to slosh to carry water in a way that the water makes a lot of noise

fuzzy blurred, unclear
unabated not in any way hindered

to swing, swung, swung by (coll.) (here): to pull in, to stop by

salvage yard yard that stores used parts

to roil to move about turbulently

solitaire card game for one person

trifecta (here): a situation where three events occur at the same time
feature story special front page article

No answer from the chickens, gathered across the wire, waiting, clucking, scratching. They seemed used to him, all eight, looking at him their sideways way, and he was beginning to think he could tell them apart.

He drove that evening to Wal-Mart and bought two bags of chicken feed and put them in the back of his Jeep and was out there that night slinging in the moonlight. He filled an old milk jug with water from the spigot at the back of Larry's house and sloshed it over in a bowl so they could drink. The egg dilemma was still unsolved.

Fuzzy days found him asleep in the Jeep while speeders went unabated on the highway below. The Jeep took longer and longer to crank. One day he swung by the auto shop at the mill and the mechanic opened the hood and whistled. "If this thing was a horse we'd a done shot it," he said. He told Silas to bring it in early next week and leave it a few days, he'd see if he could order parts from the salvage yard. "Carburetors," he said nostalgically.

After his evening patrol, Silas would roil semiconscious in his sweaty sheets waiting for the alarm to buzz so he could go the hospital and watch Larry sleep. One night he sat dozing in his guard chair and woke himself by snoring. He blinked and looked down the hall and saw a stringy-looking shadow standing watching him. Then it was gone. He rose and ran past the other rooms to the end where the hall was empty. Somebody down past a Coke machine moved and Silas said, "Wait," and began to run down the hall.

He turned the corner and nothing. More halls. Door to stairs. He eased a bit farther along the hall, then turned and went back to Larry's room, shaking his head, wondering if he'd made it all up.

The rest of the night he stayed awake.

Now, Monday, he finished the traffic. Yawning, he hoped Mrs. Ott was still having a good day at the nursing home.

In City Hall, Voncille was on the phone, solitaire on her computer. He laid his hat and sunglasses on his desk among the day's scattered paperwork and got his coffee cup and filled it at the water fountain and drank it so fast it made his neck hurt.

"That was Shannon from the paper," Voncille said when she hung up, rolling her chair over to hand him a message. "Said she wants to talk to you about your trifecta, as she called it. Reckon she figures it'd make for a good feature story. What an outstanding constable you are."

"Right. I'm headed over to River Acres."

"What for?"

"See Mrs. Ott."

"Larry's mother?"

"Yeah."

"Well. You look like you ain't slept in a month," she said. "But I'm glad you finally stopped by. If you don't go out and write some tickets, the mayor's gone have your head."

At five-thirty, at River Acres, he climbed out of the Jeep, which continued to run as it had been doing lately, like a stutterer.

Inside, Brenda was reading a magazine at her desk. "She tried to call her son on his cell phone," she said, "and when nobody answered she started getting upset."

upset *aufgebracht, verärgert*

He pictured the phone lighting up, rattling in the box in French's office, vibrating the pictures and all the other evidence.

"How is she now?"

"Little calmer. Good thing about Alzheimer's is they don't stay mad long."

He thanked her and said he remembered the way.

Entering the room he was hit by the stink of feces. Ina Ott lay flat on her back with her right hand fluttering, flies buzzing in the bright light through the window. The tiny black woman beside her was asleep.

"Mrs. Ott?" Silas took off his hat.

She looked up at him without recognition. "I've messed myself," she said. "Where's Larry?"

He saw the dark stain around the sheets at her crotch, her useless hand laying right in it.

"I'm sorry," she said.

"I'll get a nurse," he said, glad to leave the room and its smell.

"Second shift's coming on in half a hour," Brenda told him, hardly looking up. "They'll clean her."

"How long's she been laying like that?" he asked.

"I don't know."

"You what?"

"Laying's all she can do."

"She ain't got to lay in her own stink," he said.

"You don't smell so good yourself."

"If her son come up and seen her like that what would yall do?"

"Last I heard he ain't going nowhere."

"This how yall treat folks?"

Brenda gave him a sharp look. "Nigger, don't come up in here telling me how to do my job. We got forty-five old people here and we get to em best we can. Come in here all high and mighty just cause you got your picture in the paper?"

high and mighty as if a person of great importance

"Fuck this," he said and went back down the hall.

He found a closet with clean sheets and a box of disposable wipes and snatched the sheets off the rack and put the wipes under his arms and went looking for an orderly.

disposable that can be thrown away after using
wipe s.th. like a towel to clean up with
orderly person who works in a hospital who carries supplies, cleans up, or moves patients

A man standing by a broom pointed him down the hall and he pushed through a glass door in the back and found Clyde, leaning against the wall, smoking.

"You best come with me," Silas said. "Now. Mrs. Ott done had a accident."

"Chill out, bro," he said. "I'm on my break."

chill out, bro (coll.) Relax, brother!

Silas got up in his face. "You go clean Mrs. Ott up right now or I'm gone take your sorry ass back to the jail."

"For what?"

Silas plucked the cigarette from Clyde's lips and threw it down and pushed the sheets and wipes into his arms. "I'll think of something."

He stood outside her door, just in sight of Clyde, making sure he treated her right.

"I'm sorry," he heard her say. "I messed myself again."

"It's okay, Mrs. Ott. We getting you all clean now. It's somebody out there to see you."

"My son?"

"Naw, ain't him. Somebody else."

"It's not true," she said, "what they're saying?"

Clyde came out wearing rubber gloves and carrying the soiled sheets and her nightgown in a plastic bag. "You happy now, motherfucker?" he said.

Ignoring him, Silas went in and she looked better, her bed raised and the smell nearly gone, the window opened.

"Mrs. Ott?"

She turned toward him where he stood holding his hat. Her good eye widened but otherwise she showed no surprise at a big strange black constable in her room.

"I'm Silas Jones, ma'am," he said. "People call me 32."

"32?"

"Yes, ma'am."

She turned her head to regard him from another angle. Wedged between the beds, a small table held nothing but a worn-out Bible. Out the window, past the black woman still asleep and beyond the chain-link fence, cars on the highway. Her dying view.

"I may have met you," she said. "But I'm forgetful."

"Yes, ma'am. I come seen you once before, about your son. I used to be friends with him, a long time ago."

"He's okay, idn't he?"

"Well," he said.

"I called him but nobody answered."

Silas looked down at his hat. Maybe this was why police wore hats, for the distraction they provided when you had to tell somebody their daughter had not only been strangled to death but beaten and raped first, or to tell a woman her son had not only been shot but maybe had shot himself, and that if he ever came out of his coma he'd be charged with killing the girl.

"Well," he said again.

"He didn't have many friends," Mrs. Ott said. When he looked up from his hat she was watching him.

"I came to ask you about my mother," he said.

"What's her name."

"Alice Jones."

"Who?"

He took the photograph of her from his wallet and showed it to her. Alice holding Larry as a baby. Silas realized that she must have been pregnant in the picture, though she didn't show.

"Why, that's my boy," Mrs. Ott said. "And that was our maid, I can't recall her name."

"Alice," he said.

"Yes. Alice Jones. But she had to leave." Mrs. Ott lowered her voice but continued to look at the picture. "A nice colored girl, but loose. But she got herself in a family way and wasn't married. I don't know what ever happened to her. What was her name?"

loose (here): promiscuous
to get yourself in a family way (coll.) to get pregnant

"Alice," he said gently. "She died a while back. Had a heart attack in her sleep."

She reached out to touch his hand, laid there on the side of her bed. "I'm so sorry."

"Reason I came," Silas said, "was to ask you if you know who her baby's daddy was."

"What's your name again?"

"32."

"That's not a name. What did your mother call you?"

"Silas."

"I remember you, Silas. You were Larry's friend."

"Yes, ma'am, I was."

For a long time she watched him and he saw himself come and go in her eyes, she knew him then she didn't. Then, for a moment, she did again.

"Silas?"

"Yes, ma'am?"

"I'm frightened."

"Of what?"

Shaking her head. "I can't remember."

They sat. The other old woman in the bed by the window shifted in her sleep and made a low noise.

to shift to move from one position to another
to brim to fill with moisture

He watched Mrs. Ott's good eye brim, a tear collect and fall and fill one of her deep wrinkles and never emerge at the bottom. "I'm sorry, Mrs. Ott," he said and saw he'd lost her, she was looking at him as if she'd never seen him.

"Clyde?" she said.

"No, ma'am. It's Silas."

"Who?"

He sat for a while longer, finally admitting that yes, he was Clyde. He let her ask about her chickens and he began to tell her how Eleanor Roosevelt kept trying to lay with no success and how Rosalynn Carter was getting fatter and Barbara Bush had lain two eggs in one night, and finally, as the chickens moved in their pen, smudges in her memory, she closed her eyes and began to sleep. He turned his fingers to free them of her brittle grip and took, from the sheets where it had fallen, the photograph. He fitted it in her good hand and rose and left

smudge s.th. with no shape

brittle frail and easily broken

button-down with buttons on the tips of the collar

to be peeved to be annoyed

Braves Atlanta Braves
medium supreme Pizza Hut pizza for two persons

tired's all tired that's all
to fiddle to move the hands or fingers restlessly

infield the area of a baseball field enclosed by the three bases and home plate
at short at the shortstop position

scrunchie a fabric-covered elastic to hold back hair
to swipe (here): to catch in the air
line drive (baseball) a baseball hit in a straight line just above the ground
to short-hop to catch a bouncing ball
bullet grounder very fast ground ball (ball rolling on the ground)
to flip to throw quickly
second second base
invincible unable to be defeated
diamond (here): infield

her in the light from the door and went down the hall and outside to his Jeep.

He was late for dinner with Angie, her turning her cheek to catch his kiss there and leaving him standing by her open apartment door as she descended the stairs toward her car. He wore jeans and a white button-down shirt. He'd left his hat, which she only liked if it came with the uniform.

She drove, unusual for them, a sign she was peeved. Ten minutes later, he sat across from her in a booth in the Fulsom Pizza Hut while the Braves lost on the television on the far wall.

"Baby," he finally said over their medium supreme, "what is wrong?"

"What you mean?"

"You know what I mean. You all quiet."

"Maybe cause I ain't see you all week and you late and don't even call? I put on my best jeans and you ain't even say I look nice?"

"You look nice."

She shook her head. "I know I do, you ain't got to tell *me*. My point is, where are you?"

"I'm tired's all."

She lifted her pizza and took a bite and chewed slowly. "You know how I can tell when you lying, 32?"

He met her eyes. "How?"

"You start messing with that hat."

He looked to the table, where the hat would've been, and saw his fingers, fiddling with air. He put his hand in his lap and had to smile. "When else did I lie?"

"Last week at the diner. When I asked if you ever dated that girl."

Cindy Walker.

He glanced at the television. Braves changing pitchers. He was suddenly on the Fulsom City Park infield as Coach Hytower stood talking to his pitcher and Silas, at short, was looking past them into the stands, where she always sat.

Angie put her pizza down. "Well?"

"Would you stay here a minute," he said, starting to rise. "I got to get my hat."

"Sit your lying ass down, 32, and talk to me."

When Silas played baseball, Cindy had come to games, smoking cigarettes and sitting in a miniskirt with her legs crossed on the high bleachers, her hair in a scrunchie. Sunglasses on. He knew she watched him and at some point he realized he was playing for her, swiping impossible line drives out of the air and short-hopping bullet grounders to flip to M&M on second or fling over to first for the out. Sometimes he felt invincible on the diamond, white people and black both watching him, taller now, up to six feet by the eleventh grade, growing so fast he still had stretch marks on his lower back. Daring that baseball to come anywhere near, willing it to, seeing it big as a basketball when he crouched at the plate, hitting for power to all fields so everybody played back, and then he'd bunt and most times there wouldn't even be a throw, him standing on first before the third baseman or catcher barehanded the ball.

On the infield tapping his cleats with his glove to knock off dirt, he'd watch Cindy leave after the eighth inning, walk off away from town, but always look back.

Then the time where he went five for five (including a triple) and dove and caught a liner up the middle to end the game. His teammates swarmed him and carried him off the field and from his perch he saw Cindy at her usual spot, smoking, and smiled at her. She smiled back.

She'd stayed till the end.

He skipped his shower and slipped away and followed her still in his dirty uniform and caught up and walked along the rural road with her, carrying his cap and glove, a few houses back against the trees, the two of them stepping around mailboxes in the weeds and hurrying when dogs boiled out from beneath a porch to bark at them.

"You see that catch?"

"You seen me there, didn't you?"

"You like baseball?"

"No."

"For a girl don't like baseball, you sure come to a lot of games."

"Maybe it ain't the games I come to see."

He looked down. Grass stains on his pants, infield dirt. "Coach say I got a chance for a scholarship to Ole Miss."

"You lucky."

"Might go all the way, he say. Say if I focus. Keep my mind off distractions."

"That what I am?"

Yeah, he wanted to say. She was thin with small bright blue eyes that had a kind of beaming intensity, especially when she frowned at him. She had freckles tiny as sand on her nose and throat and bare shoulders, her hair blond and curly and cinched back. Even sweaty she smelled good. Her breasts were little things under her top; he kept trying not to look at them. She had a concave figure, walking with a little hook to her, her belly in, as if waiting to absorb a blow. Today she wore sandals, and he liked her white freckled feet and red toenails.

"You from Chicago?"

He said he was.

"What's it like up there?"

"It's cool." He told her about Wrigley Field, the Cubs, Bull Durham on first, Ryno on second, Bowa at short, and the Penguin, Ron Cey, on third. Bobby Dernier in center. Silas and his friends skipping school to catch home runs on the street outside the stadium, the time he'd nearly got hit by a cab going after a bouncing ball, and then his fantastic catch on the sidewalk, dodging parking meters and diving and

---

to crouch to bend down
plate home plate
to hit for power to hit for maximum distance
to play back to stand farther back
to bunt to hit the ball lightly
to barehand (baseball) to catch the ball with a bare hand
to tap to strike lightly
cleats Stollen
inning one of nine divisions of a game whereby each team has a turn at batting
five for five (baseball) five runs in the fifth inning
a triple a safe run to third base
to dive, dove, dove (here): to drop down
liner line drive (Catching a batter's ball in the air results in the batter being put out.)
perch (here): high up position
rural road country road
to boil out (here): to suddenly rush out

scholarship Stipendium
Ole Miss University of Mississippi

beaming strahlend
freckles Sommersprossen
cinched back fastened towards the back

to absorb abfangen
blow Schlag

on first on first base
on second on second base
in center in center field
to skip school schwänzen
to catch home runs to catch the ball at home plate before a runner can reach it
cab taxi
to dodge to move to the side to avoid s.th.
parking meter Parkuhr

median (strip) strip of land dividing a highway	
buddy (coll., AE) *Kumpel*	
calling vocation, dream job	

landing in the grassy median with a group of white people watching from Murphy's Bar, the old man who came out and traded him four tickets for the ball. They'd gone the next day, him and three buddies, sitting in the sun in the bleachers. They got a drunk man to buy them beer, buying him one in return, Silas knowing as he watched the acrobatics on the field that he'd found his calling.

"What else," Cindy said, "that ain't about baseball?"

He told her how the snow sometimes covered cars entirely, and about his neighborhood, how the old black men would gather in the back alley around a fire in the trash drum and pass a bottle of Jim Beam and tell stories, outdoing each other, he told her about hopping the turnstiles and catching the el train, going to blues bars where the musicians smoked weed in the alley between sets, the endless honking traffic, freezing Lake Michigan glittering under the lights and buildings blocking the sky. Chicago pizza was the best, a thick pie of it, and burritos were as big as your head.

trash drum large container for garbage

set (coll.) (here): performance

"They got shows, ain't they?" she asked.

"Like movie shows?"

"No." She puckered and frowned but kept walking. "Like Broadway. Plays."

to pucker *die Lippen spitzen*

"Yeah." He remembered seeing their titles in the *Chicago Tribune*. Sunday mornings lying on the rug waiting for Oliver to finish with the sports pages. "My momma went one time," he told Cindy, "for her birthday. Saw *The Wiz*."

"That's what I want," she said.

"You mean be a actress?"

"No. To be able to see them shows. You can't see shit here."

"You could be a actress," he said. "You pretty enough."

She gave him a sad smile like he was a simple child. She went on talking, though, said how she couldn't wait to get the hell out of Mississippi, away from Cecil and her mouse of a mother, and as they walked along the road, no houses now, a field with cows following them along the other side of the fence and his cleats clicking on the pavement, a passing car slowed and the white man behind the wheel glared out his window.

"You okay?" he called to Cindy. "That boy bothering you?"

doofus (coll., AE) idiot
to flip s.o. off to give s.o. the middle finger

"Mind your own business, doofus," she said and flipped him off. He sped away shaking his head.

"Hey," Silas said, looking back. "I best go."

"Suit yourself."

He kept walking alongside her.

"Your stepdaddy like it you walking with a black boy?"

weed (here): *Unkraut*

"What you think? He's ignorant as a damn weed. Won't even try to get a job. Say he hurt his back at the mill."

Another car, the woman behind the wheel turning as she passed to stare.

"You ever kissed a white girl?"

"Naw," he said. "You ever kissed a black boy?"

"Sure," taking his hand, leading him down the embankment and into a stand of trees.

From there, notes passed at school, their secret meeting place in the woods behind the baseball field. He was a virgin but she wasn't, and on their blanket spread over the grass they became lovers and for the second half of his junior year he'd never been happier, a great season with an average just over .450 most of the time and a secret white girlfriend watching from the bleachers. A lot of people came, he knew, to see him, the sense he was going places, even old Carl Ott sometimes.

Cindy liked beer and Silas drank with her and they hid their relationship from everyone else, Silas not even telling M&M, knowing if anybody found out they'd have to give each other up. Slipping away from his friends, from hers, like the haunted house that Halloween, the one where Larry came and brought his mask, the two of them leaving separately but meeting later, in her mother's car or in his mother's, whoever could borrow one. Going to the drive-in, her driving and letting him off by the road, him sneaking through the trees to where she parked in the back corner, the thrill of being discovered a thing she seemed to like, Silas terrified but unable to resist the hot vacuum of her cigarette breath, click of their teeth, her soft tongue, her perfect breasts, the patch of secret hair in her jeans.

Once, as they lay on a blanket on the ground, Cindy told him she'd started liking him when he came out of the woods and stood up for her when Cecil was pulling off her towel.

"He did that kind of shit all the time," she'd said. "Trying to see me without my clothes, come stumbling in the bathroom with his thing in his hand. He'd do it when he was drunk, act like he didn't remember when he sobered up."

"What about your momma?"

"How you tell your momma she married a slime? Sides, she always takes his side over mine. She, kind of, believes the worst about me. I always been trouble for her. I don't guess I help none, cussing, smoking, messing with boys."

"Messing," he said. "That what we doing?"

"What else you gone call it?"

At school one day Silas walked up to her in the smoking area, and she said he'd slapped her. Cecil. Said she was a whore. Off fucking boys.

Standing all casual so nobody would notice them.

"Your momma let him do that? Slap you?"

"She wasn't home. But now he won't let me leave the house cept for school, says he'll tell her I been trying to come on to him, like I ever would."

"Your momma believe that?"

"If he said it she probably would. They'd throw me out."

She'd always caught rides to school with her friend Tammy and now Cecil had decreed that Cindy had to come home right after

fool *Dummkopf*

tomcat *male cat*
to purr *schnurren*

such and suching *having a sexual relationship with a white girl* TF

gone *(dialect) was going to*

school, that if Tammy couldn't bring her, Cecil would come get her himself.

"I told him, 'You ain't even got a car, fool,' but he said he'd get one if it meant keeping me away from – "

"Me," Silas finished.

When he went home a few nights later, their trailer in Fulsom, his mother was waiting up in the dark living room, sitting rigid in a kitchen chair, her old tomcat, now half blind, purring in her lap.

"Silas," she said.

"What?"

"Son, you got to stop with that white girl."

He had no idea how she knew.

"Momma, what you mean?"

"Silas don't lie to me."

"We just friends."

"Son, nothing good ever come out of colors mixing."

"Momma – "

"Such and suching like you doing would be dangerous enough in Chicago, but you in Mississippi now. Emmett Till," she said, "was from Chicago."

"You the one brought us down here."

He went to the refrigerator and opened it and got out a carton of milk.

"Silas, baby," getting up, holding the cat to her chest, "you all I got. And you all you got, too. Please tell me you gone stop. Please, son?"

He said he would. Promised he'd focus on his ball, work on his grades for that scholarship to Ole Miss. He didn't mean it, though, knew he would keep seeing her, this girl who would fall asleep on their blanket in the woods, how her lips opened and he'd lean in and smell her breath, sweeter to him for the cigarettes and beer.

It was Cindy who'd said she had a plan to see him that last weekend. If he could get his mother's car, she could outsmart Cecil. On Fridays Alice worked until seven at the diner, then came home and, tired from a twelve-hour shift, went to sleep in her chair by the television. Didn't even eat. He took the car without asking.

Now, in Pizza Hut, the slice on his plate had gotten cold. The Braves had lost and a movie started and the waitress brought another pitcher of beer. He finished his and poured himself another, topped off Angie's glass. She'd been watching him with her eyes growing narrower as he talked.

"I didn't know," Silas said, "it was gone be Larry that brought her."

Angie said, "How'd she get him to bring her and drop her off?"

"Told him she was pregnant."

"Was she?"

"No. I don't think so."

But that had scared Silas. What if she had been?

"We drove to a quiet spot," he said, "and all we did was argue. I told her it wasn't gone work and she started crying and saying yes it would, we ought to just run away for good. I said where and she said Chicago. I said why didn't she go by herself, she wanted to go so bad. We went round and round, and finally I drove her back to the road led to her house. Larry was supposed to pick her up. We got there early, though, and she just slammed the car door and run off down that road, in the dark. I sat there thinking a minute, but wasn't no way I could go after her. Not with Cecil there, drinking.

"When I got home, Momma, she was waiting on me. She could tell from my face where I'd been. Never even said anything. Just went to her room and closed the door. Did something I'd never seen her do, called in sick to work at the diner. I could tell, she'd had enough. Monday she went to see my coach, but everybody else was talking about Larry. How he took Cindy on a date and she never came back. And a month later, I was on my way north, up to Oxford High School, living in the coach's basement."

Angie watching him.

"To be honest," he said, "I was glad to go. It was a whole lot better up there. Better field, school. They give you your cleats and equipment. Pretty soon I had me a girlfriend." Whose name he couldn't remember.

Angie said, "And Larry?"

Silas looked to where his hat would've been.

He said, "I forgot him. Him and Cindy both."

"Forgot him?"

"It wasn't hard. I was busy in Oxford, and Momma, in her letters, she never mentioned it."

"You let him take the blame. All this time."

"I thought she'd just run off. Thought she'd turn up sooner or later and it'd be okay."

"For twenty-five years, you thought that?"

A pleading note in his voice. "Things ain't so clear when they're happening, Angie. You're eighteen and playing ball and everything's going your way. Then all of a sudden twenty-five years've passed and the person you look back and see's a whole nother person. You don't even recognize who you used to be. Wasn't till I come back down here that I saw the mess I'd made."

"So it was Cecil who killed her?"

"That's my guess."

"Where's he now?"

"Dead. His wife, too."

He moved his hand to the center of the table. He hoped she'd place hers on top of it, but she didn't. He looked out the window where he could see their reflections, saw her watching him and focused on her profile, it was easier than looking at her eyes, seeing what she must be thinking.

"Sometimes," he said, "I think it'd be better if Larry had died."

to call in sick *sich krank melden*

pleading (here): trying to find sympathy from another person
whole nother person (dialect) completely different person

"Better for you?"
"For him."
"Yeah, but for you, too."
"Yeah. Me, too."
"Look at me," she said.
He did.
"I know this, 32 Jones," she said. "You didn't let him die, did you? Cause of you that man's still alive, and when he wakes up, if he ever does, it's gone be even worse for him. Just imagine that."
"I have been."
"Well then," she said. "What you gone do?"

He slept little, used to his night shift outside Larry's room, and at six-thirty the next morning he eased out of bed and left Angie in a nightgown in the sheets, the first time she'd worn anything to bed in a while. They hadn't made love after dinner, neither in the mood, didn't even try, just lay apart, not much more to say between them, her heart beating in her breast without him to hold it.

Outside, he closed the door and locked it, a bright September morning, sparrows shooting through her balcony with its hanging plants. He stood looking where she'd hung bird feeders, had a table and chairs set up. They'd spent many evenings out here, her serving his beer in glasses without him even asking her to, Al Green on the CD player.

He hung his badge around his neck and went down the stairs. On the road, he noticed the Jeep's blinkers had stopped working and rolled down his window and hand-signaled onto Highway 5, opting for an early morning patrol of the eastern part of Rutherford's land, cruising through the lines of loblolly pines, bumping over the washboard roads, letting himself in and out of gates with his big key ring. He was sweating by the time he got back to Chabot, around seven-thirty. He hand-signaled into the parking lot across from the mill and went up the steps and let himself into Town Hall, glad Voncille wasn't there yet. He made coffee and fussed with some paperwork, checked his e-mail. At five to eight he went out, slipping the orange vest on, crossed the parking lot and directed traffic at the shift change. He saw Voncille arrive and tooted his whistle at her as she got out of her pickup.

He wasn't hungry so he didn't make his normal visit to The Hub. He drove to Larry's house, caught between two log trucks much of the way, and slung a bowlful of feed in the chicken wire and watched the first ladies peck it up. He added water through the fence and looked in the door at the boxes where they roosted in pine straw and wondered how long it took eggs to go bad, how long before the sitting hens began to suspect that nothing good would come from all their work, just rotting shells.

He had no idea how long he'd been standing there when his radio squawked.

"Thanks for the coffee," Voncille said.
He keyed it. "You're welcome."
"You okay?"
"Yeah."
"Shannon called again."
"Yeah. I'll talk to her."
"Well, stop by and visit awhile," she said. "If you got a minute."

He hung up. Larry's grass had grown high and weedy and Silas remembered how his fists had vibrated on the lawn mower's handle, the shower of green grass out the side, Larry watching from his porch. He longed to cut it now, mow his way back to the boy he'd been and do it differently with Larry, go to the police and say, "She was with me."

What's missing out of you, Silas?

Courage, he thought.

No wonder he felt at ease among these damn chickens.

His cell buzzed and he dug it out of his pocket, walking back toward where he'd parked in the same spot each day, over his oil stain.

"Constable?"

"Yes," he said.

"It's Jon Davidson, at the hospital?"

"Hey, Jon with no *h*."

"Thought you'd want to know," he said. "Judging from the fact that the sheriff and Roy French just arrived and seemed like they was in a hurry, I'll volunteer a guess that your Mr. Ott's woke up."

to key to push the appropriate buttons

at ease comfortable, relaxed

to volunteer (here): to offer without being obliged to do so

Chapter Eleven

He'd been dreaming about him and Silas, perched in high branches. Then it was him and Wallace.

When he opened his eyes the world was too vivid and he shut them again and dreamed of wearing his monster mask, pulling at screaming girls in his barn. Later he saw the high television, first thinking he'd fallen asleep in his mother's bed at River Acres. Had she died?

He closed his eyes again and opened them in darkness. Silas had floated into the room and was telling him something, not to confess, hear? He didn't know what was a dream and what wasn't. When he woke next he seemed in a hospital now, the bed next to him empty, not even sheets. It hurt to turn his head, he felt confined, his throat so dry he couldn't speak. The window so bright he couldn't look outside. His chest ached. That seemed real. His nose hurt. His mouth felt tight. His moving toes seemed real. His curling fingers.

He closed his eyes, dreamed of an ambulance, hearing its siren, belted on a flat bed. The black girl (*Monkey Lips*) over him yelling, "Stay with us, Larry, stay with us." Overhead the high television again, the window. Fluorescent lights. Hospital.

It hurt to breathe but he was breathing faster, he felt tears tracking down the side of his face.

He woke again. He moved and a wave of dizziness flooded his head. He heard an announcement asking for doctor somebody to call extension 202. He lowered his chin and saw his bandaged chest and the tubes going into his arms. Something stuck up his nose, something hooked in his lip. He'd never been so thirsty and thought he might gag. He thought how, when Johnny Smith from **The Dead Zone** opened his eyes from his coma, the nurse wasn't surprised and Johnny thought he must've had his eyes opened before.

He faded back to sleep.

When he opened his eyes again a nurse saw him watching her and jumped. "Oh," she said.

Then a man in a blue uniform was standing in the door. Talking on a radio.

A moment later a doctor came in snapping on latex gloves and asked him his name and he tried to say it, the doctor working on the tube in his mouth.

"Get him some water," the doctor told somebody and a moment later a straw touched his lips.

"Sip it slowly," the doctor said. A suit with a stethoscope around his neck. Short gray hair. Glasses hanging on a string. Shining a light in his eyes, taking his pulse.

"How do you feel?"

Bad, he wanted to say.

"What's your name?"

"Larry," he rasped. "Ott."

"Good. How old are you?"

"Forty-one?"

"Who's the president?"

Larry coughed. "Did they find that girl?"

The doctor looked behind him. Cop in the door.

"Yes," he said.

He was feeling better, a little. The tubes in his mouth and nose were gone but his face felt hot and chapped from the tape.

More sleep, dreams, waking to find three men watching him. The doctor, leaning against the wall. Roy French in a camouflage T-shirt, holding a paper, a cigarette behind his ear. And another, older, balding man he didn't recognize. The men made the room smaller, plus the nurse now coming in, hair tied back, gloves, scrubs. She pressed a button, raising Larry's bed so he was in more of a sitting position. She held a straw to his lips and he sipped.

"Now yall don't take too long," the doctor said. "He's still weak." To Larry he said, "It's amazing you're still with us, I can tell you that. If Officer Jones hadn't sent an ambulance, if the EMTs had gotten there half an hour later, if they hadn't done everything exactly right . . ." He shrugged. "And our ER man, Dr. Israel. Just a genius."

"He was in Baghdad," French said. "Two tours over there."

"You'd been shot near the heart," the doctor said, "had a very leaky hole. Bleeding like stink."

"Officer Jones?" Larry whispered.

"32 Jones," French said. "He saved your life, Larry."

Silas.

"Least you got the place to yourself," French said, tapping the other bed. "I was in here last year for gallstones and they bunked me with this old geezer kept farting. He was deaf as a post and couldn't tell how loud they were."

"Wasn't that me?" the other man said. He was white, stocky, a tight belly in his button-down shirt and a string tie. Short hair. Pistol high on his belt, star pinned to his chest.

"There was a gentleman in here when they first brought him in," the nurse said, "but he asked to be moved."

"That's enough," the doctor said.

"If you need me," she said.

"I'll call."

She walked out of the room, leaving the door cracked. French went and closed it, nodding to the deputy outside, and came back and stood looking down.

"You know me," he said to Larry, "but you might not know this fellow here. Sheriff Jack Lolly?"

"Morning," he said, nodding to Larry.

sore hurt, painful
wrist *Handgelenk*

hoarse rough, harsh

to pull through to survive
gut the inside of the belly

spleen *Milz*
miracle *Wunder*

to manacle [ˈmænəkl] to fasten with a manacle (*Handschellen*)

Doc (coll.) way of addressing a doctor
to come to to become conscious

estimation judgment, opinion

French set the envelope and a tape recorder on the empty bed.
"We got to talk," he said.
Larry adjusted his left arm, stiff and sore, and felt something holding his wrist. He tried to look but couldn't see what it was.
His right wrist, too. Then he knew.
French picked up the recorder and clicked a button and set it down. "If you don't mind, I'm going to record this conversation. You get to be as old as me and the sheriff here, you forget things. That okay with you?"
"Yes, sir." Larry's voice hoarse.
"Now if you need a break, just say so. We got plenty of time. Doc here tells me you're gone pull through. Said the bullet just missed your heart. Hit a rib and bounced around your gut a while. Had yourself a heart attack and then your organs shut down and they took your spleen, but here you are."
"Miracle," the sheriff said. "Did you shoot yourself?"
He couldn't remember. He thought of Wallace giving him the gun. He wanted to ask why he was manacled to the bed. He tried to think and knew things were there to be remembered but where, what, were they? His mother staring off but not at anything he could see. Was that what she was looking for? All those missing things?
"I don't know," he said.
"Well," French said, glancing at Lolly. "Let's come back to that in a minute. Now, Doc here, he says the first thing you asked when you come to this morning was if we'd found Tina Rutherford."
He didn't remember that. Then he did. He remembered his old zombie mask, his father looking at it, shaking his head. His mother saying, "Oh, my Lord, Larry."
"Some memory loss is common, Mr. Ott," the doctor said. "Delirium. Just relax. Take your time."
"Can you tell me," French asked, "when was the last time you seen her?"
Larry moved his eyes – even that hurt – from French to the sheriff. To the doctor.
"Is she okay?"
"No, Larry, she ain't. She was found buried in that hunting cabin over on the west end of your land. Nine days in the ground, by our estimation. Raped – "
"What?" Larry said, coming off the bed, held back by the restraints on his wrists.
"Beaten."
"No – "
"Strangled."
Larry shaking his head despite the hurt, moving his arms, pulling at the leather belts, the sheet over his feet kicking up.
"Stay calm, Mr. Ott." The doctor there, frowning. "I told yall, it's too soon."

Larry had begun to convulse and the men blurred as they tried to hold him down.

"Nurse!" the doctor called, then, to French, "Yall have to go!" his voice spiraling away and Larry falling back into his own face, the ceiling receding, bright then distorted then . . .

When he woke he lay alone in his bandages and restraints, he thought of his mother and her ladies. Were they unfed, dead in their pen? A nurse came in and he said in his cracked voice, "Will you help me, please?"

Not looking at him. "What you need?"

"Somebody," he said, "to please feed my chickens."

They were back next time he woke. French and Lolly. Watching him.

"We've sedated you," Dr. Milton said. "If you want to do this later, I'll send these gentlemen off. It's up to you."

He shook his head. Thought it was later the same day, the men in the same clothes.

"You want them to stay?"

A weak nod.

French came to his side. "Doctor," not looking at him, "can you give us a minute?"

"Well – "

"Preciate it."

The doctor rose off the wall where he'd been leaning and opened the door. "I'll be right out here."

French clicked his recorder on again and cleared his throat, said who was present and the date, time, and place.

"How you feeling, Larry?"

He gave a weak shrug.

"We'll try not to take too long, put you out too much. The nurse in yonder said you asked about your chickens. Well, I can tell you they're all fine. It's your old schoolmate 32, he's been seeing to em. He went out to see your momma, too. She's bout the same."

"Why," Larry asked, "would he do all that?"

"Well, I don't try to understand people's motives until *after* they commit a crime." He smiled and half turned. "Now Sheriff Lolly here, he was a deputy way back when that other girl, the Walker girl, disappeared." French stepped aside and the sheriff came and sat on the bed opposite Larry.

"First thing," he said, "I'm sorry bout the restraints." He unfastened the left one, then leaned over Larry to undo the other. "That was the hospital's request," he said as Larry brought his heavy arms up to his chest and rubbed one wrist, then the other, both sweaty from the lambs wool lining.

"Not something we normally do," the sheriff said. "Specially for a man's been shot in the chest and had a heart attack in the same day. I speck you're too weak to pull them IVs out, much less get up and escape."

force the police force
to serve (law) to bring, to deliver
warrant (law) *Vollziehungsbefehl*
rookie (coll., AE) person just starting a job with little experience

to prove *beweisen*
circumstantial evidence (law) *Indizienbeweis*
unaccounted for no explanation as to where s.o. was or what s.o. was doing at a certain time
poof expression used when s.o. or s.th. has suddenly disappeared

out of his jurisdiction He is not authorized to participate in this investigation.

to ride s.o. pretty hard (coll., AE) to treat s.o. rather roughly
to convict (law) to officially declare s.o. guilty of a crime

clear (coll., AE) completely
to stumble onto s.o. to find s.o. by chance
odds the degree to which s.th. is likely to happen

to ostracize to exclude s.o. from society
to come on to s.o. (coll.) to show sexual interest
to mess with s.o. (here): to flirt with s.o., to make sexual advances towards s.o.
dairy bar restaurant that serves ice cream and other milk products

Larry nodded, still massaging his wrists.

"Anyway, Chief Inspector French yonder, he told you I was a deputy sheriff back in 1982, when Cindy Walker disappeared. Been on the force bout two years at that time, out riding around serving warrants, picking up drunk drivers, things like that. Rookie stuff. But I remember those events real good, Larry, cause it was the biggest thing to come along in my career, at the time.

"Reason we never arrested you back then's cause we never did find a body, and you never confessed. Without no body or confession there wasn't any way to prove you killed her. Just what we call circumstantial evidence. You had, if memory serves, bout three and a half hours when you was unaccounted for, which would've give you plenty of time to have took her somewhere else. But your story was you let her off and left her and went to the drive-in, was supposed to pick her up at her road. Only she never showed up. Just, poof, gone."

Larry opened his lips.

"You want to say something?"

"Can I talk . . ." He swallowed. "To Silas?"

"Who?" The sheriff looked back.

French said, "He means 32." The chief came forward. "He's not part of this investigation, Larry. This is what we call out of his jurisdiction. Why you want to talk to him?"

"Cause we used to be friends."

French nodded. "He mentioned something about that, but didn't sound like yall was friends. More like you just went to the same school."

"We *were* friends," Larry said.

"Okay. We all remember things different, I guess." He stepped past the sheriff, who eased back and lowered himself into the chair by the window. French glanced at his tape recorder. "Now I've rode you pretty hard over the years, Larry, I know. But we ain't never found nothing to let us convict you for that Walker girl or any other girls. Till now." He was shaking his head. "I reckon it ain't but a handful of people in the world knew about that cabin out in your woods – "

"I'd clear forgot it," said the sheriff.

"Cabin out in the last part of them woods you ain't been willing to sell. And then one of our men stumbles onto her, out there where, odds are, she ought to never been found. It gets me to thinking, Larry." French scratching his head as he talked. "I'm thinking, fellow with your history might've just got fed up with the world. World's a awful small place, specially here in southeast Mississippi. Maybe you just got tired of ever body thinking what they been thinking about you. Hell, maybe we all partly to blame, whole county ostracizing you. Maybe you just wanted some company, she may of even seemed like she come on to you, way these young girls dress, belly button rings, all that. Tattoos. You with your own kind of, well, local celebrity, I guess. Maybe she was messing with you, all I know. Your biggest fan. There she is, you see her at one place or another, the dairy bar, post office, Wal-Mart, young girl, pretty, long hair, and maybe you resist a while, maybe a long while.

"But then a man can only resist so long, right, once his rut gets up, and maybe you drank a passel of them Pabst Blue Ribbons we seen in your fridge, or smoked a little dope, got out of your head, and next thing you know you've taken her. Just to talk, for all I know. Little companionship. Man gets lonely. But then, you know, way girls can get, all hysterical, maybe you got scared. Maybe she hit you. Threatened you. Tries to run and you didn't mean for things to happen like they did. Maybe it was all a accident, her winding up dead. You might not even remember exactly what happened or how it happened. It's one fellow I knew, started drinking with his air force buddy and when he woke up in the morning it was a butcher knife sticking out of his buddy's chest.

"Maybe that's why you shot yourself, Larry. All that guilt, adding up. Nothing you meant to do but suddenly it'd done got out of your hands. And you can bury the past but it always seems to come back, one way or another. There's her face, on the news. In the paper. Whole damn world out looking for her and you alone know the truth."

French talking on in his calm voice, making rape, murder, logical, Larry listening with his veins full of airy drugs and his head afloat, how reasonable if he had done it, strangled the girl and buried her, how these men understood his life so thoroughly and knew how people were in the world, in their hearts, brains, what they were capable of doing when they drank a passel of Pabst Blue Ribbon beers and smoked a heap of dope, how you could stick your best buddy with a knife, how sometimes women wanted to be raped, they were asking for it, you put on the mask so it wasn't you doing it, it was somebody else doing what the women wanted anyway, French was saying that, maybe she was asking for it and he was trying as French talked to see into that space where his mother looked, where the truth of memory hid. He could feel the truth waiting for him, floating like a ghost in the room, but his brain the doctor said had been deprived of blood so there might be lapses or delirium and he remembered the mask and remembered the gun, he seemed himself the man in the mask waiting by his door for the other him to come home, watching as Larry got out of his truck and crossed the yard and came up the steps and over the porch and let himself in with his keys and then coming in the house and turning, Mask Larry marching up to Face Larry, pushing the gun against his heart and the two Larrys merging to one with one heart and it's him holding the gun to his own chest, thinking how good it would feel to confess, to please these reasonable men doing their reasonable, necessary work.

"Larry?"

He blinked French into focus. "Do you think I did it?"

French glanced back at the sheriff. "Yeah. I do, Larry. I think you done away with both girls. Tina Rutherford and Cindy Walker. The sheriff here, he does, too. We don't know why you did it, but if you want to tell me, it'd sure help us."

"I don't know why," he said. "Why I would've done that. I didn't even know that Rutherford girl. I don't know anybody except my momma and she don't know me. I used to go a week sometimes without talking to anybody except the girls in Kentucky Fried Chicken."

"Well," French said, "sometimes we do bad things without knowing the reasons, that's surely possible. Like I said, things can get outta hand so quick it's like the world's in fast-forward. But the way you feeling now, Larry? And how you felt when you put that gun to your chest and pulled the trigger? That ain't going away. It's only gone get worse. I been in law enforcement a long stretch now, and the one thing I can tell you for sure is that the only way you'll ever feel better about this is to own up and pay the price."

"Okay," Larry said.

outta (dialect) out of

stretch (here): period of time
to own up to admit you have done s.th. bad, to confess

Chapter Twelve

Silas full of dread, switching his hat one hand to the other, waiting for the hospital elevator, its third-floor light lit so long he imagined somebody must be holding the door. He knew what was going on up there now, Lolly and French coercing Larry, wheedling him, crafting a confession, French so damn smooth at what he called *interviewing* that people said he could make a stump confess to saying "timber."

Finally the elevator doors slid open and Silas stepped in, pressed "3" and the doors closed. On the third floor he excused himself between a pair of nurses holding cigarettes and lighters and hurried down the hall, Skip rising with his newspaper to meet him. A doctor talking on his cell phone, finger in his other ear.

"Hey, 32," Skip said.

"Skip." Nodding at the door. "They in there?"

"Yep. Bout twenty minutes, this time."

The doctor snapped his phone shut. "Can I help you? I'm Dan Milton, Mr. Ott's physician."

Silas offered his hand. "32 Jones."

They shook.

"The officer who found the Rutherford girl?"

Nodding, looking from Skip to Milton. "Can I go in?"

Before either could answer, he'd entered the room, Skip and the doctor saying "Wait," together, following him in.

French turned and Lolly rose from his chair, his hand on his pistol.

"Speak of the devil," French said. He pointed to the door and Skip nodded and left, but the doctor stayed.

Larry raised his head and, when he saw Silas, smiled, his eyes misted with drugs, but he still moved his hand up to his lips, covering his mouth, like he did when he was a kid, his wrist red from the restraints.

"Hey, Silas. There you are."

"Hey, Larry. Here I am." He wondered should he offer to shake his hand. "How you feeling?"

"Not too good. They say I shot myself and killed that girl, but I can't remember doing either. And now they want me to say I killed Cindy Walker, too."

"You had enough, Mr. Ott?" Dr. Milton said. "You want me to ask these gentlemen to come back tomorrow?"

Larry said, "No, sir. I'm glad Silas is here."

"Press your buzzer," Milton said, "if you need me." He glanced at French, then the sheriff, and left the room.

"Chief," Silas said. "Can we have a moment or two? Me and Larry?"

"Not right yet," French said. "But you can stay and witness our interview."

Interview.

to will *(unbedingt) wollen*	
looped on it fastened around it	
gauze thin cotton cloth used for bandaging	
to buoy [bɔɪ] to make s.o. feel cheerful and confident	
splotch spot	
cheek *Wange*	
to flex to bend repeatedly	
to get back on track (here): to return to the subject at hand	
oblivious (formal) not noticing	
to mount to increase	

"Did you come in my room at night?" Larry asked Silas. "When I was in my coma?"

"Yeah." Silas willing him to shut up, not say more, wait till they could be alone. He focused on the bed rail, long, stainless steel, one of the restraints looped on it halfway up. He felt like a kid caught in a lie.

"Sometimes."

"You was feeding Momma's chickens, too?"

"Yeah. I never did move the pen, way you do."

"Did you bring me **Night Shift**?" The men followed his eyes to the book on the table between the beds. The gauze-wrapped hand on the cover, the eyes in its palm gazing out, seeing all.

"Yeah," Silas said.

"Thanks."

"You welcome."

"Did you ever read it?"

"Yeah."

"You like it?"

"No," he said. "Horror, it ain't my thing. Too much of that in real life."

He wanted to say how Larry's versions, way back when, were better, but French cleared his throat.

"If we can end our Oprah book club, we was just telling Larry here that his guilt won't go away till he owns up to what he's done. Ain't you found that to be the case, 32?"

"Only if he's done something." Silas sensed French stiffen, heard Lolly squeak in his chair.

"Tell em, Silas," Larry said, "that we used to be friends."

"Yeah," French said. "Tell us, Silas."

"We was," he told Larry.

"Friends, huh?" French kept his eyes on Silas. "Yall meet at school?"

"No." Larry seemed stronger now, buoyed, a splotch of color coming into his cheeks. He shifted in his sheets, flexing his hands. "We couldn't be friends there cause Silas was black. We used to play out in the woods. Remember, Silas?"

"This might," French said, "be a good time to get back on track. You want to tell us what really happened to Cindy Walker, Larry?"

"Wait," Silas said.

The sheriff coughed behind them and French fixed him with a hard gaze, one that said, *Don't fuck up.*

"I took her where she asked me to," Larry said, oblivious, it seemed, to the tension mounting in the room. "And I let her out. Then I drove off."

"That's what you've been saying all these years," French said. "Tell us the rest. It's time, Larry. Like I said, it ain't going away, this guilt."

"It wasn't him," Silas said.

"Constable Jones," the sheriff now, "you want to wait in the hall?"

"No, I don't."

The room quiet except for the tick and beeping of Larry's machines. Silas aware of the chief's hot eyes on his face and the sheriff's on his back like the red dots of laser sights.

"Is there something you want to say, then?" French asked.

Here it all came. A quarter of a century bunching up on him, bearing down, a truck slamming on its brakes and its logs sliding forward, over the cab, through the window, the back of his head, shooting past him in the road.

"It was me," he said, turning away from French.

"You."

"I'm the one picked her up after Larry dropped her off. In the woods. I'm the one let her off at her road."

Larry said, "What?"

French clamped his fingers on Silas's shoulder and turned him so he could see his face. "Wait," he said. "It was *you* that Larry took her to see in 1982?"

Yes, it was him.

"You mean," French said, "he's been telling the truth all this time? And that you, in fact, were the last person to see her alive?"

Silas nodding.

"It was you?" Larry asked.

"Yeah."

"She was pregnant," Larry asked, "with *your* little baby?"

Silas had taken hold of the bed rail.

"Is that why you left?" Larry staring at him. "Went to Oxford?"

"Part of why."

"To meet her?"

Silas said, "Larry – "

"Was it a boy or girl?"

"What?"

"The baby. Your baby."

"There wasn't," Silas said, "a baby."

French pulled his hand away in disgust. "Jesus Christ."

"Roy – " Lolly said.

Larry looking puzzled.

"Larry." Silas made himself face him. "I'm the one owes you an apology. More than that. See, Cindy, she wasn't ever pregnant. She just . . . said that cause she knew you'd bring her to see me. I didn't know that's what she was doing, then. We were in love, or thought we were."

Larry saying nothing, his open face.

"That night," Silas went on, "after you dropped her off? We drove out to a field we used to go to, and we argued. She wanted to run away together, but I – " How to say it. "I had my baseball career ahead of me, and my momma was after me not to see her. It wouldn't have worked, for half a dozen reasons. So I just took her home."

Larry said, "Took her home."

"Yeah."

laser sights sights used for the aiming of firearms

to bunch up on s.o. to pile up on s.o.
to bear, bore, borne down to move down with great force

to clamp to place on s.th. holding tightly

in disgust *angewidert*

apology *Entschuldigung*

was after me constantly warned me

wait on you wait for you

aware of s.th. knowing, realizing s.th.
to streak to make a line on s.th.

high beam Fernlicht
distracted abgelenkt
to dim (here): to lower the headlights
to flinch (here): to make a sudden movement because of a bright light
bright i.e. bright light

avuncular like a friendly uncle
to conclude (here): abschließen

reef (fig.) chain of rocks or coral near the surface of water
tidal wave Flutwelle
to tumble to fall suddenly
freckled with many spots
handicap space special parking space for handicapped people
to summon to order s.o. to come
redbrick mit roten Backsteinen
numbly in a manner being unable to think or feel

to stack to pile
binder Ordner
erase board board on the wall which can be written on – The writing can be erased.

dip (here): small amount of snuff

"You got there early."

"Yeah. She didn't wait on you cause she was mad at me. She just run off down the road, in the dark."

"Where Cecil was."

"Yeah."

They stared at one another, Silas aware of what Larry must be thinking, how Cecil would have stood up as she came in the door, her face red, tears streaking her cheeks, him holding his beer, stumbling forward, toward her, yelling. Outside, Silas driving away in his mother's car, faster and faster, Larry heading there at the same moment, the two boys missing each other by a few minutes, maybe their cars even met on the dark highway, lights on high beam, both too distracted to think of dimming, both flinching against the oncoming bright.

"He killed her," Larry said.

The doctor was back in the room, tapping his watch.

"This interview" – Lolly stepping between Silas and French, putting an avuncular arm over both their shoulders – "might need to be concluded, fellows. For now."

"Wait," Larry said as French began to fasten his restraints. "We were friends. Weren't we, Silas?"

Tell the fucking truth, 32. Silas.

"You were, Larry," he said. "I don't know what I was."

Silas followed French and Lolly to the Sheriff's Department and parked next to French's Bronco. The chief got out and dropped a cigarette on the asphalt and ground it with his boot toe, looking up to where a reef of dark, swollen clouds, like a tidal wave, seemed ready to tumble over the building, wind on Silas's cheeks, the Mississippi flag snapping on its pole and the asphalt freckled with rain. Lolly hurried back to his reserved spot by the handicap space to roll up his windows and then French held the door and the three of them walked inside, Silas like so many others summoned down to this redbrick building, to be questioned. Interviewed. They stopped at the receptionist's desk, French and Lolly getting their messages, as Silas stood numbly behind.

He followed them to French's box of an office lined with filing cabinets. The CI tossed his recorder on his desk with cardboard evidence boxes stacked beneath and, overhead, a bookshelf lined with videotapes and manuals and three-ring binders. To the left a dry erase board on which his current cases were listed, Tina Rutherford first, M&M second, a string of burglaries, a car theft, a rape, and, at the bottom, Larry Ott's shooting. Silas sat in a folding chair while Lolly closed the door and French clicked on his coffeemaker. The sheriff stood with his arms on the top of a filing cabinet and took a can of Skoal from his pocket and fingered himself out a dip.

French rolled his chair from under his desk and sat, the coffee starting to drip.

"Okay," he said. "Talk."

"That's a hell of a story," French said when he'd finished, telling everything but being Larry's half-brother.

He'd poured a cup of coffee and handed it to Silas, then made another and giving it to Lolly. "But you want a little advice? If I was you? I wouldn't go too public with it. You know what I mean? Back in 1982? Might a been a good time. Then they could've made Cecil Walker the suspect. Questioned him at least. But since he's been dead awhile – "

"Cancer," the sheriff said. "If it's any consolation, he had a tough go at the end."

"And now," French went on, "here you been carrying this information around with you for a quarter-century. I understand your reasons. But considering they never found the Walker girl's body, and Ott never did no time – "

"Shit," Silas said. "Larry's done time his whole life."

"Well, you reaching into ethics here, I'd say. Or civil law one. And both of them's a tad outside our jurisdiction. But considering he never went to prison, it might be best to let sleeping dogs lie. We'll focus on the current case. If he's innocent, it'll come out."

"So none of what I've told yall changes anything," Silas asked, "about Tina Rutherford?"

"Like what?"

"Like whoever killed her's probably cashing in on Larry's reputation. If I'd killed her," Silas said, "guess where I'd bury her?"

"We know where you would," French said, "but it wasn't a lot of folks aware of that little tomb, was it? And Ott, before you busted in and started fucking everything up, he'd give what I'd consider to be a preliminary confession. What about you, Sheriff?"

"Sounded like one to me. Enough to keep him clipped to his bed. Keep Skip by the door."

"But not you," French said to Silas. "I think you'll understand why, as of now, I'm taking you off guard duty."

"Yeah," Silas said.

At the hospital, his shoulders and hat wet from rain, he stopped and talked a moment with Skip, who got up from his chair by the door.

"You early," he said. "You hear he confessed?"

"Yeah." It was the day for it. "I ain't staying."

"Can you babysit him a minute? I need a smoke."

"Go on."

Silas watched him hurry down the hall, and when he was sure the man was gone and wasn't coming back, he slipped into the room. Larry lay with his eyes closed, turned toward the window, his bandaged chest rising and falling.

Silas said, "Larry."

He shifted. Opened his eyes and peered up where Silas stood holding his hat.

"Hey," Silas said.

Larry lay watching him. Then he opened his lips and said something, his voice so quiet Silas came forward, leaned in.

"Do what, Larry?"

"All this time," he said, "she's been dead?"

"I don't know. Maybe. Probably."

"And all this time, you've been the one that dropped her off."

"I'm sorry."

"All this time people thinking it was me."

"Look," Silas said, "we can talk about that. We will. I got a lot to say to you. Hell of a lot, more than you know. But right now, it's real important that we get this mess with that dead girl cleared up. The Rutherford girl. They think you confessed to it. But we both know you didn't do it."

"How you know I didn't do it, Silas?"

"Same way I know you didn't shoot yourself."

"How? Cause you knew me for three months, twenty-five years ago? What makes you think you know anything about me now?"

"Just tell me who shot you. I got a good idea that that person may be the one that killed her."

Outside, thunder. Larry turned toward the window.

"You called me," Silas said, that note of pleading in his voice, "right before you got shot. You said it was important. What was it you wanted to say?"

"You never called back."

"I didn't get your message in time."

"Those other times."

"I'm sorry about that. But – "

"The thing," Larry said, "that I wanted to tell you that first time, when you didn't want to talk to me, was that I was sorry. About what I said, when Daddy made us fight."

"That's okay, Larry. It was a long time ago."

"But now," Larry said. "I don't know what to think. Or even if I'm still sorry."

"Fine," Silas said, "but do you know who it was that shot you? Why'd you call me?"

"32?" Skip from the door. "What you doing?"

"Nothing," Silas said. He looked again at Larry, who'd turned back toward the window, shut his eyes. Silas waited a moment, then left the room and closed the door.

"The chief just called," Skip said, a puzzled look. "You off nights?"

"Guess so."

"How come?" he asked. "What the hell?"

Silas turned to go. "Long story," he said.

He sat at a plastic table in a plastic chair in the back of the Chabot Bus, tracing his fingers up and down his Budweiser bottle wishing he had a glass. The mill crowd had gone home, loud, dirty, and he had the place to himself. He'd been wondering what you felt when you learned you've been robbed of twenty-five years of life, Larry like a convict exonerated by DNA evidence and Silas, the real criminal, caught at last.

It was 11:00 p.m. The rain had quit. The bartender, Chip, a white dude with a goatee, sat on his stool behind the counter cutting limes into wedges and putting them in a bowl and fanning mosquitoes with his knife. He'd tended bar long enough to know when to let a man alone, bringing Silas a fresh beer when he needed and taking his empties and clinking them in the garbage can. Shannon, the police reporter, had called his cell phone but he didn't want to talk to her.

Out the row of windows in front of him were more tables and chairs and, beyond, the gully overflowing with kudzu, trash caught in it like bugs in a spiderweb. Silas remembered riding the school bus as a boy, after they'd left the cabin on the Ott land and moved to Fulsom, how the landscape blurred beyond the windows as you rode, him on his way to school, baseball, his future. Maybe, before its recruitment to bar service, he'd ridden this very bus.

Now look out. Nothing but a gully full of weeds and garbage. Everything frozen. Was that what childhood was, things rushing by out a window, the trees connected by motion, going too fast for him to notice consequences? If so, what was adulthood? The bus stopping? A man in his forties, slammed with his past, the kudzu moving faster than he was?

"Hey, cop. Where's your hat?"

He looked up, ready to grumble he wanted to drink alone. But it was Irina, from White Trash Ave., standing with her hip cocked and a little snarly smile, her pale skin glistening from rain.

"Any more snakes in your box?" he asked her.

"I been scared to open it. And them boys has got it staked out, hoping whoever it was'll try again." She'd streaked red into her blond hair. She wore a short denim skirt and red cowboy boots, wet too. A low-cut tank top that showed her tattoo. Was it a pot leaf? He was wary of looking too hard. She had a lot of plastic bracelets jangling on her wrist and a cigarette in her hand and red nail polish. "Had to carry my damn phone bill down to BellSouth to pay it. Can I join you?"

He nodded to the empty chair next to him.

"Hey, Chip," she said. "Budweiser."

"You ready, 32?"

"Sure. Both on my tab."

Silas pushed the chair out with his boot and she eased into it, a snake crawling in his own mailbox now, if Angie happened in. He'd half expected to find her here. They hadn't talked since the night before, his interpreting her not calling as a point she was making. *I'm disappointed in you.* Well, who wasn't?

Irina leaned forward to look into his eyes, the low neck of her shirt inviting, the cups of a lacy black bra showing, its tiny straps. "You okay, Officer?"

neck (here): narrow part of a bottle at the top

to down to swallow

slug (coll.) small amount of an alcoholic drink

apologetic feeling that you are sorry for having done or said s.th. bad

dilated [daɪˈleɪtɪd] wider than usual
heavy (coll.) extremely unpleasant
to fool around (here): *rummachen*

to nail (here): to shoot
cunt (vulgar) vagina (here): a slut

to flip on s.o. (slang) to reveal illegal activities to the police

Chip's arms appeared between them, two bottles. "Enjoy."

"Cheers," she said, touching the neck of her bottle to Silas's.

He cheered her back and they sipped together, her putting her cigarette out in the ashtray.

"What you doing?" she asked. "Getting drunk?"

"Getting?"

"I better catch up, then." She ordered a shot of tequila, no salt, and when it came she downed it and set the glass on the table. "That's better" she said, her eyes watering. "I was on my way to a party when I saw your little Jeep outside."

"It's hard to miss."

"It's cute. Hey," she said, pushing at his arm with her knuckles, her bracelets rattling. "I got a tip for you."

"I'm off duty," he said, "but go ahead. I can always use me a good tip."

Irina took another slug from her bottle and sank even lower on the table, her breasts resting on it.

"Evelyn? She's my other roommate? She was at work when you came over, so you didn't meet her. But we got to talking the other night, the snake and all, and she gets all apologetic, something she hasn't told us, how she used to go out with this weird guy. Before she moved in with us. So one night Ev goes over to his house, and they're partying, you know, and this guy has all these guns. Pistols. A rifle in the corner."

"That's your tip?"

"Guns? Hell no. Ev's fine with guns. She loves to shoot. But the other thing is, he also has all these live snakes. In aquariums. On shelves. The kitchen table. Right in his living room. He told her he collected em."

Silas watched her as she talked. Her pupils were dilated. Weed. Maybe pills.

"So they start fooling around and she says it's weird, you know. Necking, with snakes watching. How they don't blink? So by then it's getting too heavy, she tries to stop but he won't. It starts getting ugly, she's really scared. Now Evelyn's second ex-husband, he gave her this little pistol. Single-shot. For her purse. She manages to get it out and threatens to shoot this guy if he doesn't let her go. She said for the longest time he just looks at her, this weird smile, easing his hand toward one of the pistols on his table, like daring her to shoot, and she thinks, God, she might really have to nail the son of a bitch. But finally he just calls her a cunt and tells her to get the fuck out."

"She make a complaint?"

"Not really. Evelyn's not, you know, the complaining type."

Some part Irina wasn't telling him, drugs probably. Maybe this Evelyn had thought he'd flip on her if she reported him.

Irina tapped a cigarette from her pack and he took her lighter and lit it. "She just barely got out of there. Had to call somebody on her cell phone. Come pick her up."

"So this guy. You think he mailed the snake?"

"Maybe. She admitted she left her other place cause of him. He kept riding by. Calling."

"What's his name?"

"Wallace. Wallace Stringfellow. Lives over on 7. Past the catfish farm."

He felt his pocket for a pen and scribbled the name on a napkin, stuffed it in his jeans pocket. It rang a dim bell. That guy on the four-wheeler? With the pillowcase. Wasn't that his name? Didn't Larry once say a good way to carry snakes was in a pillowcase?

"You best get on," he said. "To your party. You ain't gone be fit to drive, you keep drinking."

"You want to come?"

"Me? The Chabot constable? You sure you want me there? I can have a dampening effect for certain kinds of partying."

She was sipping her beer, using her tongue on the lip of the bottle. "I see your point."

Instead, after a few more beers, more shots of tequila, they took his Jeep to her house. She had the place alone, Marsha and her baby gone to her mother's for the week, Evelyn at the party. The roads were slick with rain and he drove carefully. She said it was cool riding drunk with a cop; you didn't have to worry about a DUI. In her yard they waded through the muddy dogs and he put his hand on the wall beside her door for balance as she felt under the mat for her keys. Inside, she clicked on the light and a room appeared and he made his way to the sofa while she went to get more beers. Place was clean enough, baby toys around, a lava lamp churling on the end table, drapes open to the night. He put his fingers to his head to stop its spinning, thinking, What are you doing, 32 Jones? You got to get out of here.

She came back with two Bud Lights and sat beside him, handed him a bottle, put hers on the coffee table and her feet in his lap. "Remove these, Officer," she said. Her boots. He got up and worked the first one off slowly and pulled at her little sock, her toes wiggling to help, her toenails red when the sock slipped free, her foot a good kind of musky. He let his gaze drift up her legs past her knees to where he saw red panties under her skirt, another tattoo (an apple with a bite out of it) high on her inner thigh. She was watching him with a sleepy smile. He started to work the second boot off and lost his balance, his momentum taking him to the door where he caught its handle. She giggled and shook her foot at him. Get back over here. He held the doorknob, looked out the window where a car passed slowly, its lights on dim. He thought how he was leaving fingerprints on the knob, on the beer bottle, too, her cowboy boots. Plus a witness just now out of sight, around the curve in the dark. He thought of Larry in his bed, thought of Angie in hers. What the hell was he doing?

"I got to go," he said.

to scribble s.th. to write s.th. hastily
dim (here): not loud, soft

dampening effect making s.th. much less lively and enjoyable

slick slippery

to wade through (here): to walk through with difficulty
mat doormat

lava lamp a lamp that contains a liquid in which colored shapes move about
to churl (dialect) to move about rapidly

to wiggle to move about

musky having a strong, unpleasant smell

momentum Wucht

lights on dim with just the parking lights on

Chapter Thirteen

Larry was flicking through channels on cable television, thinking of his mailbox. Over the years he'd repaired it half a dozen times, mornings as he left for work discovering it by the highway, askew on its post or the whole thing knocked down and splayed in the mud, sometimes magazines fluttering over the road like chickens on the loose. Once the box and post missing altogether. He knew about this, how teenagers rode along, hanging out car windows with baseball bats. Knowing it happened to others should've been a comfort, but as he'd driven on to his shop those days, he'd noticed other mailboxes still standing and known that he alone had been targeted.

He was tired. Even though all he'd been doing was sleeping, he'd never been so tired.

He was tired of buying mailboxes.

He was sitting up, holding the remote control, the lights of his room dim. Outside, tall black clouds had so walled out the sky that night had come early, but now that the lightning had been unleashed, so much, so often, the world seemed weirdly strobe-lit, at odds with itself, day and night battling for dominion like God and the devil. His television remained clear through it all, unlike his set at home, where bad weather fuzzed the picture. He stopped on a Christopher Lee Dracula film from the early 1970s. By his count he had sixty-six channels. This was cable. Not DIRECTV. DIRECTV had even more channels. Wallace had said that.

Wallace.

He was tired of having only three channels.

He aimed the remote up and switched to a talk show. Then *Bonanza*. Then news. A sitcom he didn't know. An old Jerry Lewis film. He thought of Silas again and felt his ears heat and something unfamiliar baking in his chest. He thought of Cindy. He changed the channel to where a man and a woman were selling jewelry. People out there buying it, calling on the phone. His chest hurt when he remembered Silas's face as a boy, Cindy's as a girl. The television flashed a man standing at an easel giving an art lesson. Larry closed his eyes and it was summer, 1979, the morning he'd brought paper and colored pencils to the woods along with his rifle. He and Silas spread the supplies out over a patch of bare ground and lay side by side and began to draw comic books, Larry's about one of his stock superheroes, a standard plot. More interesting, Larry stealing looks, were Silas's pages. His characters were strangely drawn, out of proportion but interesting, elongated heads and large hands and feet. No background to any scene. Just panels with people in them. He was doing a Frankenstein-like comic, a mad scientist bringing a corpse to life, and Larry noticed in a dialogue caption that his assistant's name was Ergo. Larry said it to himself. He liked it for a name. He pushed his paper aside and rolled over, flexing his hand. Silas stayed working.

"Hey," Larry had said. "How you pronounce that guy's name?" Pointing with his red pencil to Ergo. "Igor," Silas had said.

Larry opened his eyes, worried his heart might push through the staples keeping his flesh shut. The sky cracked outside. How long he'd waited on his porch, in his living room with its three channels, its puttering fire, how long he'd waited in his shop, in his father's old office chair, rereading the same books, how he'd driven from one spot to the other in his father's truck, this his life, waiting for Silas and Cindy to return, while Silas roamed the world in his cleats. And Cindy probably buried somewhere only Cecil knew. He changed channels. People singing. Soap operas. More news. Commercials. Baseball highlights. He saw Silas on the infield, cocky, acrobatic, firing a white blur to first, frozen over second base, caught in the act of throwing. He saw himself before his date with Cindy, remembered his smile in the bathroom mirror, his father's story about Cecil falling off the rope, the three of them laughing, their last good night. His window flickered. He saw himself the day of their date, talking to Cindy in the smoking area, Silas watching them from the field, saw Silas and his friends at the haunted house, saw Cindy there, they'd been together then but nobody knew, and neither offered him as much as a glance, turning their backs on him as he left with his mask. The mask. Wallace. He clicked the remote, his wrist sore, cartoons, not Bugs Bunny or Daffy Duck but some new Japanese-looking thing, something he'd missed, something else he'd missed. *Click.* Another western. *Click.* News. Iraq. Commercials. *Click.* A show about a serial killer and the serial killer who imitated him. The remote sweaty in his hand. Weather, tennis, men, women, children, dogs, airplanes, the president waving, a televangelist asking for money with his eyes tight in prayer, *click,* a king cobra rising with its hood fanned and the camera panning to show its eyeglass design. So many channels. He pressed the button again. Close-up of a mosquito among the hairs of an arm, its needle sunk in the rippling skin.

On local Channel Five, he paused on a familiar scene, this hospital, an angle from the parking lot, daylight. Then his own face at sixteen, his eleventh-grade yearbook photo. He pressed a button on the remote and a reporter was saying, ". . . recovering from a possibly self-inflicted gunshot wound to the chest in Fulsom General Hospital." The scene changed to a grainy shot of ambulance drivers hurrying a body bag over a parking lot, flashing police lights, and then a picture of a lovely, smiling girl. "Ott is a suspect in the abduction, rape, and brutal murder of nineteen-year-old University of Mississippi junior Tina Rutherford, whose body was discovered buried beneath an abandoned building on Ott's property in rural Gerald County, Mississippi. Police investigators won't comment on the story, but a deputy is presently stationed outside Ott's hospital room."

Larry sat breathing, his chest sore. The rain fell harder and the window had gone very dark until lightning lit the streaking panes. He looked to the door.

to change one's mind seine Meinung ändern, es sich anders überlegen

to vanish to disappear

to cast werfen
sedan Limousine

to shack up with s.o. (slang) to start living with s.o. who is not married to you for the purpose of having a sexual relationship
tween (dialect) between
pond Teich
to sneak up in s.th. to secretly go somewhere without being noticed
sumbitches (dialect) sons-of-bitches

"Excuse me," he called to the deputy outside. He had to call four times before the man – he'd read SKIP HOLLIDAY on his name tag – got up and peered in, a frown.

"Yeah?"

"Can I talk to Roy French, please?"

The deputy regarded him. "You change your mind?"

"Tell him," Larry said, "that I remembered something."

"Well, he's gone. Won't be back till tomorrow. Is it somebody else you want to talk to? Sheriff?"

"No. I'll wait for French."

The deputy nodded and left.

Larry was going to tell what he knew. Until today, he'd have preferred Silas. But now he would tell French how, a few nights after the Rutherford girl had vanished, he'd opened his eyes and sat up in bed, awake for no reason. He'd reached for his clock and held it out to see the time. Three-fifteen a.m. Risen from bed in his pajamas, he'd gone down the hall closing his robe, standing in his living room. For a moment he considered his pistol, but then he unlocked his front door and gone out without it. Wallace was sitting on his steps smoking, his back to Larry, head down, looking very small in the dark. The moon was low but still cast Larry's truck shadow in its light and, beside it, a sedan parked in the yard.

"Wallace?"

"Hey," he said, not turning.

"You drunk?"

"Yeah."

"It's the middle of the night."

"I done something."

"What?"

He didn't say, just inhaled, exhaled his smoke.

"How long you been out here?"

"I don't know."

"Where you been all this time?"

He didn't answer. Larry went to his chair and eased himself down, sat leaning forward with his hands folded on his knees. His bare feet on the porch floor. "Is something wrong, Wallace? What'd you do?"

He didn't answer.

"How's John Wayne Gacy?"

"Mean as ever. I moved out of Momma's house cause she's scared of him. That DIRECTV bastard's shacking up with her now. I rented me a place up near the catfish farm. Ain't got no neighbors but catfish. They got a fellow rides a four-wheeler tween the ponds but sometimes I can sneak up in there and fish."

"Like you used to fish in my creek?"

"Yeah, but now I catch one once in a while. Some big ole sumbitches in there."

"They'll let you fish on that place, you know," Larry said, "if you'll just pay a fee. Got a special pond, I heard. People take their younguns. Cost by the pound, I think."

"You know me, Larry. I'm a outlaw. Can't do it legal or it's no fun."

"You get a new car?"

"Yeah. Don't run worth a shit though."

"I had an idea," Larry said.

"You did?"

"Yeah. Would you like to learn to fix cars?"

"What you mean?"

"I mean, would you like to come work at my shop?"

Wallace quiet.

"You could be my apprentice."

"I don't believe it'd work out, Larry."

"How come?"

"Cause I ain't worth a shit."

"Why you say that, Wallace? If I could learn, anybody can. My daddy, he used to say I was mechanically disinclined. But then in the army, they taught me and I found out I was pretty good at it. Just needed a chance."

Wallace ground his cigarette out on the step. "Anybody else been by bothering you?"

"Not for a while."

"Not since me, huh?"

"You never bothered me, Wallace."

They sat a while.

"You can think about it," Larry said. "The apprenticeship."

The visit hadn't lasted much longer, and Wallace never said what he'd done, but after Larry watched him go, he'd spent the rest of the night on his porch as daylight crept through the trees like an army of crafty boys.

When French got to the hospital, Larry decided, he would talk. Tell what he'd remembered. Tell how, at first, he'd felt a kind of protection for the man who'd shot him. Who'd been his friend. But he'd thought Silas had been his friend, too, hadn't he? Maybe Larry was wrong about the word *friend,* maybe he'd been shoved away from everybody for so long all he was was a sponge for the wrongs other people did. Maybe, after all this time, he'd started to believe their version of him.

But no more.

This fellow, he'd tell French, saw him at church once. He used to come around when he was a boy. Larry saw a little of himself in him, maybe. This strange lonely kid. Maybe, to this kid, in this world Larry hadn't caught up to, Larry was even a kind of hero.

But watching its images, he was catching up to what the world had become. No more the world of green leaves where his father had carried a shotgun to school, left it in the corner by the woodstove, walking home shooting squirrels for dinner. Summers Carl Ott had

outlaw lawless person sought by the police

Don't run worth a shit. (slang) It's of poor quality.

apprentice Lehrling

to grind, ground, ground to press, to crush

to creep, crept, crept kriechen
crafty schlau

hadn't caught up to (here): hadn't found his role in this society
he was catching up to what the world had become i.e. he was adjusting to what the world was now

chigger mite (small insect) that sucks blood

cancer *Krebs*

gone shirtless and grown dark brown from the sun and found ticks in his hair and chiggers fattening with his blood. Now the land had been clear-cut. Mosquitoes infected you with West Nile and ticks gave you Lyme disease. The sun burned its cancer into your skin, and if you brought a gun to school it was to murder your classmates.

I've been lying here a long time, Larry would tell French. I got a good idea who shot me. And who killed the Rutherford girl.

He drinks Pabst beer, Larry would say. Rides a four-wheeler. He buys marijuana from a black man named Morton Morrisette, nicknamed M&M. He has a mean dog named John Wayne Gacy. He gave me the pistol he shot me with. He said girls wanted to be raped, they liked it. He came to my house and said he'd done something. I saw his eyes in the mask he wore. My mask. And it was only four people alive who knew about the cabin where that Rutherford girl was buried. Me. My mother, who can't remember anything. Silas Jones. And Wallace Stringfellow.

to unmute [ɪʌnˈmjuːt] to restore the sound
scar *Narbe*
to rake (fig.) to pass over with a rake (*Rechen*)

Larry unmuted the television. Changed channels. Tried not to think of Wallace anymore, or of Silas, or of Cindy. When he did his chest hurt in a way that had nothing to do with the bullet they'd cut out. Nothing to do with the scars raked over his heart, that sad little muscle.

to embed to fix s.th. firmly into a substance
punk (coll., AE) **out the window** (a) punk (hooligan, thug, violent teenager) out the window – The indefinite article is omitted to reflect Larry's thoughts. TF
cocked back held backwards ready to strike

Somewhere he'd read the solution to people slamming mailboxes with baseball bats. What you did, you bought a *pair* of mailboxes, a small one and a much larger one, big enough for the first to fit into, like a package. You put the smaller one into the larger and poured concrete in around it, embedding it. When it dried, you cemented the whole heavy thing into the ground on a metal post. So the next time a car roared along, punk out the window, baseball bat cocked back, let him take his swing, let him break his arm.

mutely quietly

Click. A show about polar bears. *Click*. When he got home he would cement his mailbox. A dog food commercial. He'd get a dog when he got home. *Click*. Another preacher, fine-looking suit, the man crossing a podium decorated with lilies, preaching mutely, his Bible in the air.

Click.

Chapter Fourteen

Silas woke in his clothes and boots, only a few minutes late, and stood in the shower until the hot water ran out. He spat foul mouthwash in the sink and opened and closed his lips in the mirror, his head shady with fuzz. The idea of buzzing his razor over it was appalling so he set his hat on gently and finished buttoning his shirt going out the door and took his headache to work, bumping along in the Jeep that smelled vaguely of cigarettes and Irina's perfume. The end of the night was a blur, him fleeing, her hobbling to the door in one boot, saying if he was going to be such a dud, would he at least drop her back at the party?

He was pretty sure he hadn't, though he owned little memory of getting home. At least he'd woke up in his own bed. There was a message from Angie on his cell, about eleven, asking if he was coming over. Another at midnight. Where *was* he?

It was seven-thirty when he got to Chabot Town Hall. Today being Angie's day off, it was too early for him to call her back, so he crossed the parking lot and stood wincing at the passing cars and trucks as the mill screamed at him and each bleat of his whistle jabbed a hot wire in the mush behind his eyes.

"I know that look," Marla said when he came in The Hub, still wearing his vest, already drenched with sweat. "Seen you dragging ass over the parking lot." She got up off her stool and handed him a cup of coffee. He thanked her and went to his table in the back and stripped away the vest and eased his hat off, resisted the urge to put his head down. Marla chatted with another customer but then here she came a few minutes later with two sausage biscuits on a Styrofoam plate and, more important, a bottle of Bayer aspirin. She slid into the chair across from him and pushed the breakfast across the table and opened the Bayer.

"Thanks," he said, taking three of the pills and washing them down with coffee.

"Tie one on?"

"More like knotted it."

"I remember when I used to drink."

"Problem is, what I don't remember."

"What was the occasion?"

"Guilt," he said.

Marla lit a cigarette. "Ah guilt. Opiate of the Baptists. You want to talk about it?"

"Naw. I done done too much of that. Don't seem to help much."

The bell over the door rang and she rose with her cigarette. "Well, sugar," she said, limping off. "don't be too hard on yourself. Now and again it's okay to let yourself off the hook."

But that was his trouble, wasn't it? Letting himself off the hook had been his way of life.

to balance (finance) to determine that the money received is equal to the money spent	
to churn (here): to move about in one's stomach	
shy (here): hesitant, reserved	
nozzle *Zapfhahn*	
read (coll.) (here): schedule	
dispatch the person in a police station who is in radio contact with all the police in police cars and can inform them about important events or instruct them to drive to areas where there is a crisis	
first first gear	
beat all to hell (coll.) completely damaged	
jug *Krug*	
to solidify to confirm	
rut deep mark made by tires in mud	
sprig small cluster	
to range to move around an area	
imprint mark pressed into s.th.	
whorl pattern of curved lines	

He stopped by Town Hall. Voncille was balancing the town's budget, gospel music leaking around her iPod's earbuds.

"Reckon you can write a few tickets today?" she asked.

"I'll try." He sat down at his desk, felt the biscuits churning.

"Guess who else called."

"Shannon."

"She says you're avoiding her."

He pretended to be interested in his reports.

"You ain't never been shy about talking to her before, 32. What's up now?"

Her phone rang before he could answer, and he slipped out.

He drove to Fulsom, past Ottomotive, where somebody had spray painted serial killer across the door. Two of the office windows were broken, too. The gas pump nozzles gone. Stolen. Silas kept going.

At the hospital he saw three news vans in the lot, their satellites up, reporters standing in the shade smoking cigarettes. Word was out – the killer had awakened. From here, Silas thought, it would only get worse for Larry. He pulled into the lot and radioed the Sheriff's Department, try to get a read on French's day. Dispatch told him French had gone to Oxford to interview and hopefully pick up Charles Deacon, the suspect on M&M's murder. He'd be back after dark. Did Silas want the sheriff?

"No, thanks," he said. He sat a moment longer, looking up at Larry's room.

Then he rattled the Jeep into first and eased back onto the highway. He drove out to Larry Ott Road, past the mailbox, beat all to hell. He turned in and drove to Larry's house and parked over his oily spot and got out with his feed jug, walked around the house, through the tall grass. Fed the chickens. Stood watching them, the rain having taken care of their watering. French, he knew, would talk to Larry again, try to get him to solidify the drugged-out confession. But the chief was gone and that gave Silas a day. He left the barn and walked out toward where he'd molded the four-wheeler tracks, the one with the nail in it. Wasn't anything unusual about people four-wheeling, or even doing it on Scary Larry's property. There it was, smeared now, all the rain, but he stood looking down at it, ruts through sprigs of high weeds. He began to walk the field, his pants brushed by weeds and growing wet, thinking what was he missing, ranging toward the trees and back, the barn distant now. He saw a Pabst can and stared at it a while, was looking for a stick to use as a place marker when he noticed a fresh set of four-wheeler tracks. And there it was, again, the circle imprint, the nail. Whoever this was, he kept coming back.

He saw something else, other whorls in the mud by the tracks. Footprints. This fellow had gotten off his four-wheeler here, hadn't he?

He spent another hour wandering the land, bagged the Pabst can, then thought, since he was out here, he could go see this Wallace Stringfellow. Ask him about a rattlesnake in a mailbox.

The Jeep backfired as he climbed the steep hill on 7, and when he topped it and coasted down the other side he passed the catfish farm and saw the oxygen man riding his four-wheeler between ponds. Silas waved and slowed, passing the driveway of a crumpled house up on blocks, dirty aluminum siding. Satellite dish on the roof. Dirt yard and scrubby trees. There was a mean-looking dog, some pit bull mixed with something else, Chow maybe, tied to a wooden stake, getting up and barking, pulling at its rope. Brown with pointed ears, tail down, head the size of a watermelon. No water bowl in sight, no shade. There was his angle, if he wanted it. Mistreated animal. He could use that to get to the door, maybe inside. French always said you wanted an interview subject in your office, on your turf, where you were comfortable.

But Silas wanted to see the snakes.

There was a beat-up sedan in the drive and a four-wheeler parked by the wooden added-on deck. No name on the mailbox, just its number. He cruised on by, holding his radio.

"Miss Voncille?"

"Yeah?"

"Can you tell me who lives at 60215 County Road 7?"

"Yeah, hon. Give me a few minutes."

"Thanks."

Little farther he pulled off, parked, and waited, his headache better. Thinking later he'd go get some of those tire molds from the Sheriff's Department.

"32?" Voncille on the radio.

"Yes, ma'am."

"I got a name."

"Is it Wallace Stringfellow?"

"Sure is. What's going on?"

"Might be our snake-in-the-box. I'm gone go talk to him, if he's home."

"You want some company?"

"Naw. I'll call if I do."

"Be careful."

"Yes, ma'am."

He put the radio on the passenger seat and drove back to the house and pulled into the driveway. The dog scrambled to its feet barking, its rope lashed to an old leather collar, its head low.

"Easy, Cujo," Silas said, getting out.

The dog pulled at its rope, straining its collar, frothing, batting at the air with its front paws.

Easy, boy.

Hoping the stake held, Silas eased around the patch of yard that defined the dog's orbit, unsnapping his sidearm. He circled toward the house, keeping an eye on the pit bull, aware, with all this noise, that Stringfellow would know he was coming. The yard all tracked up from cars and the four-wheeler, and it was these tracks he wanted to examine, see if they had the same circle in the tread he'd noticed in Larry's yard.

"Hey."

Somebody coming out.

Silas glanced again at the pit bull then went to the porch where Wallace Stringfellow stood shirtless and skinny, blue jeans, a cigarette smoking in one hand, cup of coffee in the other. A few Pabst cans on the rail.

"Hey there," Silas said at the bottom of the porch steps. He had to speak loudly to be heard. "How you doing?"

Not looking him in the eye. "I help you?"

"This your residence?"

Looking out toward the road, at the dog. "Yeah."

"That your animal?"

Stringfellow closed the door and stood on the porch. "Yeah. Shut up!" he yelled. "You need something?"

"Just want to talk to you, you got a minute."

"I ain't rode on the highway no more. Just off-road, like you said."

"Glad to hear it." The dog was loud. He put a hand to his ear. "Can we talk? Inside?"

The young man looked behind him, the door. He pulled on the knob.

"Ain't got time right now. I'm in the middle of something."

Silas came up the steps and Stringfellow backed away. He dropped his cigarette over the rail. He was barefooted. He looked at the cup in his hand and set it on the rail behind him, among the beer cans. "What you want to go inside for?"

"So I can hear."

"What for?"

"I just want to ask you a few questions."

"Bout what?"

"That dog."

Stringfellow looked toward the road, behind him. He shrugged and got his coffee mug and opened the door. Silas followed him in, taking a deep, silent breath, not smelling the marijuana or crack he'd hoped to, just beer and cigarettes and filth. He spotted an ashtray on the coffee table but saw no roach or paraphernalia. The room was small and shadowed, its Venetian blinds drawn, fast-food wrappers on the table. A row of aquariums along the counter, each screened at the top and containing a snake or two or three, it was hard to tell, their bodies looped and strung over limbs and coiled in the dark corners, all perfectly still, like rubber snakes.

"You a reptile collector?" Silas asked, remembering Larry saying *herpetologist,* keeping an eye on Stringfellow where he'd retreated in the corner, rubbing his coffee mug like he was rosining a baseball. When he noticed he was doing it he set it on the windowsill and pushed his hands in his pockets.

"It's a hobby," he said, pulling out a package of Camels and a lighter.

"Mind if I look?" Silas asked him. "Snakes and me, we don't always get along. This here's how I like em. Behind glass."

Stringfellow was having trouble getting his lighter to work. "Go on."

Silas went around the counter into the kitchen, scanning the room, the aquariums between the two of them, and bent, his face inches from a fat cottonmouth, lying like a big burnt arm. He could see its frozen frown, the pits under its slit eyes, flicking tongue the only sign it was alive. Through the smeared glass, Stringfellow got his cigarette lit.

"What was it you wanted?" he asked. "I'm kinda busy."

Silas moved to the next aquarium, this snake smaller, brightly banded in red, yellow, and black.

"This a coral snake?" he asked, remembering the rhyme Larry had taught him: red on black, a friend of Jack, red on yellow, kill a fellow.

"Naw," Stringfellow said. "King snake."

"Is it true they'll eat a rattlesnake? Swallow it whole?"

"What I always heard. Ain't never tried it, though."

Silas stood straight, his eyes better adjusted to the dark room, and saw a monster mask on a shelf by another aquarium, on a bookcase over against the wall. It was familiar, a zombie.

"That mask," he said.

Stringfellow followed his eyes.

"Where'd you get it?"

Fidgeting. "I don't know."

"Don't know."

"Someplace."

Outside, the dog continued to bark.

"Wait a second," Stringfellow said. "Just hang on." He was sweating now, sucking on his Camel. He crossed to the door.

"Hey." Silas hurried around the counter, following him outside, on the porch, down the steps, expecting to see Stringfellow fleeing. Instead, he was over by the dog, yelling for him to shut the fuck up.

Silas came down the steps, gripping his pistol in its holster. "Hey," he called again.

"Hang on!" Stringfellow's hands trembled as he got the pit bull by its collar, the animal growling now and snapping, focused on Silas. "I'm just gone try and get him calm!"

The dog bit backward and nipped Stringfellow's wrist. He let go but had its collar with the other hand and with the bleeding one he hit the back of its head. "You sumbitch."

"Back up," Silas was saying, coming around the porch, reaching for his radio and not finding it. He reached in his pocket for his cell phone. "Hey," he called again.

When Stringfellow unclipped the dog, it was like he'd set off a cannon. It hit the ground once then came at Silas in the air before he could draw his weapon, was on him tearing his arms and hands, growling like a motor gone haywire in its ribs. They fell hard, him pushing at the hot slick jaw and trying to keep his face away and get his hand around its throat. He closed his eyes and turned his head

pit small hole

kinda (coll.) kind of

coral snake extremely poisonous snake

King snake non-venomous snake that kills other animals by constriction

to fidget to move about nervously

hang on wait a minute

to snap (here): to try to bite s.th./s.o.
to nip to give a quick, painful bite

to unclip to unhook
to draw (here): to pull out
to go haywire (coll.) to go out of control
slick slippery

to bat at s.th. to strike s.th.	
muzzle mouth	
to snap (here): to break with a loud sound	
windpipe Luftröhre	
to latch on to grasp tightly	
to yelp to give a sudden cry of pain	
to fumble for s.th. to make awkward attempts to find s.th.	
to shiver to shake slightly	
to scrabble to scramble	
numb without feeling	
muck slimy filth	
sewage Abwasser	
thigh Oberschenkel	
to limp hinken	
made (here): reached	
jag sharp, projecting part	
mound large pile	
Taser gun that fires electrified darts to stun s.o.	
cordite an explosive used in bullets, bombs, etc.	
to blur to lose sharpness	
to lurch to move suddenly forward	

and batted at the face and then it got his arm, he felt the deep teeth. Somebody, he, was yelling, wrestling the dog in the mud, his elbow in its muzzle, a bone snapping. With his other hand he clutched the loose fur of its throat and closed his fist, felt the cable of its windpipe in his grip and latched on.

Then he heard a shot, very close, and rolled. Another shot, loud and ringing. The dog yelped, blood on its fur. It was hit. Or he was. Dog trying to get away now, but now it was Silas wouldn't let go. Using it for a shield. Stringfellow yelling, "Get him!" They'd rolled under the porch. Silas heard another shot and saw the man's running legs, bare feet. Felt cold mud in his arm. The dog was trembling and he lay behind it, fumbling for his gun. Shit smell everywhere. Another shot, mud splashing in his eyes. He clung to the pit bull, the dog shaking and biting weakly at him. Silas had his pistol now, awkward in his right hand. He put the barrel to the back of its head and fired. It shivered once and lay still. Stringfellow's footsteps over the porch, loud ringing shots as he fired into the wood yelling, "Killed my dog!"

Silas was scrabbling under the house, his left arm numb and useless, he could feel his heart pushing out blood. Overhead, the front door slammed and Stringfellow thundered over the floor still yelling about his dog. Silas crawled past pipes in the muck and more beer cans and toward the light at the other end, stink of sewage, came out the same time Stringfellow leaped from the back door holding a long revolver. He didn't see Silas behind him on the ground aiming his shivering pistol with his right arm. He fired and missed and fired again. The young man screamed and fell but got up holding his thigh and limping away, shooting blindly, a window shattering, echo of aluminum siding. Then he made the pine trees at the edge of the yard, through the bobwire, and was gone.

Silas lay breathing hard, fighting to stay awake. His mouth so dry. He looked at his arm and saw how bad he was bleeding. Saw a jag of bone, mud and straw in the wound. He set his pistol down and tried to tear off his shirt for a bandage but his strength was gone. He looked behind him under the house, past the mound of dead dog, saw his Taser flattened in the muck, saw his Jeep's tires. He pulled himself up and stood against the siding.

He remembered his cell phone but couldn't find it.

The door was open, hip level, no steps. He lay backward in it and pulled his legs inside. Holding his hurt arm, which looked like hamburger meat, he got to his knees, rising in air that smelled of cordite, using the wall to prop himself up, the room blurred. No telephone, just a cordless base on the end table. He clutched his arm, warm blood running through his fingers. He lurched across the floor and fell over a table, upsetting an aquarium, glass breaking, a rattlesnake's dry buzz filling the room. He rolled onto his back and saw the snake slide over the carpet. Saw the monster mask looking down from its shelf. He wanted to get up but couldn't let his hurt arm go. He was freezing. The snake crawling by his head.

Chapter Fifteen

After breakfast, the deputy watching as he ate, saying no, French wasn't back yet, Larry asked the nurse to put **Night Shift** in his hand and spent the afternoon wandering through the familiar stories, difficult as it was to hold the book and turn pages with one tired hand. The words were harder to see, too, from this angle, and it occurred to him that he'd been holding books farther and farther away from his eyes these last years, that he needed reading glasses. When he got out he'd make an appointment to see an eye doctor.

In the afternoon he called the deputy back in. "Yall said he'd come this evening," Larry said. "I got something he'll want to hear."

"It's been an incident," the deputy, Skip, said. "He's out investigating a crime scene. He might be a while."

"What you mean?"

"We had an officer hurt."

"Hurt?"

"Yeah. That black fellow kept coming in here? One watched you on night shift?"

"Silas Jones?"

"Yeah."

"What about him?"

"He went to see a fellow and the fellow sicced a pit bull on him and took some shots at him."

Larry knew the answer before he asked, "Was the fellow, was his name Wallace Stringfellow?"

Skip looked at him. "Shit. It's on TV already?"

"No."

The deputy watched him a moment longer.

"Is he okay?"

"Don't know. He's down in surgery now, what I'm told. Dog took a big chunk of him. Chief French and the sheriff and them, they out at Stringfellow's house now."

"Is it any way I can talk to Chief French? It's important. It's about Wallace Stringfellow."

Skip said wait and went in the hall. A moment later he came back with his radio and Larry heard French's voice crackle over it. Skip held it up for him to use. "Talk when I mash the button."

"Chief French?"

Background noise, other radios. Men talking. "Yeah, go ahead."

"This is Larry Ott. In the hospital?"

Static. "Go ahead."

"I been waiting to tell you, I think it was Wallace Stringfellow shot me. Took that girl, too."

"How you know that?"

He started telling it, Skip holding the radio with his mouth slowly opening as Larry talked, how Wallace knew of the cabin where they found the girl, his last visit, how Larry had recognized his eyes behind the mask when the fellow shot him, the voice that had asked him to die.

"Mask?" French asked. "Describe it."

Larry did, leaning up, his back sweaty. "Is Silas okay?"

More static. "I got to go," French said. "Thanks for the information. I'll be there when I can."

Later that night Larry woke and heard French outside. He and the night shift deputy spoke in low tones, then French came in the room smelling of cigarettes and sweat, wearing a black T-shirt with a pistol on it pointing at Larry. GUN CONTROL, it said, MEANS HITTING WHERE YOU AIM. He had a large plastic bag with what looked like a severed head inside. Larry's mask.

The chief set the mask on the other bed and then, gently, undid the restraint on his right wrist and came around the bed and did the same to the one on his left. He tossed them aside and sat on the other bed and took off his glasses, looking tired, and rubbed the bridge of his nose.

"What a day," he said. He reached for the mask and held it up for Larry to see, its eyes dead now, and black. "Can you identify this?"

"Yeah," Larry said. "It's mine."

French tossed the bag back and folded his arms. Larry watched it, remembered ordering it, racing his bike to the mailbox every morning hoping for the box that was so big the mailman would have to lean it against the post.

"You'll get it back," French said, "but for now we got to keep it."

"I don't want it. Just throw it away."

French's radio blared and he mumbled something in it.

When he signed off, Larry said, "How's Silas?"

"In recovery."

"Will he be okay?"

"Looks like it. Don't know if that arm of his'll be any good. That damn pit bull bout tore it off."

"John Wayne Gacy," Larry said.

"What?"

"That's the dog's name."

"*Was* his name." French put his glasses back on and felt his back pocket for a pad and wrote that down. "Now what's left of its head's on its way to Jackson to get tested for rabies and its body's on the way to the incinerator."

"How's Wallace?"

"Dead."

"What happened?"

"Watch the news," the chief said. "You'll find out."

Larry lay back.

"How would you characterize your relationship with him?" French asked. "With Wallace Stringfellow?"

"I thought he was my friend."

"You got a strange taste in friends."

"I don't know if you noticed," Larry said, "but I ain't had a lot of options."

French stopped writing but didn't look up.

"You've been the only person inside my house since they come took Momma," Larry said. "In a way, you were the closest thing I had to a friend till Wallace came."

"Yeah, well. Can you tell me about him?"

Larry thought of the show about the serial killer and the killer who imitated him. He thought of how he used to catch snakes and bring them to school. He thought about the boy in his barn, the boy in church, that grown boy coming back a decade later in a stolen DIRECTV truck. He thought about Pabst beer and marijuana. The pistol, the only Christmas present he'd gotten in twenty-five years.

"We were both lonesome," he said. "I think that's why he came to see me in the first place. I don't think he had anybody to look up to, a daddy or uncle, and crazy as it sounds, he chose me."

to look up to s.o. to admire, to respect s.o.

"You said he came seen you last, when?"

"Night before I got shot."

"Said he said he'd done something?"

"Yeah, but he never told what. But I started to figure it might've been the Rutherford girl."

"And how come you didn't report this?"

"I tried to."

"You called 32."

"He came to see me," Larry said. "Silas. After yall questioned me yesterday. All in a hurry, like he wasn't supposed to be here. He said he knew I didn't shoot myself or kill that girl. He wanted to know if I could tell him anything to help him figure out who really did it. I'd already started to put it together, that it must've been Wallace, that pistol, the cabin, but I didn't tell Silas. I didn't want to talk to him."

to figure out *herausfinden*
to put it together to find the solution to a mystery
to counsel to give professional advice

"Well, I ain't good at counseling," French said, "but it strikes me it's long past time the two of yall talked." He picked up the restraints. "I got to put these back on for tonight. But I hope we'll be able to get em off tomorrow. Once and for all."

When he left, Larry lay amid his machines, thinking of Silas, how time packs new years over the old ones but how those old years are still in there, like the earliest, tightest rings centering a tree, the most hidden, enclosed in darkness and shielded from weather. But then a saw screams in and the tree topples and the circles are stricken by the sun and the sap glistens and the stump is laid open for the world to see.

amid in the middle of

to topple to become unsteady and fall
stricken wounded
sap *Saft*
to glisten to shine
stump *Baumstumpf*

Larry thought of Wallace, what he'd done to that poor girl, raping her, killing her, burying her in the dirt. Thinking what he, Larry, might have done to stop what happened, what he could've said, thinking in a way it *was* his fault, Wallace's desires tangled and connected in his mind to what he thought Larry had done. Larry sending him home that night instead of understanding. If he was try-

to tangle to twist together in a confused way

to emulate (formal) to strive to be s.o.'s equal

to untangle entwirren

cast Gipsverband

ing to emulate Larry, wasn't it somehow Larry's doing? His fault? And what if he'd told Silas what he knew when Silas had asked him? Would the outcome have been different? Wallace still alive, Silas with two working arms?

He was still trying to untangle it when his door was pushed open by the end of a rolling bed and two nurses wheeled in a sleeping black man, his left arm in a cast.

"You got a roommate," a nurse said.

Silas.

Chapter Sixteen

When Silas opened his eyes in the dark early hours of the morning, warm from drugs, he wasn't surprised that he found himself flat on his back under a cast, by the hospital window. Beside him, Larry sat propped up in his bed, flicking through channels, not yet aware Silas was awake. For a moment Silas imagined it had always been like this, that they'd been normal brothers all the years of their rearing, both black or both white, sleeping side by side in matching twin beds. Instead here they were. Strangers. The sons of Carl Ott, injured, bandaged, like survivors of an explosion.

Except for the flickering TV, it was dark in the room, Skip still stationed by the door. Silas moved his heavy arm, suspended in traction over his chest, his fingers tingling, hot at the ends. In recovery they'd told him it would take a while, some hard rehab, those years of pitching, the broken elbow, the damage he'd done then, and now this: his elbow not only broken again but crushed, the tendons torn, muscles ripped, steel screws and pins holding it together. Yet he stood a chance of, eventually, getting most of the arm back, most of the control of his hand. Writing, things like that, would be the hardest. But he was lucky, he'd been told. Lucky Wallace had missed him with his .38 Special, having fired, in all, six times, hitting the dog once. "You got in a fight with a big-ass pit bull," the ER doctor had said. "Judging from its bite radius, it's amazing you're alive." "Yeah," Silas had mumbled. "You should see the other dog." He remembered Angie's worried pucker in the ER lobby. He couldn't tell if her sniffing was allergies or crying, but he was glad she was there, holding the hand that still worked.

After surgery, he'd asked the nurse to put him in with Larry Ott. She'd had to call French, and to Silas's drowsy surprise, he'd okayed it.

Now Larry stopped his surfing on the late news, Channel 6, the cute redheaded anchor. She bid the listening world good day and led with what she called "a story of local violence and justice. Chabot Constable Silas Jones," she reported, "nicknamed '32,' while investigating a tip about a man who'd put a rattlesnake in a local woman's mailbox, stumbled instead into a snake den himself." Exterior shots of Wallace's house – there was Silas's Jeep – and then inside shots, the aquariums, that big-ass cottonmouth, the king snake, the rattler. "When Constable Jones attempted to question the suspect, now identified as Wallace Stringfellow, of Chabot, Stringfellow allegedly set loose his dog, a part pit bull, part Chow mix, on the police officer." Stills of the dead dog lying in the mud, big as a grown hog, stills of bullet holes in the porch floor. "The officer was seriously injured and the dog killed when Stringfellow allegedly fired at the officer during the attack."

---

rearing das Großziehen

to suspend to keep in a hanging position
in traction (medical) with the fractured bone being slightly pulled by a special device to help the healing
to tingle to feel as if small, sharp points are sticking into your skin
tendon Sehne
screw Schraube

pucker the act of pushing the lips forward

drowsy sleepy

anchor the main newscaster in a news program
to bid, bade, bidden (here): *wünschen*

snake den area where a lot of snakes are together

allegedly angeblich

still still photo
hog pig kept on a farm

What Silas remembered most vividly was that zombie mask. How different would their worlds have been if he'd followed Larry across the road toward his mother's Buick way back when, that long-ago haunted house? What if he'd just reached out and took Larry's shoulder, said, "Wait"?

The anchor was saying that Chabot Town Hall employee Voncille Bradford, unable to reach Constable Jones on her radio, notified the Gerald County Sheriff's Department, who dispatched two cars to the scene. "Deputies found Jones unconscious in the house and bleeding seriously," the anchor said. "There was also a three-foot-long diamondback rattlesnake near his leg. Deputies were able to subdue the snake without incident and Jones was taken by ambulance to Fulsom General Hospital, where he's reportedly in stable condition.

"The house's occupant, Wallace Stringfellow, fled into the woods and was pursued by deputies. After a brief gun battle, Stringfellow allegedly took his own life before deputies could apprehend him. No other injuries were reported.

"But here," she said, her nostrils flaring the way Silas had always liked (he saw now because it reminded him of Angie), "is where the story takes a surprising turn. Deputies, searching Stringfellow's property, discovered not only illegal drugs and drug paraphernalia but surprising evidence in another case."

The television switched to French's badly lit face, a hasty news conference outside Stringfellow's house. "Searching Mr. Stringfellow's residence," French said, "we found a wallet that belonged to Tina Rutherford."

"Rutherford is the Gerald County Ole Miss student," the anchor filled in, "who, missing for eight days, was discovered by Constable Jones last week, brutally murdered and buried in a hunting cabin on the property of local business owner Larry Ott. Ott has been a suspect in the murder since."

Back to French.

"We can't comment on these findings yet – "

"Does this," a reporter called, off camera, "clear Larry Ott?"

"As I say," French repeated, "we can't comment yet."

"Not such a quiet rural community these days," the anchor finished.

"We'll keep you updated as this story develops. And now to Afghanistan, where – "

Silas felt for the button that raised the top half of his bed. When he began to move, Larry muted the television.

"You're a hero," he said, watching Silas.

"Hey," Silas said, better sitting up. "Ain't we a pair?"

Larry looked back at the television and clicked the sound back on and began to surf channels again.

Silas lowered his chin and thought about how to say what he needed to say. He had no idea where to begin.

"Larry," he said, "it's something I need to tell you. Some *things*."

Larry continued to click. "Go ahead."

"Could you turn that TV off?"

Larry ignored him.

"Well"- Silas turning toward him – "seeing as you still attached to your bed, you ain't got much choice but to listen."

Which Larry did. Partway through, he muted the television. A few moments later he turned it off and the room was dark except for the watchful gray and green eyes of their machines. Talking, Silas could see how still Larry was as he heard about the picture of Alice holding him and about Silas's visit to River Acres. He sat without moving until Silas stopped and it was the end, the end where the two lay now with their injuries side by side in a hospital, both of them silent, neither moving as the moon pushed the shadows of the room along the floor and walls with its soft yellow light. Silas felt flattened by the truth, or the telling of it, his lungs empty and raw and the spaces behind his eyes throbbing.

"We're brothers," he said.

"Half-brothers."

"Did you know?"

"No," Larry said, then, "Yes. Ever since yall got in our truck that morning, I knew something. Then when Momma give yall them coats . . ."

Silas remembering Larry's breezy mother, so different than now, saying how Alice should have no trouble accepting the coats because she'd never minded using other people's things.

"He wished you'd been the white one," Larry said.

Silas thinking how Mrs. Ott had driven away and Silas had put on his coat and zipped it to his neck and buried his hands in the pockets, which were lined with fur. But his mother had continued to stand in the freezing air, holding the coat she'd been given, looking at it. "Ain't you gone put it on, Momma?" he'd asked as they started to walk, her carrying the long gray coat as if someone had handed her a dead child. At some point Alice slipped one arm and then the other into the coat's sleeves, she buttoned its buttons, starting at the top. Silas had followed her, still not seeing what an emblem of defeat, shame, loss, hopelessness, the coat was. With such gaps in his understanding, he saw very clearly how the boy he'd been had grown to be the man he was.

"You think it was better," Larry said, "living with him?"

"No," Silas admitted. "I speck it wasn't." Then he said, "It wasn't easy without one, either. I used to wish I was you, all that land, all them guns. That warm house, that barn."

"Bet you don't wish it now," Larry said.

Silas didn't know how to answer but it didn't matter. Larry was thumbing his buzzer.

The nurse walked into the room. "Yes?"

---

attached to verbunden mit

raw (here): painful
to throb to pulsate

breezy casual, carefree

defeat Niederlage
emblem (here): symbol
gap Lücke

speck (dialect) suspect

Chapter Sixteen

trouble *Umstand, Aufwand*

paperwork forms that have to be filled out

"How much trouble would it be," Larry asked her, "to move me to another room?"

She blinked and then closed her mouth. "You. You want to change rooms?"

"Yeah. Please start whatever paperwork you have to. I'll pay whatever extra it costs. I just want my own room. Please."

"Well, he's out tomorrow," the nurse said, nodding to Silas, "he'll be gone before we could move you. But if you want me to go to the trouble of starting the paperwork – "

"I do," he said.

Chapter Seventeen

Where Larry's only visitors had been law enforcement officials, Silas had a stream. Not long after Larry asked to change rooms, a pretty black girl in a paramedic outfit came in, smiled quickly at Larry then went to Silas's bed, her fragrance settling over Larry like a whiff of honeysuckle bush. He'd requested that a nurse draw the curtain between the beds, so now he heard but didn't see.

"Baby," she said, "you okay?"

"Yeah," Silas said. He cleared his throat.

"I'm sorry," she said, "bout the way I been."

"You ain't been no way," he said, "but right."

Rustling, sheets moving.

"Look at your arm."

"It's a mess ain't it."

"They gone put you on disability?"

"Say they are."

"Full pay, 32?"

"Say so."

"I'll believe that when I see it."

They talked about the dog, the girl telling him she was glad she hadn't been the first responder. She didn't know what she'd have done, something happened to him. He kept assuring her he was fine. She said she knew a great rehab tech, she'd make sure 32 hooked up with him, he'd get his arm back, wait and see. Then their voices lowered and Larry figured they were talking about him. He had the television on overhead, not too loud. Though Silas had a remote control on his bed, too, and though they shared the set, Larry maintained control. There were other sounds and he knew they were kissing.

A moment later she stuck her head around the curtain. She had a high pretty forehead and big eyes, a little smile.

"Larry?" she said.

"Yes, ma'am."

"I'm Angie Baker." She came forward and touched the back of his hand where it lay in its leather belt. Her nails weren't painted; he could tell she bit them. She looked into his eyes so frankly he glanced away. "I'm 32's girlfriend," she said, bending to get back into his sightline.

"You the one who found me," he said.

"32 sent us."

"I thank you," Larry said.

"I just wanted to say," the girl said, "that I'm sorry for all you been through. Silas told me. And I wanted to tell you if you ever wanted to come to a church, the Fulsom Third Baptist on Union Avenue would welcome you."

Larry didn't know how to answer. It was a black church. Finally he said, "Does Silas go there?"

to drift off	to fall asleep
bouquet [buˈkeɪ]	bunch of flowers attractively arranged
for evidence	als Beweismittel
to ensue	(formal) to follow
to flush s.th.	to put s.th. into a toilet and let the water flow down into the sewage system
the bunch of them	the whole group
spiffy	(coll., AE) well-dressed, attractive
ruddy	red and healthy-looking in the face
more TV	i.e. more TV interviews
divider	i.e. the dividing curtain
aside from	besides
ammo	(coll.) ammunition
one-hitter	small, slender pipe for inhaling marijuana or other drugs one time

"You ain't got to worry about Silas," she said. "You can't get his black ass anywhere near a church. Less you shoot somebody in one."

She stayed much of the night, was there when Larry drifted off.

Next morning she was gone, replaced by a heavy woman with a bouquet of daisies, nodding to Larry as she got water for the flowers and tidied the room. Silas called her Voncille and thanked her for sending the deputies after him. And for the flowers.

Then a man Larry recognized as the mayor of Chabot came and joked could Silas still wave cars with that cast on? And could he learn to use his right arm to aim the radar gun and his right hand to fill out his reports? But all joking aside, the mayor said, they sure were proud of him.

Later a couple of other deputies came in and talked with Silas. They'd taken Wallace's snakes for evidence, and there'd been a moment of dark comedy when a heretofore unseen boa constrictor slid across the kitchen floor and was shot to death. They'd also found an aquarium of rats, food for the snakes, in a back bedroom. A debate had ensued over what to do with them. Let them go? Flush them? They'd decided to turn them over to a local pet store, the bunch of them currently in the back of Deputy Parvin's Bronco.

Leaving, the deputies both nodded to Larry.

French came by around nine, looking spiffy and wearing, for the first time, to Larry's knowledge, a shirt with buttons on it and khaki pants. He looked rested and ruddy as he stood at the end of the curtain between them, where he could see them both.

"Gentlemen," he said.

Silas said, "You must got more TV today."

"So do you," the chief said. "On your way out. That pretty anchor wants to talk to you."

"First," Silas said, "can you undo Larry?"

"I can," said French, coming down Larry's side of the divider, undoing the right restraint and then rounding the bed to do the left. "I apologize for that," he said.

Larry rubbed his wrists and looked past the chief at the television, a cat food commercial.

"Well." French moved around the curtain to Silas's side. "We got a fellow doing your traffic."

"Thanks."

French reached past him and pulled the curtain aside, Larry swept into view, his eyes on the TV.

"I'm gone talk to yall both a minute," French said. "Mr. Ott, will you turn that thing off."

Larry clicked it off.

French said aside from the Rutherford girl's wallet, they'd recovered eleven firearms at Wallace's place, pistols, rifles, shotguns and ammo. Also, most of an eight ball of cocaine, pills, an eighth of marijuana and a pipe and a one-hitter.

That sounded about like Wallace, Larry thought.

French went on. The zombie mask had a spot of blood on it that matched Larry's blood, which, bolstered by Larry's testimony, left little doubt that Stringfellow had pulled the trigger. Also, because of the information from Larry, Stringfellow had been linked to M&M, so they could now investigate that case in light of this new evidence. French's guess? Wallace had shot M&M, too.

"Now you fellows," French said, looking one to the other, "have got some history. But what else we got is a whole shebang of reporters and cameras, even CNN, and now Fox News. They all want the story, when each of you gets out, and I don't see no reason to hold things back now. The parents have been told, and they send their apologies to Mr. Ott," nodding to Larry. "And their thanks to you, 32. But I warn you both against getting too personal. They'll sink their teeth into anything you give em, try to make this a damn human interest story. I don't know about yall, but I don't want no humans interested in me."

Not long after, Silas was taken away in a wheelchair, discharged, saying as the nurse rolled him out the door, "I'll come see you, Larry."

Now the nurse appeared with another wheelchair, this one for Larry.

"Your room's ready," she said.

"Never mind," he said. "I'll stay here."

Chapter Eighteen

Angie had brought his cowboy hat and two of Marla's hot dogs. She couldn't stop touching him as she drove him to the Chabot Town Hall, and he finally took her nondriving hand in his good one and held it. His arm, in a cast and sling, hurt like hell and he was tired, but it felt good being out of the hospital and into his hat. He'd just come from a meeting with Shannon, the sole reporter he intended to speak to about any of this. Let her scoop CNN and Fox. They'd met at the diner and she'd recorded his story, growing more excited as he talked, already writing, her photographer moving around the room, standing on chairs, squatting. The article, Shannon said, scribbling, would run Thursday. "It just might get me a Pulitzer," she'd said. "Will Larry Ott confirm all this?"

"You'll have to ask him," Silas had said.

Angie was chatting, and he could tell she was happy. Their plan was for him to go by his office and then to her place where she was going to put him to bed and baby him for the next few days.

She pulled into the parking lot across from the booming mill. "You want me to come with you?"

"Naw," he said, opening the door. "I speck the mayor's gone reprimand me, and I wouldn't want you to see that. Might lose all respect for me."

"Might?" she said. "I'll be here when you ready."

Mayor Mo and Voncille were waiting in the office, her at her desk, him at his. Neither spoke as Silas came in, taking off his hat with his good hand. He tossed it on his desk and turned his chair around the way he usually did for town meetings and sat down. They were both watching him in a way he couldn't decipher.

"Let me go first," Silas said. "I got something to say."

"About what?" The mayor looked down at his legal pad. "Neglecting your traffic duty? Putting us in the hole in our little budget with a whopping, what, three citations in the last three weeks? Harassing the receptionist at River Acres? Enormous ER bills? I could go on, you know," tapping his pad.

"He's always been a list maker," Voncille said.

"All of it," Silas said. "Look – "

Mayor Mo tossed the pad behind him and stood up. "What are we going to do with him, Voncille?"

"You could fire him," she said. "But who'd you get to replace him on that salary?"

Silas looked from her to him.

"Only thing I can think to do," the mayor said, "is hire him some part-time help. What you think, Voncille?"

"Yeah," she said, smiling now. "I been working up an ad for the paper. 'Somebody' " – quoting from her own pad – " 'to direct traffic,' for starters."

Silas didn't know what to say.

"Mr. Rutherford," Mayor Mo said, "has authorized it. He thinks we'd all be better served with you doing more patrols. What he called real police work."

5 "He said that?"

"He did. And I told him we might start thinking about getting you a better vehicle, too. Next year. Maybe, what, a new used Bronco?"

Silas sat looking from one of them to the other. "Thank yall," he finally said, "but I can't take none of it. Not yet. You got to wait till 10 the paper comes out."

"Why?" the mayor asked. "What's in the paper?"

"You just got to wait," Silas said. He got up. "For now, thank yall. I need to go home and get to bed."

He convalesced the rest of the day and into the evening, Angie pam-
15 pering him, propping his arm up with her big throw pillows, bringing him his grilled tenderloin in bed, taking the day off from work in case he needed anything. He sat studying her little catfish as it probed along the bottom of the tank. That night they watched movies in bed and slept close and he woke in the dark thinking of Larry.

20 The next day, he asked Angie to take him to Larry's house and then by the hospital. She helped him dress, lingering at his zipper, and they took her Mustang with her hand on his knee.

At the hospital she helped him with the box of mail he was carrying. Tough with one hand.

25 "You want me to come up with you?" Angie asked, balancing the box for him.

"Naw, thanks," he said. Standing in the parking lot by her car. "I just don't know what to say up there."

"You ain't got to say anything," she said. "Just go and sit with him.
30 See what happens."

He did just that, came in the room and sat on the edge of the bed. Larry wouldn't look at him, just gazed at the television, which was showing the Cubs on WGN, losing, as usual. He'd put the box of mail on the foot of Larry's bed but Larry wouldn't acknowledge it.

35 "I used to go there," Silas said, pointing to the television. "Wrigley Field. When I was a boy."

Larry raised his arm and changed the channel. Geraldo.

"Yeah," Silas said. "They ain't no good anyway."

"I'm still feeding the first ladies," he said. "Getting them eggs. You
40 know what I do? Take em to Miss Marla over at The Hub in Chabot. You know that place? She calls em 'free-range eggs.'

"Need to hire somebody to cut your grass, it's getting pretty high. I'd do it myself but, you know." Raising his sling.

He sat for nearly an hour and then pushed himself up. "Okay," he
45 said. "I'll see you tomorrow. Bring the mail."

---

to convalesce to spend time recovering from an illness or injury

tenderloin best quality steak
to probe (here): to examine, to test the outer limits
close close to s.o.

to linger to hesitate for a moment

tough (here): difficult

to acknowledge anerkennen, würdigen

free-range out in open fields

Chapter Eighteen

penance *Buße*

At River Acres he sat with his knees crossed so he could rest his cast on it. Motherfucker was heavy. His elbow ached all the time, but he'd decided to stop taking the Lortabs. He didn't fool himself: the pain was penance. Were his visits to Mrs. Ott more penance?

As she sat in her chair, gazing at him as if he were a broom, he dug up memories, telling her about him and Larry and them chickens, how that one afternoon long ago, when they'd been let to be themselves, they'd bounded through woods and over grass, invincible boys, snagging grasshoppers out of the air and capping them in jars with air holes nailed in the lids, overturning logs for the fleeing beetles and cockroaches they yielded, stealing spiders out of their webs, taking the jar to the chicken pen where the birds zipped right over –

to bound to run with long steps
to snag (coll., AE) to capture
cockroach *Kakerlak*
to yield to produce
to zip (coll.) to run quickly

"Who're you?" Mrs. Ott asked.
"Silas," he said, hefting his arm.
"Oh," she said. "Who?"

to heft to lift s.th. heavy

Later he stood with the Jeep ticking behind him, watching the Walker place. Kudzu and privet had overtaken most of it, given the house another layer of mystery. Something moved past his foot and he looked down, a slender black pipe slid away from his boot. He caught his breath. The weeds twitched and it was gone. He took off his hat and stood holding it, looking where her window was, behind its boards and vines, and wondered was her ghost in there, leaving a trail of smoke dissolving as she passes one room to the next.

to twitch to make sudden movements

trail of smoke *Rauchfahne*
to dissolve *sich auflösen*

rag old cloth

Next day he tore the Sheriff's Department seals off Larry's front door and stuffed them in a garbage bag. Behind him Angie, in a head rag and old jeans, came up the porch carrying a bucket with a brush and Ajax in it. She got to work cleaning the blood from the floor and Silas went to the gun cabinet and started moving catalogs and junk mail to the kitchen table. It took him a while to get the cabinet clear and dusted, and then he went out to Angie's Mustang and opened the trunk. He came back in the house, past her on her knees, wearing rubber gloves and scrubbing and humming, and went down the hall.

to scrub to rub s.th. clean

For a moment he held the old rifle, which Angie had helped him clean that morning. It seemed lighter than it used to. He took its walnut forearm with his gimpy fingers and worked its lever with the other hand, the smooth ratchet sound, smell of gun oil, and admired its craftsmanship, the checkering on its stock, its blueing in which he could see his reflected face, the nearly faded etching of a hunting dog on its forearm. Holding it for a moment he was a boy again, the world the world it had been a long time ago, a world full of unknowns, a world full of future and possibility, but then he reached and set the rifle down stock first in the green velvet oval and fit its barrel in its green velvet groove and it stood there, a thing returned to its rightful place. Silas inhaled, a man now, full of unknowns yet, but, maybe, with some future still ahead. Some possibility. He looked a moment longer, then turned and went up the hall to where his girl was standing up, pushing her hands into the small of her back.

forearm front wooden grip under the barrel
gimpy (coll.) crippled
to work (here): to move up and down
to admire *bewundern*
craftsmanship (here): level of skill in making s.th. by hand
stock (here): the wooden part held to the shoulder behind the barrel
faded almost gone
etching (here): picture carved into the wood
groove long, narrow channel cut into s.th.

Chapter Nineteen

Silas had visited four days in a row. Larry didn't know what to say to him so he said nothing. He enjoyed the visits, saw that Silas was nervous but liked that he came so often, liked, in fact, that he was nervous. Not talking was easy when you had no idea what to say and, he supposed, it was his right. Yesterday his mail had included some new books, **Lonesome Dove** and some John Grishams. Silas had also brought him a change of clothing, khakis and a chambray shirt. A pair of work boots Silas had put in the closet. It occurred to Larry that Silas had been in his house, going through all his things. Without being asked, he brought Larry's checkbook so Larry could pay bills. He was getting the shop mail, too. As if anticipating all Larry's questions, Silas would chatter about how the chickens were, which always led to Larry's mother, her condition the same. He asked if Larry knew when he was going home but didn't seem to need an answer.

On the fifth day after Silas's release, Dr. Milton came by on his rounds and listened to Larry's back and chest and examined his wound, looking better, the skin around it less bruised. He changed the bandage, then shone a light in his eyes and asked questions and poked him here and there and seemed satisfied. He said Larry's wound looked good, and that his heart sounded decent enough but that he should change his diet, eat less fat and more salad. He should exercise.

"Get up and walk the halls," Milton said.

"I didn't know I was allowed."

"You are," the doctor said. "You are allowed." He was frowning. "I want to say congratulations to you, but that's not right. Not for what's happened to you. Yours is a unique situation, Mr. Ott, and I can't imagine what it must have been like. But I'm glad it seems to be over now."

"When can I go home?"

The doctor turned in the door. "Couple more days? I just want to keep an eye on that gunshot."

Dr. Milton gone, Larry buzzed the nurses' station and the one who'd been so cold to him came in.

"He said I can go for a walk."

She nodded, lowering his rail. His catheter had been removed a couple of days ago, and she set his empty bedpan on the table. She helped him to his feet and took his elbow as he eased off the bed.

"Thank you," he said.

"You're welcome. You need me to go with you?"

He told her he thought he could make it.

He walked the halls in his hospital robe, wondering was the doctor right. If it was really over. When he came to the elevator he rode down. He stepped out and stood for a moment in the lobby, the glass doors across the room filled with news vans and people in suits standing in groups. Waiting for him. None were looking now, none saw him.

---

chambray light fabric with white and colored threads

to anticipate vorausahnen

release Entlassung

bruised with colored marks that were the result of injuries

to poke stupfen

couple (of) a few

lobby foyer, large area inside the entrance of a theater, hospital, hotel, etc.

Women and men both, several with cameras. Silas would've already talked to them, given his story, so now they were waiting for him, for Larry. The elevator door began to close and he stepped back in.

That night at ten, most of the nurses on their break, he slipped out of bed. Winded from dressing, he left his room and walked to the elevator and waited for the doors to open, wondering was this a crime. He didn't have his keys, wallet, or phone, sorry now he'd not asked French for them.

His pants felt big and he tightened his belt. He came out of the elevator in a warm darkness, an exit sign glowing in the distance. He heard someone cough in the dark gift shop and lowered his head and walked as fast as he could past the volunteer at the information desk, the old man putting on his glasses. Then, just as quickly, Larry was outside, over the sidewalk, not looking up, approaching two orderlies lighting cigarettes. He nodded and they nodded and averted their eyes, stepping off the sidewalk, out of his way.

The news vans had shut down, the reporters and cameramen probably at the motel. He put his hands in his pockets and walked as fast as he could across the parking lot, leaves scratching over the cracks and snagging on sprigs of grass. The night wind was cool, him alone with his shadow crazed by the overhead lights, each with its orbit of bugs.

Wishing Silas had brought him a cap, Larry stepped onto the sidewalk that went alongside the highway south toward the center of Fulsom. But that was a good two miles away, past fields and woods, past neighborhood after neighborhood with old-timey gas-burning streetlamps and flower boxes, kids standing in the yards to watch him pass, dogs barking on their leashes. There were no taxi services in Fulsom. Were their rental car places? But how would he pay? If he could just get to his shop he'd be okay. That was beyond the town center, two and a half more miles.

Long walk.

He was out of the flooded light and passing a grove of pine trees, lamps ahead but dark now. He wondered again was it really over. Scary Larry. If anything would really change. Earlier that evening, before he'd busted out, he watched the news where the local anchor announced that Wallace's death had been ruled a suicide, that Silas "32" Jones was recovering at home, and that local business owner Larry Ott had been cleared of Tina Rutherford's murder. Wallace Stringfellow was now believed guilty of killing the girl and, possibly, Morton Morrisette, whose body Constable Jones had discovered twelve days before.

Larry limped over the uneven sidewalk in the dark breadth of trees, his legs stiff, holding his hand over his heart. He felt in each beat a labor he couldn't remember and wondered what that meant. Sweat covered his face and drenched his back. His breathing was harder and he was beginning to feel pricks of pain in his chest.

He went on.

Chapter Nineteen

Silas was holding a bottle of pain pills, trying not to take one, when his cell phone buzzed on the counter across the room, its light reflected in Angie's fish tank. Currently on night shift, she'd been unable to get someone to trade with her and had left him alone for twelve hours. She'd been doting over him so much it reminded him of his mother, which he'd found himself not minding.

Now he heaved off the sofa, muting the television and setting the remote alongside the phone.

"Yeah?"

"Constable Jones?"

"Hey, Jon with no *h*."

"How you feeling?"

"I'm not too bad. What can I do for you?"

"Well, I'm looking at my computer here, and it don't say nothing about his being discharged, but there he went. Just walked out the door. And they make you ride a wheelchair, too. Every time."

"Wait, Jon. What you talking about?"

"Larry Ott. I think he just checked himself out."

Ten minutes later, Silas came down the steps of Angie's apartment snugging his hat then adjusting his sling, his jacket arm hanging loose. He had a bottle of water in one pocket and a plastic bag in the other. It was awkward opening the Jeep door with his right hand and more awkward getting in. When he turned the key the starter ground a few moments longer than healthy and he smelled gas. He waited a moment and tried again and the engine sputtered to life. He'd discovered he could keep it between the ditches by working the pedals with his right foot, steering with his left knee and shifting with his right hand, a rhythm, like anything else. Soon the Mississippi night hummed by outside his windows, bug, bird, frog, the wind on his face. His elbow hurt but otherwise he felt alert, clearheaded. He passed the hospital going east and slowed, Larry would've come this way, heading home.

And there he was, limping along, his shadow tethered to his feet and elongated by the streetlights.

Silas slowed and leaned across the seat and cranked down the window.

Larry's face was pale and covered in sweat.

"Need a ride?" He opened the door.

Without an answer, Larry climbed in, nearly panting. He leaned back and closed his eyes.

"You want to go to the hospital?"

Larry shook his head. "Home?" he whispered.

"That might not be exactly legal," Silas said, "but home it is."

They rode a while, Larry's breath slowing. Silas offered the water bottle and Larry took it. After a while he opened it and drank most of it.

---

to trade *tauschen*
to dote over s.o. to take care of s.o. with excessive affection
to heave (here): to raise yourself with difficulty

to check out (here): to tell the reception you are finally leaving – The appropriate papers are then filled out and signed.

to snug to cause to fit tightly
awkward (here): somewhat difficult
to grind, ground, ground (here): to make a sound like s.th. rubbing on hard surface
to sputter to life to make a series of short explosions and then start
ditch long channel dug along the side of a road
to work (here): to manipulate
to shift *umschalten*

to tether to s.th. (fig.) to tie to s.th. (especially a horse)
to elongate to make longer
to crank *ankurbeln*

to pant to breathe heavily

hardware store *Eisenwarengeschäft*
slash *Schrägstrich*
manicure-pedicure having to do with cutting and treating fingernails and toenails
joint (coll., AE) a not very reputable business
to plaster (here): to completely cover

strip mall (AE) line of shops and restaurants
content satisfied

six i.e. 1976

to cock to raise to one side

to bump (here): to ride up and down on an uneven road
gloom partial darkness

yep (coll., AE) yes, indeed
to bounce to run with springing steps

They passed through the quiet Fulsom town square, the hardware store now a tanning salon slash manicure-pedicure joint. The drugstore a video rental place with a going-out-of-business sign in the window. Two closed barbershops, their poles plastered with stickers and graffiti. A block east, centered in a streetlight, a bent dog was eating something in the middle of the road and backed up as they passed. A box of chicken.

Then they were passing strip mall after strip mall. Larry seemed content to ride, his eyes shut, as the buildings fell behind and the night closed them in, though both knew that outside the windows were acre after acre of loblolly pine, fenced off and waiting for the saws.

After a while Larry's breathing had slowed. He opened his eyes, finished his water, then looked around the Jeep. "What model's this? Seventy-five?"

"Six."

"Four cylinder."

"Yeah."

Silas had been driving slowly, he realized, like he used to with Cindy, not wanting to let her go, say good night. On those nights he'd wanted to hold on to her forever.

"Your carburetor," Larry said, cocking his head. "Sounds like it needs rebuilding."

"So I been told."

After a few more minutes, Silas signaled and turned and bumped by Larry's mailbox where the familiar gravel ground beneath them and the familiar trees slid from the gloom of the headlights into passing night. A deer flashed across the road in front of them, gone so quickly Silas had barely raised his foot from the pedal. He slowed anyway. One meant two or three and yep, here came the second, bouncing over the gravel.

They passed the old Walker place a moment later, the overgrown driveway. You couldn't see it, but if you could all you'd see was privet and kudzu. The land had a way of covering the wrongs of people.

"You reckon," Silas said, "if I was to bring this old Jeep in, you might look at that carburetor for me?"

Larry took a moment to answer. "I don't know how long it'll before I open," he said. "They told me I need to take it easy a while."

"I reckon that's true."

Silas stopped in front of Larry's house, the old Ford truck waiting where Larry had left it. Larry opened the door and climbed out with his water bottle and stood a moment, the only light the light from the headlights. "I thank you for the ride."

"You welcome," Silas said. "But wait. I near bout forgot." He handed Larry the plastic bag, his wallet, keys, cell phone.

"Thanks, Silas." Larry closed the door.

Silas waited as he made his way slowly up the walk. Halfway to the house, he turned over his shoulder. "Silas? I suppose you could bring the Jeep by here tomorrow. I got tools in my truck yonder."

"I'll do that," Silas said.

They looked at each other for another moment, and then Larry turned and went on, laboring up the steps, opening the bag, letting himself in, flicking on the light. Through the pane, Silas watched his back stiffen in surprise, seeing before him his house made ready, washed of blood and smelling like Angie. Silas thought of the lilies she had left on the table, the gift basket filled with fruit. The cinnamon candles. Larry didn't know it yet but his refrigerator was stocked (a couple of the beers gone, replaced by Marla's hot dogs). He didn't know that Silas had had satellite television installed. He didn't know Silas had taught himself to drive the tractor in a one-armed way, and that he'd been pulling the chickens to fresh grass and that there were two dozen eggs waiting.

Silas put the Jeep into first and eased off the clutch and began to roll. It was country dark, as Alice Jones had called these nights, the absence of any light but what you brought to the table. He sped up, his eyes focused on what was before him, and drove toward home.

And not too long after the Jeep's lights had faded and the night grown darker yet, after a dog had barked somewhere far away and another answered, Larry rose from his chair on the porch and went in and walked down the hall and stood staring at the rifle. Shaking his head. Then, one by one, he passed through the rooms of his house and clicked off the lights, the last lamp the one by his bed. What he thought before falling asleep was that he needed to call Silas in the morning, tell him to stop at the auto parts house, get a carburetor kit for the Jeep. He, Silas, knew the model.

to labor up (here): to walk up with great effort
pane *Fensterscheibe*

cinnamon *Zimt*
to stock to provide a supply of s.th.

first i.e. first gear
to ease off to slowly raise
clutch *Kupplung*

to fade (here): to slowly disappear

house shop

Additional Notes

"TF" indicates the commentary is by the author.

page	line	
8	17	**stabbed** (fig.) with pointed objects pushed up
	27	**smokestack** vertical exhaust pipe – Larry used the sardine can to keep out the moisture. TF
	31	**Model 8-N** tractor produced by Ford between 1939 and 1952
	41	**dewy** *taufeucht*
9	2	**trailer hitch** hook at the back for connecting agricultural implements
	3	**tack room** (here): room where farm tools are kept
10	17	**board bed liner** the flat surface behind the cab of the pickup consisting of boards
	19	**running board** narrow platform beneath the doors
	20	**wrench** *Schraubenschlüssel*
	20	**socket** *Steckschlüssel*
	21	**ratchet** *Ratsche*
	31	**Eleven boys** (soldiers) **dead in Baghdad.** – a reference to the Iraq War (2003 - 2011) initiated by President George W. Bush
	33	**to detach** to remove
	37	**to splatter** to splash noisily
	39	**tilted** not straight up but to the side
	39	**red flag** If raised, it indicates to the mailman that there's outgoing mail.
11	5	**book-of-the-month** recently published book that has been selected by the Book-of-the-Month Club
	21	**chief investigator** trained official who works for the sheriff's office – It is the task of this officer to investigate a crime by interviewing suspects and seeking evidence at the scene of a crime.
	44	**patch** small area
	45	**strand** long, thin piece
13	5	**badge** *Abzeichen*
	12	**three-point turn** a turn into the opposite direction by moving back and forth three times
	14	**box turtle** North American land turtle
	25	**whitetail deer** North American deer
	27	**loblolly pine** a pine in the south-eastern United States (*Pinus tidae*)
	31	**blue jay** (*Cyanocitta cristata*) bright blue bird found in the eastern United States
	32	**.45** large caliber pistol
	37	**Oxford** city in northern Mississippi
	37	**Ole Miss** University of Mississippi

Additional Notes

page	line	
14	2	**bitterweed** a common low-growing weed
	3	**hood** (car) *Haube*
	4	**to slant down** to go downhill
	8	**Bronco** Ford SUV
	18	**you owe me** You will have to compensate me for my having to direct traffic for you.
	19	**to roger** (radio communication) to say you have understood a message
	34	**woodpecker** *Specht*
	35	**Indian hen** American bittern (*Botaurus lentiginosus*)
	37	**bullfrog** *Ochsenfrosch*
15	28	**sidearm** pistol
	29	**to veer away** to suddenly change direction
	47	**cottonmouth-moccasin** water moccasin – poisonous viper native to the south-eastern USA
16	4	**vista** panorama
	4	**cypress** ['saɪprəs] *Zypresse*
	5	**parliamentary** (fig.) snattering and arguing with each other
	11	**ID** identification
	16	**Chevy** (Chevrolet) **Impala** popular low-priced car manufactured by General Motors
	19	**vanity plate** license plate for a car with numbers and letters you have chosen – There is an extra charge.
	20	**second base** in baseball: field position at the second of four bases
	20	**shortstop** in baseball: field position between second and third base
	36	**to swear out a warrant** (law) to get a judge to approve the arrest of a suspect
	39	**to write a ticket** to give s.o. a notice for driving too fast or parking illegally
	39	**roadkill** dead animal hit by a car or truck
	40	**presumably** *angeblich*
	43	**.22 bullet** small caliber bullet
	44	**impact** *Zusammenstoß*
	45	**Top rolling papers** ™ paper used for rolling your own tobacco or marijuana cigarettes
	46	**shake** (slang) cocaine in powder form
	47	**fedora** soft hat with a brim
	47	**snagged** caught
17	1	**to back-burner** (coll., AE) to no longer consider a priority
	3	**upwind** in the opposite direction from which the wind is blowing
	15	**Vietnam** a reference to the controversial Vietnam War, 1964 - 1972
	17	**close-cropped** cut short
	20	**Doe** as in 'John Doe' to mean the average American

Additional Notes

page	line	
17	20	**tucked-in** folded into s.th.
	21	**Glock 9 mm** popular semi-automatic pistol originally manufactured in Austria
	21	**you have the right to remain silent** the so-called Miranda warning whereby anybody arrested has the right to remain silent according to the Fifth Amendment of the U.S. Constitution, which stipulates that no one must incriminate himself/herself
	26	**catfish** an edible freshwater fish that also eats dead animals
	44	**I shall return** (humorous) a reference to a quote from the American General, Douglas MacArthur when he was forced to leave the Philippines during World War Two
18	6	**Game & Fish** department concerned with protecting game and fish and issuing licenses to hunt and fish
	13	**to grunt** to make a low, short sound in your throat
	26	**EMT** emergency medical technician – a person trained to provide basic emergency medical services before and during transport to a hospital
	31	**weird** [wɪrd] strange
	33	**Nicorette gum**™ gum with nicotine to help smokers who want to stop smoking
	43	**button-down** shirt that has buttons at the tips of the collar
19	5	**deputy** assistant to the sheriff
	28	**benefits** pay
	31	**BlackBerry**™ brand of smartphone
	34	**hon** (coll.) honey – (here): informal form of address to s.o. you know well – no racism intended TF
	35	**cubicle wall** high wall with three sides as often installed in offices to separate employees
	41	**to turn the double** (play) baseball: to manage (the team on the field) to put two players out for one ball hit by the opposing team
20	4	**credit union** cooperative association that makes small loans to its members and offers the usual banking services to them
	4	**the mill** i.e. the sawmill company
	5	**hub** *Mittelpunkt*
	5	**IGA**, Independent Grocers Alliance – It offers a franchise to small, independent supermarkets.
	6	**Wal-Mart** name of a large international chain of retail stores
	21	**ATM** automated teller machine (*Geldautomat*)
	23	**wet county** county that allows the sale of alcoholic drinks
	24	**dry county** county that forbids the sale of alcoholic drinks
	32	**last stand** (fig.) last defensive position in a battle – Cf. Custer's Last Stand, otherwise known as the Battle of Little Big Horn in 1876, in which the U.S. Army suffered a major defeat at the hands of several Native-American tribes
	39	**to gnash** [næʃ] to grind
	48	**master cylinder** the small container that holds the brake fluid

Additional Notes

page	line	
21	1	**Freon**™ gas or liquid used for air conditioners
	11	**his highness** (ironic) *seine Hoheit*
	18	**silent partner** person who owns a part of a business, but does not directly run it
	19	**get-out-of-jail-free pass** (ironic) card in the game of Monopoly that allows a player to escape punishment in jail
	20	**premeditated murder** *vorsätzlicher Mord*
	24	**reality** a reality show
	31	**Norman Bates** pathological killer in movie director Alfred Hitchcock's 1960 film *Psycho*
	35	**the usual suspects** a reference to the words spoken by Captain Louis Renault at the end of the 1942 film *Casablanca*: "Round up the usual suspects."
22	15	**The Birds** 1963 Hitchcock horror film about birds that suddenly attack human beings
	18	**drive-in** open-air movie theater where you can watch a film from your car
23	30	**accelerator** *Gaspedal*
	31	**to backfire** *fehlzünden*
	40	**tune-up** *Inspektion*
24	5	**sparse** rare
	9	**Building on his right . . .** Normally, you would use a definite article before "building." Why does the author leave it out?
	9	**Radio Shack** chain of radio and electronics stores that has since gone bankrupt
	22	**.32, .41** 32 cents or 41 cents a gallon – prices in the early 1970s before the oil crisis
	22	**ethyl** tetraethyllead (no longer used)
	28	**pump handle jack** device for raising a car by moving a handle up and down
	29	**creeper** low platform with small wheels which you can lie on to work under a car
	29	**drop light** light hanging down from the ceiling
	34	**wrench** *Schraubenschlüssel*
	34	**socket** *Sockel*
	37	**bearing** *Kugellager*
	37	**shocks** (coll.) shock absorbers (*Stoßdämpfer*)
25	20	**flag up** the small red metal flag on the side of the mailbox that is pushed up to tell the mailman there is mail inside to be sent
	22	**federal crime** a crime that is committed against a law of the U.S. Federal Government as opposed to a state crime which is a crime committed against a state law – The crime committed here is a federal crime because the mail service is a part of the U.S. Federal Government.
	30	**PR** public relations
	31	**Buford Hayse Pusser** (1937 - 1974) Sheriff of McNairy County, Tennessee, famous for capturing and killing gangsters and mobsters
26	12	**light** flashing light
	22	**Airstream** brand of luxury trailers

Additional Notes

page	line	
26	25	**crystal meth**, methamphetamine – recreational drug that elevates mood and increases alertness
	27	**to cruise** to drive at a steady speed
	31	**Chevy Vega** subcompact car produced by Chevrolet from 1970 to 1977
	42	**Heinz 57s** i.e. all kinds – a reference to the brand of ketchup, other condiments, and canned food known as *H. J. Heinz 57 Varieties*
27	15	**crew cut** short haircut
	16	**mullet** haircut with the front and sides short and the back long
	16	**BB gun** a gun for children that shoots small pellets
	19	**biddy** (coll.) tiny
	39	**snake-of-the-month club** a reference to the Book-of-the-Month Club which formerly selected, on a monthly basis, a book thought to be of special merit and sent it to its members
28	33	**diamondback** large, deadly rattlesnake
29	22	**Oxford** small city in northern Mississippi, the site of the University of Mississippi
30	16	**Tupelo** small city in northern Mississippi
	26	**Meridian** small city in east-central Mississippi
	42	**We ... like you said?** One of the many examples in the novel of a sentence with a question mark at the end to indicate the intonation of Southern speech. TF
31	3	**fume** harmful smoke
	5	**frigid** extremely cold
	8	**Salem's Lot** 1975 Stephen King horror novel about a village in Maine in which the residents become vampires
	22	**to rattle** to move with a series of loud noises
	39	**soul shake** (handshake) a handshake with three positions that is often used by African Americans as a form of greeting
	43	**acre** 1 acre = 4,050 m^2
32	1	**furnishings** furniture, carpets, curtains, etc.
	17	**redistricting** As a result of several Supreme Court decisions, especially in 1971, *Swann versus Charlotte-Mecklenburg Board of Education*, public schools were required to ensure that there was racial balance in all schools, either by redistricting or by transporting students to other schools (busing).
	20	**principal** (AE) *Schulleiter*
	26	**to hurl**, **to curve** (fig.) to rush
33	47	**Buick** luxury car made by General Motors
34	45	**to pick at s.th.** (here): to eat small pieces of food
	46	**tilapia** African freshwater fish
	46	**mahimahi** flesh of a dolphin
35	5	**saltine** thin, crisp cracker with salt

Additional Notes

page	line	
35	36	**crud** hardened dirt
	40	**plier** *Zange*
	40	**Channellock** American firm that makes tools
	41	**ball-peen hammer** hammer with a rounded head
	42	**wiggler** a socket with an extension that allows you to get into tight spots TF
36	1	**GoJo** American firm that sells dispensers with a special soap to wash hands covered with oil and grease
	5	**Sprite, Mr. Pibb, Tab, orange Nehi, Coca-Cola** soft drinks sold in the USA
	8	**cylinder of a key** a cylindrical lock into which a key is inserted
	15	**to clink** (here): to allow the bottles to hit each other
	21	**to knock** to make a series of loud noises
	21	**tie rod** part of the steering system directly attached to the wheel
	29	**MG Midget** small British two-seater sports car that was produced from 1961 to 1979
	30	**about time** (coll.) about the time
	31	**to unlatch** *entriegeln*
	33	**Afro** hairstyle, especially favored by African-Americans in the 1960s and 1970s, whereby the hair is allowed to grow into a large round shape – It often reflected the desire to demonstrate Black pride.
	34	**fist comb** large comb often worn in an Afro
	42	**rim** edge
37	9	**up and down the chart** i.e. in all possible variations
	38	**to frame** *einrahmen*
	45	**intake manifold** metal section between the carburetor and the cylinders of the engine
	48	**gunned it** (coll.) pressed down on the accelerator to speed the engine while disconnected to the clutch
38	3	**to race** to speed the engine without its being connected to the clutch
	25	**lockblade knife** pocketknife whose blade is locked into place when unfolded
	26	**Marlin .22 lever action** small-caliber rifle made by the Marlin Firearms Company – Bullets are inserted into the chamber with a lever under the rifle.
39	2	**Camel** American brand of cigarettes
	16	**tangle** twisted mass
	38	**free lunch** In many public schools in America free lunch is provided for children whose families cannot feed their children properly.
	43	**short Coke** small bottle of Coke
	44	**Lays** an American brand of potato chips
40	4	**yo** (dialect) your
	20	***Phantasm*** 1979 American horror film that includes zombies
	29	***Dawn of the Dead*** 1978 American horror film

page	line	
40	31	**Animal House** 1978 American comedy about a fraternity (*Verbinding*)
	31	**John Belushi** (1949 - 1982) American comedian and actor
	31	**Saturday Night Live** American late-night comedy and variety show that in its early years already had a cult following (1975 to present)
41	22	**airborne** up in the air
42	32	**The Shining** 1977 horror novel by Stephen King about a haunted hotel – later made into a film (1980)
	38	**heavy-set** broad and heavy
44	6	**patch** small piece of s.th. to cover a hole
	7	**droppings** excrement
	39	**pine tree** *Kiefer*
45	3	**gauge** [geɪdʒ] measurement used for the diameter of the barrel of a shotgun (*Schrotflinte*)
	3	**twelve-gauge** a relatively large size for a barrel – A twenty-gauge shotgun has a relatively small barrel, however both are much louder than a .22 caliber firearm.
	13	**Piggly Wiggly** American supermarket chain, mostly in the Midwest and South
	43	**cartridge** a more correct term for a tube or hull containing gun powder with a bullet on it – The bullet is the front part that is shot through the barrel.
	43	**.22 long** a longer form of the .22 cartridge that has a greater range and more impact
46	25	**to clink** to make a sharp ringing sound when hitting s.th.
48	10	**to ribbon up and down** (fig.) to seem to move along like a ribbon (*Schleife*)
	34	**Shaft** novel and film (1971) with black private detective, John Shaft, as the hero – A number of film sequels were made.
49	27	**to sweep** to move from one side to the other and then stop
	32	**to slant** to hang down at an angle, to slope
50	14	**whip-poor-will** medium-sized bird active at night
	14	**cricket** *Grille*
	24	**heel** bottom part of the inside of your hand
	42	**Conan the Barbarian** fantasy hero created by Robert E. Howard in 1932 and since that time this hero has been used for films and comic books
	42	**Harlan Ellison** (1934 -) American writer of science fiction and fantasy stories
	43	**Louis L'Amour** (1908 - 1988) American writer of Western novels
	45	**the Book-of-the-Month Club, the Doubleday Book Club, the Quality Paperback Book Club** book clubs that selected books for their readers to buy
	47	**TV Guide** bi-weekly magazine that provides information about upcoming TV programs
51	4	**Bayer** [beɪər] **aspirin** a brand of aspirin produced in the USA after 1917 when the patent was confiscated by the US Government from the German company of the same name
	7	**Comet** an American brand of powdered cleaning agent
	9	**Head & Shoulders** an anti-dandruff brand of hair shampoo

Additional Notes

page	line	
52	3	**slab** thick, flat piece of wood
54	4	**air ratchet** ratchet that operates with compressed air
	5	**power window** electrically operated window
	6	**fuel injector** *Einspritzmotor*
	17	**DIRECTV** American company that provides television and radio services to subscribers via satellite reception
	36	**Boz Scaggs** (1944 -) American singer, songwriter, and guitarist
	39	**Pabst Blue Ribbon** American brand of beer
55	36	**Maglite** American brand of high-power flashlight with an aluminum body
60	10	**Model 94 lever-action .33** large-caliber Winchester hunting rifle manufactured until 2006
	14	**pump shotgun** shotgun with a handgrip that can be slid back and forth in order to eject a spent round of ammunition and then insert a new round into the chamber
	26	**TG&Y** a chain of variety stores, especially in the South, that went bankrupt in 2001
	46	**rubber worms, broke-back minnow, Snagless Sallys, silver spoons, plugs** the name of various artificial baits
62	3	**presumably** *vermutlich*
	7	**treble hook** a special hook that has three hooks
	19	**Night Shift** collection of horror and fantasy short stories by Stephen King published in 1978
	22	**to shoulder-strap** to place the strap around your shoulder
	35	**runner** (baseball) person who has successfully batted the ball and is now running from base to base in the hope of reaching home base
	35	**on first** (baseball) on first base
	37	**thwack** short, loud sound
	40	**Atlanta Brave** a member of the professional baseball team in Atlanta, Georgia, the Atlanta Braves
63	2	**grunt** short, low sound in the throat
	22	**laundry machine** washing machine
64	20	**pigtail** *Zopf*
	25	**to zip** to quickly fly by
65	19	**uneven** not parallel
66	40	**magnolia** *Magnolie*
68	40	**Vicks** an American brand of medication that is spread on the chest for s.o. with a chest cold or asthma
69	45	**Chevy** (Chevrolet) **Nova** compact car made by General Motors
71	14	**Story of King Solomon** Cf. the Judgment of Solomon, 1 Kings 3:16-28
72	5	**rump** behind

Additional Notes

page	line	
72	12	**punch** hitting with the fist
73	5	**tangled** twisted together
	23	**She [Marla] bore an uncanny family resemblance to Roy French but damn if that woman couldn't make a sausage biscuit.** Marla is white and French and Marla are cousins. TF
	36	**BC powder** a pain reliever with aspirin and caffeine sold mostly in the South
74	2	**to stub out** to put out the rest of a cigarette by pushing it on a hard surface
	6	**ICU** intensive care unit
	21	**BIC** a brand of disposable cigarette lighters
75	12	**exposed** open
	14	**Interstate** an American company that markets car batteries
76	35	**trailer hitch** (here): connection (*Kupplung*) between a tractor and the trailer (used as a pen [enclosure])
77	11	**grainy** containing small bits of grain
	38	***Eerie*** published 1966 to 1983, and ***Creepy*** published 1964 to 1983 and again after 2009
	39	***Fangoria*** first published in 1979
	45	***Field & Stream***, founded in 1895, ***Outdoor Life***, founded in 1898 – magazines about outdoor life, hunting and fishing
78	38	**Polaroid camera** brand of self-developing camera – The manufacturer went bankrupt in 2001.
	44	**G. I. Joe** doll for boys in the form of an action hero or military soldier
79	8	**Joliet** city 64 km south-west of Chicago
	14	**South Side** part of Chicago south of the Chicago River that includes middle- and working-class residents – Some parts of the South Side have a reputation for having a lot of crime.
	16	**Bradford pear** a tree often planted in cities
	18	**wading** i.e. shallow
	20	***Good Times*** TV sitcom (1974 - 1979) about a poor black family, the Evans, that live in a Chicago housing project – J.J. is the nickname of one of the sons.
	38	**probation** the action of allowing s.o. to leave prison earlier on the condition of good behavior and regularly reporting to a probation officer
	38	**violation of probation** the act of doing s.th. that is in contradiction to the rules and regulations of probation – Owning a firearm would be an example of a violation.
	44	**bail money** money paid to a court during a trial instead of waiting in jail *(Kaution)*
80	11	**Greyhound Lines, Inc.** the largest intercity bus service in the USA
	21	***Sports Illustrated*** sports magazine published since 1954
	34	**Flip Wilson** (1933 - 1998) black comedian and actor – In the early 1970s, Wilson hosted his own show, "The Flip Wilson Show."
	48	**clanging** characterized by loud, metallic ringing sounds

Additional Notes

page	line	
80	48	**Beale Street** street in Memphis famous for jazz clubs and restaurants
82	30	**Cardinals** – the St. Louis Cardinals, a professional baseball team based in St. Louis, Missouri
	30	**Bob Gibson** (1935 -) former black pitcher for the St. Louis Cardinals
84	8	**Nikes** [ˈnaɪkiːz] athletic shoes made by the American firm Nike, Inc.
88	36	**Star Wars** 1977 science fiction film
	36	**Smokey and the Bandit** 1977 action comedy film
	39	**Hattiesburg** city in southern Mississippi
89	26	**James gang** group of outlaws including Jessie and Frank James, active in Missouri in the 1870s and 1880s
	26	**The Long Riders** 1980 western film about the James gang
	38	**place mat** *Platzdeckchen*
90	44	**double-play** (baseball) when the team in the field manages to get two players from the opposing team out after the ball has been batted by a member of the opposing team
91	9	**The Amityville Horror** 1979 horror film about a haunted house
94	26	**Tarzan of the Apes** 1912 novel by Edgar Rice Burrows (1875 - 1950) about a white child who is raised by apes in Africa
95	30	**Cooter Brown** legendary Civil War character in the South who was always drunk
97	7	**to prickle** to give the sensation of many small pins
98	13	**Bee Gees** British pop music group consisting of Barry, Robin, and Maurice Gibb – They were especially popular in the 1960s, 1970s, and 1980s.
	14	**"Stayin' Alive"** 1977 disco song by the Bee Gees from the *Saturday Night Fever* soundtrack
100	26	**the movie family fleeing the house in Amityville and its devils** – the plot in *The Amityville Horror*
	40	**Ford Fairmont** mid-size car produced by Ford, 1978 - 1983
102	29	**to stab at s.th.** (here): to push down several times
	31	**door lock** the protruding button inside at the bottom of the window that can be pushed down to lock the door
	38	**to straddle s.o.** to stand before s.o. with the legs spread apart
104	29	**But because Cindy's body had never been recovered** . . . Cf. the principle of *corpus delicti*: No one can be accused of murder if the body of the murder victim cannot be found.
	41	**Camp Shelby** army training center near Hattiesburg
105	1	**motor pool** *Fuhrpark*
	8	**Private First Class** army rank after serving a year or more
105	8	**serial number** identification number
107	39	**Lord** My God.

Additional Notes

page	line	
108	26	**Hannibal Lecter** a cannibalistic serial killer in the 1991 horror film, *The Silence of the Lambs*
109	11	**el train:** Chicago Elevated: *die Hoch- und U-Bahn von Chicago*
	14	**blue jay** *Blauhäher*, **brown thrasher** *Toxostoma rufum*, **redbird** northern cardinal *(Cardinalis cardinalis)*, **sparrow** *Spatz*
	16	**armadillo** *Gürteltier*
	16	**to snorkel** to move along, breathing as if using a snorkel
	20	**the treetops stitched out the stars** (fig.) The treetops were like sewing needles that caused the stars to appear.
110	4	**Love's Baby Soft Perfume** perfume manufactured by Dana Classic Fragrances, USA
	5	**Suave shampoo** brand of shampoo manufactured by Unilever
	5	**Certs** breath mint manufactured by the American firm, Mondelez International
	7	**First Baptist Church** part of the Southern Baptist Convention – They do not believe in infant baptism, but immersion in water as a young person or adult. A lot of churches, including Baptist churches, organize a "Haunted House" on their property or in the church just for fun. People in scary costumes jump out at you. TF
	16	**strobe light** *Stroboskoplicht*
	32	**Figuring it out.** – Trying to deal with the situation.
	46	**to crackle** to make a series of short, sharp sounds
	47	**. . . didn't signal him** [Larry] **over as he** [Larry] **sat with his brights on . . .**
112	21	**monitor** a piece of equipment that records information
	37	**ventilator** a device placed over the mouth to aid breathing
113	9	**Diprivan**™ propofol – a sedative that is often administered intravenously in intensive care
	25	**NASCAR** National Association for Stock Car Auto Racing
	35	**Oprah** the black host of the immensely popular talk show, *The Oprah Winfrey Show*
114	24	**Wheel of Fortune** American TV game show, 1975 - 1989
115	4	**Eleanor Roosevelt** (1884 - 1962) wife of President Franklin D. Roosevelt
	9	**Rosalynn Carter** (1927 -) wife of President Jimmy Carter
	11	**Ladybird Johnson** – Claudia Alta Johnson (1912 - 2007), wife of President Lyndon B. Johnson
	38	**to sizzle** to make a hissing sound as if burning
117	10	**SUV** sport utility vehicle
	40	**pillowcase** Silas is wondering if Wallace is a member of the racist organization, the Ku Klux Klan that often meets with its members disguised with a pillowcase over the head and bed sheets.
118	42	**arc** high, curved shape
119	24	**hulk** very large object
	27	**to worm your way through s.th.** to twist and turn through s.th.

Additional Notes

page	line	
119	38	**coil** *Spirale*
	43	**to erase** to remove
122	9	**to tick itself cool** a reference to the radiator fan that automatically continues to turn to cool the engine water after the engine has been shut off
	41	**ESPN**, sports network, **HBO**, network that features movies and original TV series
	42	**Skinemax** nickname for the network Cinemax, which often shows softcore pornography
123	48	**GED** General Educational Development – a series of tests, if passed, result in a certificate that is equivalent to a High School Diploma
124	11	**to do away with s.o.** to murder s.o.
126	13	**Ford Explorer** SUV manufactured by Ford
127	6	**John Wayne Gacy, Jr.** (1942 - 1994), a.k.a the Killer Clown, serial killer and rapist who murdered at least 33 teenage boys and young men between 1972 and 1978 in Cook County, Illinois. He was executed by lethal injection.
	24	**antifreeze** *Frostschutzmittel*
	36	**fucked up** (vulgar) deformed
128	17	**electric rabbit** It is used to get dogs in a race to chase after.
131	23	**zippered** closed with a zipper (*Reißverschluss*)
	24	**Sucrets** brand of small candy for a sore throat
	26	**Baggie**™ plastic bag to store food
	47	**You plain or peanut?** M & M is also a candy that is "plain" with chocolate or "peanut" with a peanut in the middle.
132	20	**TV dinner** frozen ready-made meal
	21	*How The Grinch Stole Christmas* 1966 cartoon TV film based on the children's book of the same name by Dr. Seuss
	23	*A Christmas Story* 1983 American Christmas comedy film
	37	**wicker seat** *Rohrstuhl*
136	16	**God did work in His own time** . . . Cf. Ecclesiastes 3:1-4
	36	**Mobile** city in south-west Alabama
	43	**tire rotation** changing the position of the tires to lessen the wear of the treads
137	1	**Holy Rollers** (negative) any Protestant sect whose members hold very emotional services in which people jump around in ecstasy and sometimes start speaking in strange tongues because of being supposedly filled with the Holy Spirit
138	4	**shadowed** i.e. his hat making him appear to be under a shadow
	12	**Jackson** capital of Mississippi
	27	**extension cord** *Verlängerungskabel*
	28	**to trailer in** to transport with trailers (*Anhänger*) connected behind
	29	**Tyvek**™ artificial fiber often used for coveralls
	36	**spot-lit** lit by a spotlight

page	line	
139	38	**Spanish moss** (*Tillandsia usneoides*) a flowering plant that grows upon larger trees such as live oak
140	1	**Amazing Grace** extremely popular Christian hymn published in 1779, with words written by the English poet and clergyman John Newton (1725 - 1807) – It's themes are forgiveness and redemption.
141	4	**to crack** to make a sharp sound
	39	**war in Iraq** war (2003 - 2011) initiated by President George W. Bush to remove Saddam Hussein – The claim that Saddam Hussein had weapons of mass destruction proved to be unwarranted. The war has only made Iraq and the Middle East even more unstable.
144	16	**nostalgically** because by the end of the 1990s most cars had fuel injection and no longer carburetors
148	43	**to fling over to first for the out** to throw the baseball to the first base player on the same team before the batter from the opposing team who hit the ball can reach first base – If this play is successful, then the batter must leave the infield and can't continue to run to the other bases to possibly score a run for his team.
149	43	**Wrigley Field** baseball park in Chicago, home of the Chicago Clubs
	43	**the Cubs** the Chicago Cubs, a professional baseball team
	43	**The following were players for the Chicago Clubs in the 1980s:** **Bull Durham** Leon "Bull" Durham (1957 -) **Ryno** Ryne "Ryno" Dee Sandberg (1959 -) **Bowa** Lawrence Robert Bowa (1945 -) **Penguin, Ron Cey** Ronald "The Penguin" Charles Cey (1948 -) **Bobby Dernier** Robert Eugene Dernier (1957 -)
150	10	**Jim Beam** American brand of bourbon whisky
	11	**to hop the turnstile** to jump over the turnstile (*Drehkreuz*) at the entrance to the el train to avoid paying the fare
	16	**burrito** tortilla folded with a filling of meat, cheese, or beans
	21	**Chicago Tribune** largest daily newspaper in Chicago
	24	**The Wiz: The Super Soul Musical "Wonderful Wizard of Oz"** an African-American version of L. Frank Baum's 1900 children's novel **The Wonderful Wizard of Oz** as a musical – it was first performed in 1974.
151	7	**an** (batting) **average just over .450** an incredibly good batting average
152	19	**Emmett Till** black teenager who was murdered by vicious white racists in Mississippi in 1955 because he supposedly flirted with a white woman – The murderers were acquitted. This example of the miscarriage of justice and blatant racism became a *cause célèbre* that added impetus to the civil rights movement.
154	22	**Albert Leornes "Al" Green** (1946 -) American black singer, songwriter and record producer of soul music
	42	**pine straw** mulch consisting of pine needles
156	15	**curling** bent in a curve

Additional Notes

page	line	
156	27	**The Dead Zone** 1979 supernatural thriller novel by Stephen King – The protagonist, John Smith, suffers a head injury that results in his remaining in a coma for nearly five years. When he awakes, he acquires the power to see things other people don't.
157	24	**Baghdad** capital of Iraq
	31	**gallstone** *Gallenstein*
157-167		What Sheriff Lolly and French are doing is coercing a confession. In addition, Larry is hardly, mentally or physically, able to make any kind of statements about the accusations; indeed in the second interview he's under sedation. Besides Sheriff Lolly and French have neglected to give the so-called Miranda warning *before* the interrogation: a reminder of the right to remain silent according to the Fifth Amendment of the U.S. Constitution, and the right to have the counsel of an attorney. Even if a lower court accepted the confession, it would be rejected as inadmissible by a higher court. Students are encouraged to research the 1966 Supreme Court decision, *Miranda v. Arizona*.
160	45	**belly button** *Bauchnabel*
163	24	**speak of the devil** Cf. the saying: "Speak of the devil and he doth appear."
164	23	**Oprah book club** the book discussion part of the American talk show *The Oprah Winfrey Show*
166	40	**string** series
	44	**Skoal** a brand of dipping tobacco, also known as moist snuff (tobacco that is sniffed)
169	6	**wedge** slice of s.th. thin at one end and longer and round at the other
	30	**to streak** (here): to color with thin lines
	33	**to jangle** to make a sound as when two metal parts hit each other
	35	**BellSouth** telephone company
170	7	**tequila** [təˈkiːlə] strong alcoholic drink made in Mexico
171	31	**Bud Light** Budweiser Light – a brand of beer with fewer calories and less alcohol than normal Budweiser
172	20	**Christopher Lee (1922 - 2015) Dracula** Christopher Lee was a British actor who starred in a number of Dracula films from the 1950s to 1970s.
	26	***Bonanza*** TV western series from 1959 to 1973
	27	**Jerry Lewis** (1926 -) American actor, comedian, singer, film producer, and film director
	33	**a man standing at an easel giving an art lesson** Cf. Robert Norman "Bob" Ross (1942 - 1995) an American painter best known for his TV show, *The Joy of Painting*
173	4	**to crack** to break open
	22	**Bugs Bunny, Daffy Duck** popular comic book and film cartoon characters, especially in the late 1930s, 1940s, and 1950s
176	3	**West Nile fever** disease caused by a mosquito – Only a small percentage of the infection has serious consequences.
	4	**Lyme disease** or Lyme borreliosis – an infectious disease caused by bacteria of the Borrelia type from a tick bite – If not treated promptly it can cause serious health problems.
177	18	**to jab** to push s.th. with a pointed object

Additional Notes

page	line	
177	38	**opiate of the Baptists** – that Baptists constantly fear being sinful and need to wash away their sins
178	2	**earbud** small earphone inserted into the ear
179	40	**easy** Take it easy. Relax!
	40	**Cujo** 1981 horror novel by Stephen King that was made into a film in 1983 – It involves a dog, Cujo, that is infected by rabies and then begins to attack and kill people.
180	41	**looped** forming a closed circle
	41	**to string, strung, strung** (here): to hang
	41	**coiled** in tight circles
181	35	**to growl** to make a low sound in the throat
182	14	**awkward** (here): clumsy, not able to use properly
	27	**to shatter** to break into small pieces
184	10	**gun control** laws that restrict the sale and use of firearms – Gun control is a major issue in the United States. Some people believe everyone has the right to own firearms. They claim that this right is expressly stated in the second amendment of the U. S. Constitution: "The right of the people to keep and bear arms shall not be infringed." The National Rifle Association is a powerful gun lobby that has made it difficult for legislation to be passed by Congress that restricts the use of firearms. Individual states have a great deal of leeway as to how to limit the sale and use of firearms. Only fully automatic weapons are prohibited by Federal law. What does French's T-shirt tell us about him?
187	13	**rehab** rehabilitation: special physical exercises to improve bodily motion
	20	**.38 Special** Smith & Wesson revolver using a .38 caliber cartridge
188	38	**Afghanistan** After 9-11 the United States, along with Great Britain, invaded Afghanistan in an attempt to remove Taliban influence. NATO joined in 2003. The war was officially declared ended in 2014. It has turned out to be an illusion, as acts of terrorism have continued to this day, and the Afghanistan government has proved unstable.
191	4	**to settle on s.th./s.o.** to come to rest on s.th./s.o.
192	5	**daisy** Gänseblümchen
	46	**eight ball** (slang) 1/8 ounce, 3.5 g
	46	**eighth of marijuana** 3.5 g of marijuana
193	9	**CNN** American international news channel
193	9	**Fox News** American-based cable and satellite news channel that tends to have a conservative bias
194	11	**Pulitzer Prize** American award given to newspapers, magazines, online journalism, literature, and musical composition for outstanding achievement
	29	**legal pad** (AE) yellow, lined paper fixed at one end
195	14	**to pamper** to take care of s.o. very well
	15	**throw pillow** pillow used as decoration
	22	**Mustang** moderately-priced sports car manufactured by Ford
	33	**WGN** local TV channel in Chicago

Additional Notes

page	line	
195	37	**Geraldo** Geraldo Rivera (1943 -) talk show host – He often appears on Fox News.
196	3	**Lortab**™ a medicine that reduces severe pain
	8	**invincible** not to be defeated
	27	**Ajax** American brand of cleaner
	34	**walnut** wood of a walnut tree
	39	**the world the world** The repetition of "the world" is on purpose. TF
197	6	**Lonesome Dove** 1985 western novel by Larry McMurtry
	6	**John Grisham** (1955 -) American bestselling writer and lawyer best known for his popular legal thrillers
200	4	**pole** (here): a long, slowly rotating cylinder with horizontal red, blue, and white stripes – It is traditionally placed outside a barbershop.

Worksheets: From Chapter to Chapter

Chapter 1 (p. 8 – p. 12)

Character: Who is in the focus of attention? Larry or Silas?
_____

Setting: Is the focus of the chapter on the past or the present?
_____

Content: Note down the aspects of this chapter that are of special significance.
_____
_____
_____

Language: Note down five phrases that you find important for talking about this chapter.
_____
_____
_____
_____
_____
_____

Chapter 2 (p. 13 – p. 30)

Character: Who is in the focus of attention? Larry or Silas?
_____

Setting: Is the focus of the chapter on the past or the present?
_____

Content: Note down the aspects of this chapter that are of special significance.
_____
_____
_____

Language: Note down five phrases that you find important for talking about this chapter.
_____
_____
_____
_____
_____
_____

Chapter 3 (p. 31 – p. 47)

Character: Who is in the focus of attention? Larry or Silas?

_____

Setting: Is the focus of the chapter on the past or the present?

_____

Content: Note down the aspects of this chapter that are of special significance.

_____

_____

_____

Language: Note down five phrases that you find important for talking about this chapter.

_____

_____

_____

_____

_____

Chapter 4 (p. 48 – p. 57)

Character: Who is in the focus of attention? Larry or Silas?

_____

Setting: Is the focus of the chapter on the past or the present?

_____

Content: Note down the aspects of this chapter that are of special significance.

_____

_____

Language: Note down five phrases that you find important for talking about this chapter.

_____

_____

_____

_____

_____

Chapter 5 (p. 58 – p. 72)

Character: Who is in the focus of attention? Larry or Silas?

_____

Setting: Is the focus of the chapter on the past or the present?

_____

Content: Note down the aspects of this chapter that are of special significance.

_____

_____

_____

Language: Note down five phrases that you find important for talking about this chapter.

_____

_____

_____

_____

_____

Chapter 6 (p. 73 – p. 87)

Character: Who is in the focus of attention? Larry or Silas?

_____

Setting: Is the focus of the chapter on the past or the present?

_____

Content: Note down the aspects of this chapter that are of special significance.

_____

_____

_____

Language: Note down five phrases that you find important for talking about this chapter.

_____

_____

_____

_____

_____

Chapter 7 (p. 88 – p. 106)

Character: Who is in the focus of attention? Larry or Silas?

_____

Setting: Is the focus of the chapter on the past or the present?

_____

Content: Note down the aspects of this chapter that are of special significance.

_____
_____
_____

Language: Note down five phrases that you find important for talking about this chapter.

_____
_____
_____
_____
_____

Chapter 8 (p. 107 – p. 119)

Character: Who is in the focus of attention? Larry or Silas?

_____

Setting: Is the focus of the chapter on the past or the present?

_____

Content: Note down the aspects of this chapter that are of special significance.

_____
_____
_____

Language: Note down five phrases that you find important for talking about this chapter.

_____
_____
_____
_____
_____

Chapter 9 (p. 120 – p. 137)

Character: Who is in the focus of attention? Larry or Silas?

_____

Setting: Is the focus of the chapter on the past or the present?

_____

Content: Note down the aspects of this chapter that are of special significance.

_____

_____

_____

Language: Note down five phrases that you find important for talking about this chapter.

_____

_____

_____

_____

_____

Chapter 10 (p. 138 – p. 155)

Character: Who is in the focus of attention? Larry or Silas?

_____

Setting: Is the focus of the chapter on the past or the present?

_____

Content: Note down the aspects of this chapter that are of special significance.

_____

_____

_____

Language: Note down five phrases that you find important for talking about this chapter.

_____

_____

_____

_____

_____

Chapter 11 (p. 156 – p. 162)

Character: Who is in the focus of attention? Larry or Silas?

_____

Setting: Is the focus of the chapter on the past or the present?

_____

Content: Note down the aspects of this chapter that are of special significance.

_____

_____

_____

Language: Note down five phrases that you find important for talking about this chapter.

_____

_____

_____

_____

_____

Chapter 12 (p. 163 – p. 171)

Character: Who is in the focus of attention? Larry or Silas?

_____

Setting: Is the focus of the chapter on the past or the present?

_____

Content: Note down the aspects of this chapter that are of special significance.

_____

_____

_____

Language: Note down five phrases that you find important for talking about this chapter.

_____

_____

_____

_____

_____

Chapter 13 (p. 172 – p. 176)

Character: Who is in the focus of attention? Larry or Silas?

_____

Setting: Is the focus of the chapter on the past or the present?

_____

Content: Note down the aspects of this chapter that are of special significance.

_____

_____

_____

Language: Note down five phrases that you find important for talking about this chapter.

_____

_____

_____

_____

_____

Chapter 14 (p. 177 – p. 182)

Character: Who is in the focus of attention? Larry or Silas?

_____

Setting: Is the focus of the chapter on the past or the present?

_____

Content: Note down the aspects of this chapter that are of special significance.

_____

_____

_____

Language: Note down five phrases that you find important for talking about this chapter.

_____

_____

_____

_____

_____

Chapter 15 (p. 183 – p. 186)

Character: Who is in the focus of attention? Larry or Silas?
_____

Setting: Is the focus of the chapter on the past or the present?
_____

Content: Note down the aspects of this chapter that are of special significance.
_____
_____
_____

Language: Note down five phrases that you find important for talking about this chapter.
_____
_____
_____
_____
_____

Chapter 16 (p. 187 – p. 190)

Character: Who is in the focus of attention? Larry or Silas?
_____

Setting: Is the focus of the chapter on the past or the present?
_____

Content: Note down the aspects of this chapter that are of special significance.
_____
_____
_____

Language: Note down five phrases that you find important for talking about this chapter.
_____
_____
_____
_____
_____

Chapter 17 (p. 191 – p. 193)

Character: Who is in the focus of attention? Larry or Silas?

___

Setting: Is the focus of the chapter on the past or the present?

___

Content: Note down the aspects of this chapter that are of special significance.

___

___

___

Language: Note down five phrases that you find important for talking about this chapter.

___

___

___

___

___

___

Chapter 18 (p. 194 – p. 196)

Character: Who is in the focus of attention? Larry or Silas?

___

Setting: Is the focus of the chapter on the past or the present?

___

Content: Note down the aspects of this chapter that are of special significance.

___

___

___

Language: Note down five phrases that you find important for talking about this chapter.

___

___

___

___

___

___

Chapter 19 (p. 197 – p. 201)

Character: Who is in the focus of attention? Larry or Silas?
_____

Setting: Is the focus of the chapter on the past or the present?
_____

Content: Note down the aspects of this chapter that are of special significance.
_____
_____
_____

Language: Note down five phrases that you find important for talking about this chapter.
_____
_____
_____
_____
_____
_____

Worksheets: Chronology of Events

In this section you can rearrange the events in the novel in chronological order (such events as when Silas and Larry become friends, when Silas leaves Chabot, when he returns, the events that occur before the disappearance of Cindy Walker and the murder of Tina Rutherford, when Wallace Stringfellow appears for the first time, etc.).

1966/1967	Silas/Larry: born in Chabot
1970s	
1980s	
1982	Summer: Cindy missing

Worksheets: Chronology of Events

1980s	
1990s	
2000s	

2008	End of August: Tina Rutherford missing
2008	Eight days later: monster in the house/brutal assault on Larry
...	

Historical Timeline

May 18, 1896
The U.S. Supreme Court upholds a Louisiana law requiring segregated railroad facilities, as long as equality of accommodation is assured. In effect this principle of "equal but separate" is considered to apply to all aspects of interaction between whites and Blacks. It would take more than 150 years before the Supreme Court overturns this decision as unconstitutional.

June 3, 1946
The U.S. Supreme Court bans segregation in interstate bus travel in *Morgan v. Virginia*.

April 9, 1947
Civil rights groups organize the first Freedom Rides to test compliance with bus integration law.

July 26, 1948
President Harry S. Truman signs an Executive Order 9981 ending segregation of the armed forces.

1949
Federal law bars discrimination in federal service positions.

May 17, 1954
The U.S. Supreme Court rules in *Brown v. Board of Education* that school segregation is unconstitutional and so overturns the principle of separate but equal in *Plessy v. Ferguson* (1896).

1955
C. Vann Woodward (1908 – 1999) publishes **The Strange Career of Jim Crow**, a history of racial segregation that becomes the Bible of the civil rights movement.

August 28, 1955
Fourteen-year old Emmett Till is beaten to death in Money, Mississippi for speaking too familiarly with a white woman. The accused killers are acquitted in their trial. – national and international outrage

December 1, 1955
In Montgomery, Alabama, a bus boycott begins after Rosa Parks is arrested for refusing to give up her seat on a bus to a white man. Buses are no longer segregated after December 21, 1956.

1956

November 13, 1956
The U.S. Supreme Court rules in *Gayle v. Browder* that segregation in Montgomery's buses is illegal.

---

compliance with the law obeying the law

to acquit (law) to declare s.o. not guilty of a crime

outrage great anger

1957
September 1957
President Dwight D. Eisenhower orders federal troops to enforce school desegregation in Little Rock, Arkansas.
September 9, 1957
The Civil Rights Act, the first civil rights law since Reconstruction, prohibits preventing persons from voting. The Southern Christian Leadership Conference is founded by Martin Luther King and Bayard Rustin.
September 24, 1957
President Eisenhower sends federal troops to Little Rock, Arkansas to allow 9 blacks to enter high school and prevent further rioting and obstruction by Governor Faubus.

1960
To Kill A Mockingbird is published and becomes an immediate bestseller.
1960 - 1970
Black migration: by 1970 more than half the nation's blacks reside outside the South.
February 1, 1960
Black students stage a sit-in to protest segregated lunch counters in Greensboro, North Carolina.

1961
May 1961
White and African Americans, sponsored by the Congress on Racial Equality, the so-called Freedom Riders, travel through the South to protest racially segregated interstate bus stations.

1962
September 30, 1962
Riots erupt after James Meredith becomes the first black student to enroll at the University of Mississippi. Two people are killed.

to erupt to suddenly break out
to enroll to register as a student

1963
May 3, 1963
Police in Birmingham, Alabama use dogs and fire hoses to attack civil rights marchers. Images of brutality are televised around the world.

hose *Schlauch*

June 11, 1963
Governor George Wallace stands in the door of the University of Alabama to prevent a black student from enrolling. President Kennedy sends the National Guard and Wallace gives in.
June 12, 1963
Civil rights leader Medgar Evers is slain in Jackson, Mississippi.

to slay, slain, slain to kill

August 28, 1963
Martin Luther King, Jr. leads 250,000 Americans in the March on Washington, D.C. He delivers his famous "I Have a Dream" speech.

Historical Timeline

eulogy speech that praises s.o.

to wring, wrung, wrung (here): to obtain with great effort

unmerited undeserved

redemptive freeing you from sin

poll tax a tax placed on voting

to ensue to follow

to club to hit with a club (*Knüppel*)

trek long and hard walk

September 15, 1963
Four schoolgirls are killed when a bomb explodes at the Sixteenth Street Baptist Church in Birmingham. In his *Eulogy for the Young Victims of the Sixteenth Street Baptist Church Bombing* Martin Luther King stated: "And so my friends, they did not die in vain. God still has a way of wringing good out of evil. And history has proven over and over again that unmerited suffering is redemptive."

November 22, 1963
President John F. Kennedy is assassinated in Dallas, Texas.

1964

January 23, 1964
The 24th Amendment prohibits poll tax that made it difficult for African Americans to vote.

June 20, 1964
During the Freedom Summer, one thousand civil rights volunteers go to Mississippi. Three civil rights workers in this program, Goodman, Schwerner, and Chaney are brutally murdered. It is the basis of the 1988 film *Mississippi Burning*.

July 2, 1964
President Lyndon Johnson signs the Civil Rights Act, which outlaws discrimination in public accommodations, employment, and adds protection for voting rights.

July 1964
The worst race riot since WW II breaks out in New York City for six day after a Black teenager is killed by a policeman on July 16. Race riots ensue in Philadelphia, Chicago, and Jersey City.

August 20, 1964
President Lyndon Johnson signs the Economic Opportunity Act.

December 10, 1964
Martin Luther King, Jr., receives the Nobel Peace Prize.

1965

February 21, 1965
Malcolm X is shot and killed in New York City. He believed blacks should have a separate society.

March 7, 1965
Civil rights marchers in Selma, Alabama, are clubbed and gassed by police.

March 9, 1965
Under the protection of federal troops, civil rights marchers complete the trek from Selma to Montgomery.

August 10, 1965
President Johnson signs the Voting Rights Act which prohibits discriminatory voting practices.

August 6-11, 1965
Riots in the Watts section of Los Angeles result in thirty-four people dead and $35 million in property damage.

1966
The Black Panthers are founded, which later become involved in many violent confrontations with the police.

June 26, 1966
At a civil rights rally in Mississippi, Stokely Carmichael launches the Black Power movement – for integration but black self-determination.

1967
Carl Stokes is elected as first black mayor of a major city: Cleveland, Ohio. Black mayors are also elected in Newark, N.J. in 1970, Los Angeles and Atlanta in 1973.

June 12, 1967
The Supreme Court in *Loving v. Virginia* strikes down laws that prohibit inter-racial marriage.

July 1967
Riots in Newark and Detroit leave many dead and neighborhoods in ruins.

October 2, 1967
Thurgood Marshall is sworn in as the first African American justice of the U.S. Supreme Court.

to swear, swore, sworn s.o. in to require that s.o. promises to uphold the laws of the US before taking office

1968
February 29, 1968
The Kerner Commission warns that America is becoming "two societies – one black, one white – separate and unequal" and was the cause of riots in Watts, Cleveland in 1966, Newark and Detroit in 1967, and Washington, D.C. in 1968.

April 4, 1968
Martin Luther King, Jr., is assassinated in Memphis, Tennessee.

April 11, 1968
President Johnson signs the Civil Rights Act of 1968 that prohibits discrimination in the sale and renting of housing.

May 2 - June 24, 1968
The Poor People's Campaign brings fifty thousand demonstrators to Washington.

1970
Race riots erupt in several cities, including Philadelphia, New Orleans, New Bedford, Massachusetts, and Hartford, Connecticut.

1970 -1973
More blacks migrate to the South than to the North.

October 13, 1970
Angela Davis is arrested and charged with murder, kidnapping, and conspiracy. The case prompts an international campaign to free her. Two years later, she is found not guilty.

Historical Timeline

caucus special political group with a specific goal

to spark (fig.) to cause to suddenly start

gap Lücke

charge formal accusation
affirmative action a policy giving minorities an advantage when applying for a position or for admission to a university

bid attempt

1971
The Congressional Black Caucus is founded.
April 20, 1971
In *Swann v. Charlotte-Mecklenburg* the Supreme Court rules that busing is a legitimate means of achieving desegregation in schools.

1972
Shirley Chisholm becomes the first African American in history to seek the Democratic party's presidential nomination.

1973-75
The United States experiences the worst economic recession in decades.

1977
February 1977
The television mini-series "Roots," based on Alex Haley's best-selling novel, is watched by a record 130 million viewers, sparking a national debate about race and African-American history.

1978
The Black unemployment rate is nearly 2.5 times higher than whites; this is the largest gap since the federal government began keeping such statistics.
Allan Bakke's charge of "reverse discrimination" against the University of California, Davis, Medical School weakens affirmative action policies when the Supreme Court rules in *Regents of the University of California v. Bakke* that he had been denied "equal protection of the laws" as required by the 14th Amendment.

1980
May 1980
African Americans in Liberty City, Florida riot after police officers are acquitted for killing an unarmed black man.

1982
Alice Walker publishes **The Color Purple**, which received the American Book Award and the Pulitzer Prize.

1983
Harold Washington is elected the first black mayor of Chicago.

1984
Jesse Jackson makes the first bid for the Democratic party's presidential nomination, receiving about 3.5 million popular votes in the primaries.

"The Cosby Show" about a middle-class black family starts on TV. It becomes the most popular regular program on television.

1985
September 1985
The U.S. Census Bureau reports that one out of three African Americans is living below the poverty line.

1988
Jesse Jackson seeks the Democratic presidential nomination for a second time.
March 22, 1988
Overriding President Reagan's veto, Congress passes the Civil Rights Restoration Act that expands non-discrimination to private institutions receiving money from the government.

1989
Douglas L. Wilder is elected governor of Virginia and becomes the first African American elected governor of any state.

1992
Carol Moseley-Braun becomes the first African-American woman elected to the U.S. Senate.
April 29 - May 1, 1992
The acquittal of four Los Angeles police officers accused of using excessive force on black motorist Rodney King sparks the largest, most costly urban rebellion in U.S. history.

1997
New York police officers beat and sexually assault the Haitian immigrant Abner Louima. The case calls attention to the problem of police brutality.

to assault to attack and beat

1999
August
The NAACP calls for a national boycott of vacation spots in South Carolina in an attempt to force the state government to remove the Confederate flag from the dome of its statehouse.

2000
January 17, 2000
More than forty-six thousand protesters march on the state capitol at Columbia, South Carolina, to protest the Confederate battle flag flying atop the statehouse dome.
December 2000
Condolezza Rice is appointed by President-elect George W. Bush to serve as national security advisor. She becomes the first African American and first woman to serve in this position. She later becomes Secretary of State after Colin Powell resigns.

2001

January 20, 2001

General Colin L. Powell is sworn in by President George W. Bush as Secretary of State. He becomes the first African American appointed Secretary of State.

April 2001

Cincinnati police fatally shoot an unarmed black youth, Timothy Thomas – the fourth African-American male killed by Cincinnati police in five months. The killing sparks a week of rioting, forcing the governor to call in the National Guard.

September 11, 2001

Terrorists attack New York's World Trade Center and the Pentagon using hijacked commercial airliners; over three thousand die in these attacks.

October 2001

U.S. and British forces invade Afghanistan.

2002

January 29, 2002

President George Bush identifies Iraq as part of the "axis of evil," and vows that the United States "will not permit the world's most dangerous regimes to threaten us with the world's most destructive weapons."

October 11, 2002

Congress authorizes an attack on Iraq.

2003

March 20, 2003

The war against Iraq begins.

June 23, 2003

In *Grutter* v. *Bollinger,* the Supreme Court upholds (5-4) the University of Michigan Law School's policy of using race as one of many factors in making admissions decisions. In a separate but related ruling, the court votes 6-3 to strike down the University of Michigan's undergraduate affirmative action policy.

2004

November 4, 2004

George W. Bush is re-elected

2007

One the worst financial crises since the Great Depression of the 1930s begins.

---

to vow to solemnly promise

ruling (law) decision

2008
November 4, 2008
Barack Obama becomes the first president of the United States with roots in Africa.
African Americans are appointed to a number of important positions in the Obama administration. He is re-elected in 2012.

African Americans still earn less than two-thirds the income of whites; the jobless rate of African Americans is 11 percent in October, almost double that of whites. Seven in ten African American babies are born to a single mother.

2012
February 26, 2012
Trayvon Martinan, a 17 year-old African American from Miami Gardens, Florida is fatally shot by George Zimmerman. Zimmerman is acquitted.
One year later the political movement Black Lives Matters is established to fight against police violence directed at Blacks.

2014
August, 2014
After a Black teenager is shot dead by a white policeman, rioting breaks out in Ferguson, a suburb of St. Louis, Missouri.

2015
June 17, 2015
Dylann Roof opens fire and kills nine people during a prayer meeting at a historic African American church in Charleston, South Carolina. It is an example of a hate crime.

2016
July 7, 2016
Micah Xavier Johnson, a Black Army Reserve veteran of the war in Afghan ambushes a group of policemen in Dallas, Texas. Five officers are killed and nine injured. Apparently angry about the shooting of Black men by police officers and wanting to revenge himself by killing white people and white police officers, he is killed the next morning with a bomb.

August 14, 2016
Gov. Scott Walker of Wisconsin activates the Wisconsin National Guard to assist local law enforcement following a night of violence in Milwaukee that began hours after a Black police officer, Dominique Heaggan-Brown, fatally shot a fleeing armed man, 23-year-old Sylville Smith, who was also Black, on Milwaukee's north side the day before. Ironically, the same officer is later fired from the Milwaukee

police force on November 28, 2016 after being charged with sexually assaulting a man.

September 20, 2016
Rioting breaks out in Charlotte, North Carolina after a Black man is shot dead by the police.

2017

January 5, 2017
In Chicago four black teenagers are arrested after the videotape they made while torturing a white teenager with mental disabilities is revealed.

Some Useful Literary Terms

Allegory: a narrative in verse or prose form in which specific characters and actions represent abstract ideas or moral qualities – An allegory can be literal, or real, and have symbolic levels of meaning.

Alliteration: the repetition of consonant or vowel sounds at the beginning of words

Allusion: a reference to a person, place, event, or written work such as the Bible that the author expects the reader to recognize

Anaphora: the repetition of the same word or words at the beginning of successive phrases, clauses, or sentences

Antagonist: the character or force that opposes the protagonist or hero in a conflict

Archaism: a word or expression that is out of date

Argumentation: writing or a speech that tries to convince the reader of the logic and merits of a particular viewpoint by giving specific reasons and examples.

Characterization: the means used by the author to develop the character, e.g. by description, what the character thinks or says, how he/she reacts or speaks, and how the other characters react or describe the character; the character may be superficially described or flat, or made to seem very real and complex: round.

Climax: the turning point of the story, the crisis, after which there seems to be no other possible way for the plot to continue – The part of the plot before the climax is often called **rising action** and that after the climax **falling action.**

Coming of age story/novel, *Bildungsroman*: a literary work in which the protagonist experiences events that lead to greater maturity

Commentary: The author or narrator inserts his or her own comments or views.

Complication: the point in the story at which the conflict is introduced, thus giving the plot a new impetus

Conflict: the clash between opposing forces – It can involve ideas, persons, the forces of nature and be in the mind or external.

Dénouement: the part of a story when all questions are answered, secrets are revealed, conflicts are resolved – It is also called the **resolution** or **outcome**. If the story still leaves some questions unanswered, we speak of an **open ending**.

Description: The author tries to give the reader a mental image of what can be seen, felt, or heard by giving concrete descriptions, often to create a certain atmosphere.

Dialogue: what the characters actually say

Diction: the choice of words used by the author to produce a certain effect on the reader

Doppelgänger: look-alike or double of a living person or an apparition

Dramatic Irony: when a character says something without realizing the true significance of what was said, however, it is obvious to the reader

Euphemism: the substitution of a mild or less negative word or phrase for a direct one, as in the use of "to pass away" instead of "to die"

Exposition: the part of a story, usually at the beginning, that gives essential background information for an understanding of the unfolding plot

Flashback: a scene in a story that interrupts the action to show what happened in the past

Foil: character who is the opposite of another character in order to point up the strengths or weaknesses of the other character

Foreshadowing: anything that hints that something, usually bad, is going to happen later

Frame Story: a story with a framework, for example a narrator who, from a later point of time, describes what happened in the past, or a story within a story

Hyperbole: an exaggeration

Imagery: vivid sensory details that arouse certain emotions of feelings in the reader

Irony: when the author or a character means the opposite or what he/she actually writes or says

Local Color: using details that make a particular region vivid to the reader – also known as **regionalism**

Masking: often used to describe the servile behavior and manner of speaking used by Black slaves when interacting with their white masters – During the period of segregation that continued into the 1960s this type of behavior could still be witnessed on the part of Blacks when dealing with whites.

Metaphor: a direct comparison between two apparently different things, ideas, or persons without using *as* or *like*, i.e. She had rose lips.

Motivation: the force that drives a character to take a certain course of action

Mood: overall atmosphere of a work

The Other: a concept that has its origin in psychology – It describes the tendency of a dominant group to look upon different cultural or religious groups as strange and different, even inferior. For example, British colonizers often considered indigenous people under their control, in Africa, India, Australia, or New Zealand, as barbarous and uncivilized. **Othering** is the process of putting the stamp of **the other** on a person or persons.

Paradox: a statement that seems to be contradictory

Personification: giving human or even animal qualities to objects or things

Plot: the plan and arrangement of related incidents within a story

Plot Twist: a sudden unexpected change in the direction of the plot that may lead to a surprise ending

Point of View: the manner in which the author presents the events and characters in a story
1. first-person narrator: the story is told by a character in the story, the "I" in the story – The narrator can be an adult who relates what occurred in the past as a child.
2. limited third-person narrator who focuses on one character
3. omniscient third-person or an all-knowing observer who can describe and comment about everything and everyone in the story

Polysydeton: a rhetorical device whereby a conjunction, often *and*, is used repeatedly – It is frequently used in the Bible or by the American writer, Ernest Hemingway.

Protagonist: the main character in a story on whom the action centers

Register: the kind of language used in a specific social setting – Examples of register are vulgar, slang, colloquial, and formal. The kind of register used often reflects the social status of the character or may be purposely used in the wrong context or setting.

Repetition: repeating a word or phrase in a sentence to produce an effect

Sarcasm: the use of ironic remarks to show you dislike s.o.

Satire: the use of sarcasm or irony to show the moral weakness of people, an idea, a movement, a country, etc.

Setting: the surroundings, location where the action takes place

Simile: a direct comparison between two basically different things, ideas, or persons using *as* or *like*, i.e. She had lips like a rose.

Southern Gothic: a literary genre that derives from the Gothic literature of English literature in the 18th century – It centers on eccentric characters, the mysterious, violent crimes, images of ghosts and witches, and evokes the sinister atmosphere of a decaying Southern aristocracy. Examples of Southern Gothic can be found in the writings of Edgar Allan Poe, Flannery O'Connor, Harper Lee, William Faulkner, and Truman Capote.

Stock Character or Stereotype: a character with typical characteristics who keeps reappearing in literature, such as the jealous husband, the all-knowing but silent butler, the absent-minded professor, the hypocritical preacher, the naïve American

Stream of Consciousness: often considered the same as **interior monologue** – the thoughts and impressions of a character which are set down just as they occur in his/her mind

Suspense: the feeling of uncertainty and anxiety as the plot rises towards its climax

Surprise Ending: an unexpected ending that is not anticipated

Symbol: anything that has a meaning in itself, but also stands for something larger than itself

Topos, plural **Topoi:** a traditional theme or motif, such as the jealous husband, young lovers, good overcoming evil, the servant of several masters (picaroon) who is able to trick them all, the beautiful woman who bewitches all men, the mad scientist, the devil buying souls

Selected Additional Reading

To Make Our World Anew, A History of African Americans from 1880, edited by Robin D. G. Kelly and Earl Lewis, Oxford University Press, New York, 2000

Still Fighting the Civil War, the American South and Southern History by David Goldfield, Louisiana, State University Press, Baton Rouge, 2004 – excellent survey of the Southern mentality still overshadowed by the Civil War and Jim Crow

To Kill A Mockingbird by Harper Lee, Diesterweg, Braunschweig, 2014

Go Set a Watchman by Harper Lee, 2016

Black Like Me by John Griffin (1961), Diesterweg, Braunschweig, 2009 – In the early 1960s a white journalist dyes his skin black to find out what it's like to be Black in Louisiana and Mississippi.

A Lesson Before Dying by Ernest Gaines (1993), Diesterweg, 2009

The Help by Kathryn Stockett, Penguin, 2010 – novel about Black maids and how they confront racism in Mississippi in the early 1960s

Scottsboro, a Novel by Ellen Feldman, W. W. Norton and Company, New York, 2008 – a historical novel about the trials of the Scottsboro boys in the 1930s

A Rose for Emily short story by William Faulkner – an example of Southern Gothic that deals with the decadence of the Southern aristocracy

Désirée's Baby short story by Kate Chopin – classic story about the absurdity of racism

The Invention of Wings by Sue Monk Kidd, 2014 – wonderful historical novel about the Grimké sisters, two daughters of a plantation owner in antebellum South Carolina, who reject slavery and go North to join the abolitionists and fight for women's rights

Property by Valerie Martin, 2003 – powerful novel about antebellum Louisiana

Poachers: Stories by Tom Franklin, William Morrow and Co., Inc., New York, 1999

Hell at the Beech by Tom Franklin, William Morrow and Co, Inc. New York, 2003 – Tom Franklin's first novel about the violent and bloody Mitcham Beat war in Alabama at the end of the 19th century

A Good Man is Hard to Find, a collection of short stories by Flannery O'Connor, Harcourt, Brace and Company, New York, 1955 – major Southern writer, strongly influenced by Catholicism, who emphasized violence and the grotesque – Cf. her novels as well

Native Son by Richard Wright, Harper and Row, New York, 1940 – classic novel that examines the disastrous effects of racism on African Americans

Almos' a Man by Richard Wright – short story published in 1961 that deals with Black masculinity. It has also been made into a film.

Invisible Man by Ralph Ellison Random House, New York, 1952 – classic novel about Black identity that addresses the problems of racism in the first half of 19th century America

Between the World and Me by Ta-Nehisi Coate, Spiegel and Grau, New York, 2015 – autobiography in the form of a letter that deals with the destructive effects of racism from a historical perspective

The Fire Next Time by James Baldwin, Dial Press, New York, 1963 – two essays that deal with racism and religion

Selected List of Films about the South or Racism

To Kill a Mockingbird (1962): film version of the novel

Crash (2004): The various facets of racism is one of the main themes in this film about Los Angeles.

Almos' A Man (1977): TV film based on a short story by Richard Wright

Mississippi Burning (1988): film about two FBI agents investigating the murder of three civil rights workers in 1964

A Lesson Before Dying (1999): film based on the novel by Ernest Gaines – A young African American in Louisiana in the late 1940s is executed for a crime he didn't commit.

The Autobiography of Miss Jane Pittman (1974): film based on the novel by Ernest Gaines – the sweep of African-American history from slavery to the Civil Rights Movement

A Raisin in the Sun (1961): a film about how an African-American family deals with racism in Chicago

Roots (1977): TV series about the history of African Americans

In the Heat of the Night (1967): with Rod Steiger and Sidney Poitier – A Southern sheriff overcomes his prejudices and eventually comes to respect and accept the help from a Black northern detective.

Guess Who's Coming to Dinner (1967): drama about a mixed marriage

Django Unchained (2012): violent film about racism and slavery before the Civil War

Twelve Years a Slave (2013): Before the Civil War a free Black in the North is sold into slavery.

Belle (2013): The daughter of a Black slave and a Royal Navy Admiral is raised by her aristocratic great-uncle in 18th century England.

Driving Miss Daisy (1989): film about a Black chauffeur and his Jewish white employer, Miss Daisy – The film deals with anti-Semitism and racism in the South from the 1940s to the civil rights movement.

Selected List of Films about the South or Racism

The Defiant Ones (1957): with Tony Curtis and Sidney Poitier –Two escaped convicts chained together, one white, one Black learn to get along to avoid capture.

The Help (2011): excellent film about racism in the South in the early 1960s

The Secret Life of Bees (2008): Set in South Carolina in 1964, Lily Owens, a 14 year-old girl is taken in by Black sisters, who run a successful honey business.

Lincoln (2012): film about the last four months of Abraham Lincoln's life as he seeks passage of the 13th Amendment to abolish slavery

Oh, Brother Where Art Thou? (2000): excellent satire of Southern culture and society in the 1930s

Fruitvale Station (2013): film about a young Black man shot by a policeman

Birth of A Nation (1915): at the time of its release an immensely popular historical film about the Civil War and Reconstruction – very racist and pro-Ku Klux Klan

Additional Material

The Detective Story

The detective story can be characterized by the following paradigm, beginning with Poe's tales and continuing well into the 20th century.

> A story in which a mystery, often involving a murder, is solved by a detective. The traditional elements are an apparently insoluble crime, uncooperative or dim-witted police, the detective (often an amateur) who may be an eccentric, the detective's confidant who helps to clarify the problems, a variety of suspects and carefully laid red herrings to put the reader off the scent, a suspect who appears guilty from circumstantial evidence, and a resolution, often startling and unexpected, in which the detective reveals how he has found out the culprit. The good detective story displays impeccable logic and reasoning in its unravelling.

dim-witted rather stupid
confidant trusted friend
scent Spur

culprit (formal) guilty person
impeccable perfect
to unravel (fig.) to clear up

[quoted from **A Dictionary of Literary Terms** by J.D. Cuddon, Penguin, London, 1979, p. 182]

The first Western detective story with all of it conventions is considered to be Edgar Allan Poe's trilogy of Dupin detective stories, published between 1841 and 1844. It should be pointed out, however, that Voltaire already published a tale, **Zadig**, in which the philosophical protagonist makes use of observation and logic to solve problems.

A number of French writers then began to publish full-length novels: Emile Gaboriau's **L'Affaire Lerouge** (1866), **Le Crime d'Orcival** (1868) and **Monsieur Lecoq** (1869). Fortuné du Boisgobey wrote stories in a similar vein, e.g. **Le Crime de l'Opéra** (1880). The first English detective novel was Wilkie Collins' **The Moonstone.** The publication of the Sherlock Holmes tales at the end of the Victorian era produced a cult-like following that opened the floodgates to a wide range of the detective stories. Especially noteworthy are G. K. Chesterton's **Father Brown Stories** (1911), and post WW I writers such as the English writers Agatha Christie, Dorothy Sayers, and the American writer Earl Derr Biggers (1884 - 1933), whose novels about the sympathetic Chinese-American detective, Charlie Chan found a vast readership. The Belgian writer Georges Simenon's (1903 - 1989) stories centering on Inspector Maigret are even popular today. American writers such as Dashiell Hammet, and Raymond Chandler introduced the "hard-boiled" detective story that featured a cynical "private eye" and a dialogue that reflected the speech patterns of America's criminal class. Hollywood used many of the stories by the hard-boiled school of writers as the basis for films in the 1930s and 1940s as well as those of writers such as Doyle, Biggers, Christie, and Chesterton. ITV and the BBC have also produced excellent quality TV productions of the aforementioned authors, beginning with Sir Arthur Conan Doyle.

In recent years both a writer from Sweden and Sicily have commanded the attention of fans of detective stories with an emphasis on social criticism. Henning Mankell's (1948 - 2015) Inspector Wallander, and Inspector Montalbano, created by Andrea Camilleri (1925 -), deal with the seamier side of society. Camilleri's stories are especially steeped in the history, culture, and language of Sicily. The well-crafted film versions are best watched in the original language to fully appreciate the somewhat decadent atmosphere of a southern European culture and the cadences of the Sicilian dialect. It's astounding how, in a similar vein, the local color of the deep South is made vivid by Tom Franklin in his crime novel, **Crooked Letter, Crooked Letter**.

The American South

by Prof. Dr. Horst Tonn

Laid back and idyllic, friendly and welcoming to strangers – that is how the Southern United States is seen by many. Life seems slower there than elsewhere, more relaxed and enjoyable. Geographically, the South reaches from Washington, D.C., to Florida and to Louisiana and Arkansas in a westerly direction. The region attracts many tourists because the climate is mild and one finds beautiful beaches and luscious semi-tropical landscapes. Moreover, cities like Atlanta, New Orleans and Memphis boast a lively music scene (jazz, blues, country), ethnic variety and Southern cuisine. "Dixie", as the South is also called, retains some traces of the long gone splendor of the old plantation South and it promises the pleasures of a unique way of life.

But there is another side to the story. Throughout its history the South has been a region riddled with immense poverty, racial conflict and rural backwardness. Much of the region is politically very conservative, if not reactionary. In the so-called "Bible Belt" religious fervor is widespread. In many parts of the rural and small-town South many people are poor and without social protection. Work in agriculture is seasonal with low pay. For those who have work in industry, wages are below what is standard in other parts of the country and trade unions are weaker or non-existent. Mississippi is the poorest state in the United States. It relies more on federal aid than any other state. High unemployment, lack of health care, a weak educational system and political corruption are commonly observable in many parts of the South.

The South continues to be shaped by its history of slavery, racial conflict and its attempt to gain independence from the U.S. during the Civil War (1861-65). After slavery, racial segregation was the rule throughout the region until the 1960s. Blacks and Whites would go to different schools, eat in different restaurants, travel in separate train compartments and use separate rest rooms and other public facilities. In addition, Blacks were systematically excluded from the right to vote. This did not change until the 1950s when Blacks began to fight for their civil rights. In Montgomery, Alabama, a boycott of the public bus system sparked similar protests in other parts of the region. In 1955 Rosa Parks refused to give up her seat on a bus to a white passenger. Martin Luther King's famous speech "I Have A Dream" (1963) powerfully expressed the demands of what by then had become a national movement. With the Civil Rights Act of 1964 segregation as a legalized system was abolished but other forms of discrimination and racism continue to this very day. There are many ways by which racism has become systemic. Bad schools and the high cost of a college education prevent Black students from reaching their potential. Banks refuse loans to Blacks who want to buy a home or start their own business. City governments build roads or impose zoning laws which destroy ethnic neighborhoods and enforce separations along the color line. Blacks in urban ghettos remain cut off from basic needs: public transportation, jobs, education, libraries or sports facilities. And, as the many cases of police violence in the recent past have shown, Blacks have good reason to fear even routine encounters with police officers.

to enforce *durchführen, vollstrecken*

encounter *Begegnung, Zusammentreffen*

Race and Ethnicity

by Prof. Dr. Horst Tonn

In David Mamet's play *Race* (New York, 2010), the Anglo-American lawyer Jack observes: "Race. Is the most incendiary topic in our history. And the moment it comes out, you cannot close the lid on that box." (pp. 44 f.) No doubt, race and racism continue to be persistent and painful aspects of American life to this very day. While there has been considerable racial progress, especially as a result of the civil rights movements of the 1950s and 1960s, Blacks and other racial minorities in the United States continue to be culturally and economically marginalized. Statistics on infant mortality, rates of imprisonment, access to higher education and unemployment show invariably that minorities are disproportionately affected in all of these areas. It does not come as a surprise then that Black leaders like Colonel West stress the fact that "the problem of the twenty-first century remains the problem of the color line" (**Race Matters**; New York, 2001, p. xiv).

It is important to understand that individuals and groups **do not have** racial/ethnic attributes. Instead, such attributes **are assigned or given to** them. Societies define and articulate the characteristics of racial and ethnic groups. Race is a social process rather than a given state of affairs. Hazel Rose Marcus and Paula M. L. Moya describe this process as "doing race" – an ongoing activity that is continuously performed and acted out in all spheres of social life (**Doing Race**; New York, 2010). Blackness in American society (like other racial identities) can then be seen as a set of physical and cultural traits that are either attributed to one particular group from outside or the group itself chooses certain attributes for self-description. Racial and ethnic characteristics are neither essential nor unchangeable. The example set by the civil rights movement or the slogan "Black is beautiful" can be a source of racial pride while racist stereotypes humiliate and exclude members of racial minorities.

Race can then be understood as an idea or an ideology that has evolved over time. From a historical perspective, modern racism has its root cause in colonialism's greed for territories, natural resources and cheap labor. The idea of race was invented to separate people into different groups and to legitimize relationships of domination and exploitation. During the colonial period in the United States, new forms of slavery and indentured servitude were developed. At first African laborers worked and lived under similar circumstances as indentured European workers, then slavery became institutionalized during the 17th century and the "color line" emerged. In the 19th century the anti-slavery movement (abolitionism) and the Civil War (1861 - 1865) changed the legal status of Blacks fundamentally. And after World War II, the civil rights movement brought significant changes for race relations and racial identities in the United States. But despite all the progress that has been achieved, racism continues to plague the relations between African-Americans and Anglo-Americans to this very day. Most recently, a series of shocking incidents of police brutality against Blacks hit the headlines. The killing of Michael Brown in Ferguson, Missouri, in the summer of 2014 was only one among many similar cases.

despite *trotz*

You are a detective investigating the crimes in the novel. Jot down questions, clues, and answers as you read it. For example:

| Question |

Who is the person wearing the monster mask at the beginning of Chapter One?